ELIGION:

*Writings*

# VOLTAIRE ON RELIGION:

## Selected Writings

TRANSLATED AND INTRODUCED BY

## KENNETH W. APPELGATE

Frederick Ungar Publishing Co.
New York

*Copyright © 1974 by Frederick Ungar Publishing Co., Inc.*
*Library of Congress Catalog Card Number: 74-127204*
*Designed by Irving Perkins*
*ISBN: 0-8044-5975-4*

*Printed in the United States of America*

# CONTENTS

# PREFACE

Two centuries ago Voltaire, relentless enemy of the evils of injustice, intolerance, superstition, fanaticism, and ignorance, mounted an extensive literary assault on the institutions and beliefs he held responsible for those evils. His personal campaign *écraser l'infâme* to crush the infamy aroused Western Europe to the realization of the profound abuses and absurdities that he so powerfully illuminated. In the succeeding two hundred years—caught up in a movement the impetus for which stemmed in a large part from Voltaire—Church, state, and law effected revolutionary reforms. It was no mean achievement in the face of seemingly impossible odds, in an age when even the thought of attacking the entrenched and monolithic Establishment, possessed of a monopoly of education and of the terrifying Inquisition, meant the tortures, if ferreted out.

The religious polemics that are here translated constituted part of a major weapon against the Establishment. They cannot be dismissed simply as polemics; they must be esteemed powerful generators of an historical force that exalted humanitarianism, that helped push Western Europe further out of the Middle Ages toward the modern era.

Voltaire wrote for the lay public of France. As he did with the writing of history and of science, so he did also with his religious writing; that is, he popularized it. His *rogatons* (odds and ends) on religion were not just for a select few nor for burial among unpublished manuscripts. Writing for the public, he sought to create an impact, an effect; he set out to shock, to hurt, to injure. But the ultimate goal was to heal, to cure, and if possible, to introduce the concept of a "natural" religion, purged of hierarchy and wealth. Voltaire, finding a large appreciative audience for his caustic wit and satire, attained the impact that he intended. With it came great popularity but also the powerful enmity of Church and State.

Voltaire pulled no verbal punches; neither did the defenders of orthodoxy. They excoriated him as an atheist, Deist, mystic, blasphemer, bigot. No derogatory adjectives were spared. He was labeled vain, irreligious, iconoclastic, sacrilegious, impious, intemperate, scabrous, scandalous, malicious, scurrilous, sarcastic. Name-calling apparently was effective in the English-speaking world which, with the exception of the Deists, seems to have attributed little or no historical significance to Voltaire's essays on religion, rather preferring to regard them as not quite respectable religious diatribes, unworthy of translation. Thus in English they are rarely to be found, if at all, and readers of English read *about* Voltaire but seldom *what* he wrote on religion. Through a censorship of silence they have missed an important literature in the history of successful attack on powerful, reactionary, and oppressive institutions and ideas.

Voltaire was partisan; so were his critics. The controversy generated over him has lasted with varying intensity into the present day on many questions. Among them are: do Voltaire's remarks on religion belong only to the past, as is often asserted? Have they no meaning to the "modern" world? Was Voltaire merely an iconoclast, a reckless destroyer who had nothing constructive to offer? Was he an atheist? These and other questions can better be answered after reading Voltaire himself.

Following is a bibliography of sources and references employed in the process of the present translation:

*The Complete Works of Voltaire*

*Oeuvres Complètes de Voltaire,* vol. 29, 33, 34.

Kehl, 1784–1789, Imprimeurs de la Société Typographique, 70 volumes; Life of Voltaire by Condorcet; Edited by Beaumarchais, Marquis de Condorcet and Decroix.

*Oeuvres Complètes de Voltaire: The Miscellany,* vol. 20 and 21.

Edition de Ch. Lahure et Cie.; Imprimeurs à Paris: Librairie de L. Hachette et Cie., Paris, 1859, 35 volumes. This edition is based upon the *Edition Beuchot*; Paris, 1829–1840, with Beuchot's footnotes.

*Oeuvres Complètes de Voltaire: The Miscellany,* vol. 22 and 23.

New edition with text that conforms to the *Edition Beuchot* enriched with the most recent discoveries, general and analytical tables, appendix and a life of Voltaire by Condorcet; Edited by Louis Moland.

Librairie des Garnier Frères, Paris, 1877–1885, 54 volumes (with plates).

This edition is usually referred to as the *Moland* edition.

*The Works of Voltaire,* a Contemporary Version in English.

Revised and Modernized. Notes by Tobias Smollet; New Translations by W. F. Fleming; Critique and Biography by J. Morley, Introduction by Oliver H. Leigh; St. Hubert Guild, New York, about 1901 1903, 42 volumes. This set has none of the Miscellany but does contain in volumes 5 through 14 a translation of the *Philosopher's Dictionary* (Dictionnaire Philosophique) in which are numerous references to the same subjects that appear in the following translations.

*Biblical references*
(used for the purpose of following Voltaire's biblical quotes):

*Biblia Sacra*

Vulgatae Editionis, Sixti V Pontifici Maximi Jussu Recognita et Clementis VIII auctoritate edita est; prolegomenis Ferdinandi Koph Sacrae Theologiae Doctoris; Venetiis ex typographia Balleoniana MDCCLXV.

*The Soncino Books of the Bible*

Hebrew text with English translation by the Soncino Society edited by A. Cohen with commentary by R. T. Friedman, J. J. Slotki, S. Goldman, V. E. Reichert, S. Fisch; London, Soncino Press 1945-1951, 14 volumes.

*Holie Bible*

By the English College of Doway; approbatio, Guilielmus Estis, Bartholomeus Petrus, Georgius Colvenarius, Sacrae Theologiae Doctor and professors in the Academy and University at Doway; printed at Doway by Lawrence Kellam at the sign of the holy lamb; MDCIX.

*The Holy Bible*

Containing the Old and New Testaments; Translated out of the original tongues; with the former translations diligently compared and revised by His Majesty's special command; Oxford; Printed at the University Press London: Humphrey Milford Exford University Press. Amen Corner; Prefatory Note by Henry A. Redpath, M.A., July 1902.

This is the King James Version of the Bible. Since it is more familiar to English readers than the other versions, Voltaire's references to biblical books, characters, and places in the nomenclature of the *Vulgate* have been converted to the King James usages—except where he seems to be paraphrasing or willfully misquoting.

*Septuagint Bible*
Translated by Charles Thomson; Edited and revised and enlarged by C. A. Muses; Falcon Wings Press, Indian Hills, Colorado, 1954.

*The New English Bible* with the Apocrypha; Oxford and Cambridge, 1970.

*Previous Translations of the Materials Translated in This Volume*
With three exceptions, a considerable search failed to turn up any previous English translations of the materials here translated. Briefs of twenty chapters taken from *An Important Study of Lord Bolingbroke*, which contains thirty-eight chapters, were published in *The Deist,* volume 2, London, 1819, under the heading of *An Important Examination of the Scriptures.* This particular source, available in the rare book collection of the Huntington Library, San Marino, California, cannot be considered a sufficient representation of the total of the *Important Study.*

*The Questions of Zapata,* translated from the French "by a lady," London, 1840?, 28 pp., and *Two Addresses*: against *Atheism* and *Superstition,* delivered in London in 1765, translated by C. H. J., published by J. Haywood, Manchester, 1900, 31 pp., are in the library of the British Museum. The present translator had no access to either at the time of translation. Although the three above publications and others may exist here and there in out of the way places, it is apparent that they would be available to very few persons.

# INTRODUCTION

## i

Few could have anticipated that François-Marie Arouet (1694–1778) would become, among the *philosophes* of the Age of Enlightenment, a foremost critic and foe of established religion. Parisian-born of a bourgeois family, he was the youngest of five children, two of whom did not survive. His mother, née Marguerite Daumard, died when he was seven, leaving to the father, François Arouet, the task of rearing Armand the older brother, an older sister who was a substitute mother, and the weak, sickly François-Marie. He was not expected to live and all his life complained of ill health. To all appearances his should have been a conventional, uneventful middle-class life, as his father certainly wished; but it turned out otherwise. As time went on he became one of the most controversial figures in history. Even the date of his birth, his legitimacy, and his place of birth became a matter of controversy.

The Arouets were not an ordinary bourgeois family, having a number of highly placed social connections: the Abbé Chateauneuf was godfather to François-Marie, who formed a lifelong friendship with the son of the Duke of Richelieu, the godfather of Armand Arouet. A stimulating intellectual atmosphere characterized the Arouet *ménage,* that is, until Armand, who had been sent to a

Jansenist school, began to enforce a rigorous Jansenist austerity on the family. From that time a rift between the two brothers widened into outright enmity made certain when the senior Arouet sent François-Marie to a school conducted by dedicated enemies of the Jansenists, the Jesuits of the Collège Louis-le-Grand, who influenced the boy toward the views of the *libertins*, that is, the freethinkers.

From the age of ten to nineteen, the youthful Arouet read the classics in Latin and Greek, French history, and religious literature. He also learned about Jesuit and Church politics, for which he conceived a dislike. At the same time, an early precocity blossomed into a talent for poetry and witty epigram, greatly admired by the Fathers of the *collège* who, in his school days, regarded him as impervious to religious and moral discipline but amenable to instruction in good taste. Nevertheless, a continuing affection for the Jesuits was established in the mind of their pupil, who now entered into a world filled with acrid theological disputation among Jansenists, Socinians, Deists, Gomarists, Molinists, the Protestant sects, and the Roman Church.

Introduced by his godfather into a society of freethinkers known as the Temple, he began to confirm the opinion of the *collège* that, though brilliant, he was undisciplined. He refused his father's request that he enter the law, squandered money on riotous living, and consorted with versifiers, wits, and other undesirables. His relations with his father deteriorated to the point that the elder Arouet sought a *lettre de cachet*, an order for the commitment of his nineteen-year-old son to the Bastille.

But Arouet relented, and François-Marie, after a short retirement from Paris occasioned by a satire launched against a successful competitor for an Academy award in poetry, went everywhere and met everyone. Now twenty, he followed the social path that led him in the next few years to the court of the Regent, the Duc d'Orléans, and ultimately to that of Louis XV and his queen, Maria Leszczynska. During this time he encountered Jean-Baptiste Rousseau, the poet, in Holland; after eleven days they became lifelong enemies. He visited Lord Bolingbroke, the English Deist, at his home near Orléans, a visit that may have initiated or furthered the young Arouet's interest in Deism and organized criticism of religion.

There was to be little quiet in the life of the cadet Arouet who, after 1718, supplanted the name Arouet with one of his own invention, "de Voltaire." Perhaps the "de" satisfied a desire to be aristocratic, perhaps the "Voltaire" dissociated him from Armand. He never explained why nor how he made up the name. The Regency exiled him from Paris because of a scurrilous poem that he did not write and then imprisoned him in the Bastille from May 1717 to April 1718 for satirical verses that he did write. At this time the tragedy *Oedipe* (Oedipus) gained him fame in Paris. True to his middle-class training, he was building a private fortune compounded of stipends from the royal court, an inheritance from his father, profits from commercial ventures, investments in stocks, and money-lending.

The new Voltaire exhibited an errant behavior and an insatiable appetite for publicity, whether good or bad, that created enemies, disgusted his friends, and occasioned glee among the many waiting for him to get his just desserts. After three particularly undignified public encounters with an actor, an undercover agent, and an aristocrat of dubious quality, he was again lodged in the Bastille in April–May 1726, but was released to leave France for England.

In England until 1729, Voltaire was characteristically vigorous. He learned to read, write, and speak English, considering these skills necessary for understanding the literature and for communicating with Englishmen whom he admired: Locke, Pope, Newton, Samuel Clarke, and the many Deists: Bolingbroke (whom he had visited in France and whose name he later used for the *Important Study*), Shaftesbury, Tindal, Woolston, and Collins. The works and ideas of these men Voltaire is sometimes accused of having used without acknowledgment, a controversial point that is discussed further on.

Voltaire arrived in England already considerably steeped in

Deism, in the new scientific thought, and the conviction that there should be no restraint on the individual's right to examine objectively and to express himself on all human institutions and thought, including government and religion. By this time he had read with approval Locke, Fénelon, Montaigne, Montesquieu, and Bayle, and had published his *Henriade.* As a consequence, he was known and accepted by the English, including Alexander Pope, who appreciated his work.

That his English experience had a powerful impact is attested by the *Homilies,* which have a London date line and were published in France forty years later, in 1767 and 1769. In them, Voltaire assumes the posture of an Englishman addressing his fellow countrymen. The influence of Newton's physics and Clarke's astronomy was very important, for Voltaire was determined that the irrational and absurd ideas of the world, dogmatized in religious literature, must give way to the scientific findings of physics and astronomy. To that end he set out to popularize the new science (in which he was an amateur) and to apply its findings to biblical criticism as exemplified in the *Second Homily.*

Voltaire is generally acclaimed as the first popularizer, as the first in modern times to lay before the public scientific knowledge that challenged the Church's monopoly of erudition, and the first to set up modern methods of historical criticism and historiography, which he carried over into the analysis of religion, as in the *Important Study.*

Returning to France in 1729, Voltaire resumed his old place in Parisian life, complete with critics and enemies. As usual, he was active in the theater and in writing poetry and new tragedies, among them *Zaïre,* and *L'Histoire de Charles XII* (The History of Charles XII). But he was also composing *Les Lettres Philosophiques* (The Philosophical Letters) which praised English freedom of the individual. They were badly received by Cardinal Fleury, prime minister for the Regency. For despite Voltaire's efforts to have their publication confined to England, they appeared in

France in 1734. Hearing of the issue of a new *lettre de cachet*, he fled into voluntary exile, taking up residence with Mme. du Chatelet on her estate at Cirey, an easy distance from Lorraine, beyond the jurisdiction of the king of France.

Thus began what is commonly referred to as Voltaire's Cirey period, from 1734 to the death of Mme. du Chatelet in 1749. There were many interruptions: travel, a stay at the court of Frederick II, and a return to the French court with great royal favor—abruptly lost when Voltaire remarked in English to Mme. du Chatelet when she lost a considerable sum at the court's gaming tables that there had been cheating.

At Cirey Voltaire relaxed, received guests, and gave dinners at which he read his poetry and excerpts from the yet-to-be published *Le Siècle de Louis XIV* (The Century of Louis XIV). With his guests he acted parts in *Mérope* and *Zaïre*. There was a continuous round of pleasure and display of the volatile Voltairian temperament. The wonder is that he and the scholarly Émilie du Chatelet found time to engage in a prolonged and intensive study of science and religion.

It was at Cirey that Voltaire and his partner gathered the evidence and formed the convictions expressed in his religious polemics, a few of which appeared in published form in the 1750's,[1] were produced in quantity in the 1760's, and tapered off in the 1770's. He and *la belle Émilie* researched and studied the Scriptures, the history of the Church, the literature of early Christian apologetics, hagiography, and the history of the Jews. They relied heavily upon the Benedictine Dom Calmet's 120 volumes of *Commentaries*, exact and critical in their treatment of the Old and New

---

[1] *Le Sermon des Cinquante* (The Sermon of the Fifty) was written probably about 1746–1749 and read by Voltaire at the court of Frederick II in 1751; the first date of its publication is uncertain. Beuchot says that this was Voltaire's first attack on Christianity. The *Sermon* was of such a nature that Voltaire attributed it to La Mettrie, an atheist in residence with Frederick, who died in the spring of 1751. Acknowledgment of authorship (Voltaire was suspect) would have meant the Bastille or worse. Mme. du Chatelet is said to have kept the manuscript under lock and key.

Testaments. Each compiled an *Examen* (examination or study) of the Scriptures, but Voltaire prided himself on widening the scope of his religious study to include the Muslim, Chinese, and Hindu religions, whereas Mme. du Chatelet continued to treat only of Christianity and Judaism. But it was the Voltairian style, the talent for caustic, satirical, and witty expression that commanded reader interest. He was the fighter who throve on publicity; and, surviving Émilie by nearly thirty years, he received the credit for the work of the partnership.

Voltaire, saddened by the death of Mme. du Chatelet, who had been mother, mistress, protector, and balance wheel as well as fellow scholar, turned to a life of heightened activity and complexity. Now in his middle fifties, he maintained during the remainder of his life a voluminous correspondence all over Europe with persons of all estates, with Frederick II, Catherine II, Benedict XIV, Mme. Pompadour, and statesmen and ordinary citizens of many nationalities. *Le Siècle de Louis XIV* and the *Essai sur les Moeurs et l'Esprit des Nations* (Essay on the Manners and Spirit of Nations) were completed. For a man of his age who constantly complained of ill health, he displayed an extraordinary, tireless energy.

Now a man of considerable wealth, he acquired Les Délices, an estate near Geneva, but, being unable to get along with the city fathers who disapproved of his theater and his remarks, he crossed over into France to lease Ferney, an estate a half-hour's distance from Geneva. This put him in an excellent position to protect himself from either the government of France or that of Geneva. It was here that Voltaire established his principal residence during the last twenty years of his life.

Ferney became the object of pilgrimage from all over Europe, for Voltaire was now an international celebrity. He received his guests in the manner of an aristocrat and dressed the same way. He was an actor constantly on stage, displaying with appropriate gestures the proper emotion. The goings-on at Ferney became the

talk of Europe; whether slander, praise, or just gossip, it was
publicity that the old man (crossing the sixties into his seventies
and eighties) sought and loved.

Despite the demands on his time made by his many involve-
ments, the patriarch of Ferney pursued his now prime objectives:
*écrasez l'infâme* (crush the infamy) and to improve French society.
He took it upon himself to broadcast the barbarous injustice done
Jean Calas and his family—Protestants—by the *Parlement* of Tou-
louse. The *Parlement* had condemned Calas and had him broken
on the wheel for the murder of his son who had converted to
Catholicism; the family, its property forfeited to the state, was in
desperate straits. Voltaire's investigation of the case proved the
*Parlement* wrong. Calas was vindicated posthumously, and his
possessions were returned to the family. This affair, and a number
of others in which he intervened, established him as a molder of
public opinion and created a French public waiting to see what was
to come next.

Next to come was a stream of polemics on religion—the result
of his and Mme. du Chatelet's work at Cirey—despite the attempts
of the government and Church to suppress them and to prevent
their distribution. A considerable number were published in
pamphlet form in the 1760's after Voltaire had turned seventy. He
maintained that the public would always purchase a pamphlet for a
few sous rather than pay out francs for weighty tomes; therefore, if
he had a message to reach the public in his campaign *écraser l'infâme* (to crush the infamy of ignorance, superstition, bigotry,
and fanaticism), he would issue it in pamphlet form. Moreover,
pamphlets could be printed serially or periodically with revisions or
new points of view. The essays here translated appeared originally
in pamphlets and were later incorporated in a complete collection
of his works, begun by Voltaire himself and expanded greatly
since.

But there was a price to pay. In visits to Geneva and Paris his
health began to break under the strain of public adulation in the

streets and at the theater. In spite of the fact that he was eighty-
three or eighty-four, he kept hard at work till all hours, drinking
quantities of coffee and using opiates to see him through. He died
in Paris at eleven at night, May 30, 1778. He was refused burial in
consecrated ground in Paris because his signed confession of faith
was unacceptable, and his nephew, Abbé Mignot, transported his
body to the Abbey de Scellières in Champagne, where it was
buried. The official permitting the burial was discharged from his
post.

Voltaire wrote, "They wanted to bury me but I outwitted them";
it seems he was right in two ways. An enthusiastic mob brought his
body back to Paris during the French Revolution for interment in
the Panthéon. His works, especially *Candide*, have been translated
in many languages and new biographies of him in English have
been published as recently as 1966 and 1969. It may be that
interest in Voltaire's works reaches a peak in periods of
triumphant liberalism and fades during eras of reaction, but
Voltaire will live on as long as there is an interest in crushing *l'infâme*.


## ii


Voltaire on the subject of religion, together with some of his correspondence on many subjects, is collected in that section of his
*Oeuvres Complètes* that the Hachette and the Garnier Frères (Moland) editions label *Mélanges*. Two, among others of his disquisi-
tions on religion, *The Bible Finally Explained* and *The History of
the Origin of Christianity*, run to nearly book length. In these
Voltaire expanded his discussion and criticisms without adding sig-
nificantly to the principal ideas incorporated in the briefer works
here translated.

Considering the number of biblical stories the credibility of which it is possible to challenge, Voltaire limited himself to a relative few, with the consequence that he becomes repetitious. Under different titles, the same themes are recurrent in many pamphlets: Abraham and Sarah, Moses in Egypt, Noah and the Ark, the bloody rivalry among the Jewish kings, the competition among the prophets. In the New Testament he makes much of the flight to Egypt, the confusion in the Gospels, and points out that there are sources for the life of Jesus and Mary other than in authorized biblical literature.

He charges the Church Fathers of the early centuries with religious inventions and innovations that have no foundation either in the life of Jesus or the Old and New Testaments. He condemns the usurpation of the imperial authority of Rome by the popes, and denounces the bigotry, superstition, ignorance, and fanaticism of the Christians that impelled them to a constant and bloody persecution of one another. In peroration, Voltaire pleads for a true religion (on the model of Deism) that devoid of power structure, politics, and wealth—worships a God of mercy, humanity, and tolerance.

Voltaire summarizes his thoughts on these themes and several others in the texts selected for translation. *Zapata's Questions* are given first place because they contain the essence, a distillation of the Voltairian sharp, mocking, satirical (hence provocative) analysis of the Scriptures and Christianity. In this respect he sometimes seems to become carried away with himself, he is *l'enfant terrible,* making witticisms that have a *double entendre* or are of questionable propriety or exceed what many would consider to be the bounds of normal restraint.

In the five *Homilies* that follow there is set forth his concept of God, of a true, "natural" religion that he calls "theism," in which all the evils of Christianity and Judaism are swept away. *An Important Study by Lord Bolingbroke* is a more intensive analysis, and at greater length, of Voltaire's favorite subjects, the Old and the New Testaments, the Church Fathers, and the Roman Catholic papacy. Here also are extensions of his proofs of the viciousness of bigotry, hysterical sectarianism, and the corruption of the Church by wealth and power.

Finding little good in Judaeo-Christian dogma, belief, and practice, Voltaire contradicts the greatness of those personages, secular or ecclesiastical, whom the Church honors and reveres; conversely he praises those men, particularly the Roman emperors, whom the Church declares to have been persecutors of Christians. Diocletian, whose wife was Christian, was a tolerant emperor who finally had to take action against the lawless Christians threatening the security of the Empire. Julian the Apostate, to whom Voltaire was particularly devoted, is pictured as the victim of the malignancy of the Christians because he reinstated the Roman religion under which the Empire was formerly vigorous and successful, as compared to its ultimate precarious state of ill health, for which the intolerant Christians were criminally responsible. To Voltaire, Constantine and Theodosius and their offspring were murderous monsters, guilty of a long list of crimes against God and man. Yet Constantine and Theodosius were sainted by the Church.

In contrast to strife-torn, inhuman, and intolerant Christianity, Voltaire has some interesting points to make with the virtues of other religions. The Roman, he says, was tolerant of every sectarian group; all that it asked of an individual or any society was loyalty to the state. Islam sheds no blood over doctrinal disputes, adhering uniformly to the one god and his prophet who neither claimed godhood nor was ever regarded as god. Brahmanism is the purest of all religions in its acceptance of the literature of the *Vedas* that prescribe peace and serenity as the greatest of man's goals.

Whether or not Voltaire believed these statements, or was qualified to make them, is beside the point. The romanticizing and idealizing of whatever cause he adopted was a part of the Voltairian mystique. Furthermore such statements were undoubtedly calculated to infuriate "good" Christians while conditioning sympathetic readers to use their reason and common sense in examining Christianity and Judaism.

# iii

The task at hand, *écraser l'infâme,* required the use of every wile, technique, device, and skill at the command of the philosophe-poet-dramatist-historian, Voltaire. *Zapata's Questions* are dramatized with an imagined author and setting, leading to a dramatic end which does not obscure its Voltairian source. Fiction is employed frequently in other instances, with Voltaire unmistakably on stage no matter what the name of the character in which he casts himself. In the five *Homilies* he is an Englishman preaching to Englishmen in a vein that he feels certain will appeal to Deists; in the *Important Study* he is English; as the translator and editor of Lord Bolingbroke's précis of his own *Works,* he carries on an indirect dialogue with "milord" in extensive footnotes. These essays are a limited sampling of the many religious polemics in which Voltaire is the central figure, manipulating a puppet *dramatis personae* whose names and sites are sometimes real, but more often supplied by Voltaire's always fertile imagination. Given his great sense of drama, his ebullient, pixie temperament, and his evident desire to please himself as well as the public with his writing, it would seem that such literary adventures should come as no surprise.

Perhaps Voltaire was too free and easy with the names and the works of others. Judgments that amount to accusations of fraud, plagiarism, and expediency have been pronounced upon him. N. L.

Torrey[1] maintains that Voltaire abused the name of Bolingbroke
and blamed other English Deists for his work in order to gain
greater freedom from French official censorship. He also believes
that Voltaire's work was not original, in that he adapted or
adopted outright the work of Woolston on miracles, Annet's
analysis of Paul, Tindal on the subject of the prophets, and that
his Greek quotations are all from the *Codex Apocrypha* of Fabri-
cius. But to oppose such a viewpoint there is Voltaire's *Lettres à
S.A. Mgr. le Prince de*** (Letters to His Highness the Prince of
Brunswick-Lunébourg)[2] in which he reviews at length those "who
have spoken ill of the Christian religion," from the precursors of
Rabelais to his own contemporaries in France, England, Italy, and
Germany. To quote Gustave Lanson: "England matured, armed,
and excited Voltaire, but she did not create him."[3]

Henry St. John, Viscount Bolingbroke, and Voltaire were well
enough acquainted; Voltaire visited Bolingbroke in France and
received financial assistance and aid from him in London in 1726
and 1727. Bolingbroke, Secretary of War 1704–1708, and
Secretary of State in 1710 under Queen Anne, suffered political
defeat in 1735. He went into exile on his French estate at Argeville,
where Voltaire visited him on occasion until the Englishman's
death in 1751. Their relationship resembled that of patron and
client, with Voltaire the suitor. As a result of an offer to dedicate
the *Henriade* to him in 1727, although he already had accepted the
dedication of *Brutus*, Bolingbroke suspected Voltaire's sincerity
and "verbiage." Voltaire may not have been aware that he was
held suspect for, in defense of Bolingbroke's *Letters on History*
that was attacked by Warburton, he published in English *Défense
de Milord Bolingbroke, par le Docteur Goodnatured Wellwisher,
Chapelain du Comte de Chesterfield* (Defense of Lord

---

[1] N. L. Torrey, *Voltaire and the English Deists*, New York, 1930. See also N. L.
Torrey, *The Spirit of Voltaire*, New York, 1938.

[2] One of the *Miscellany*.

[3] Gustave Lanson, *Voltaire*, New York, 1966, p. 36, in response to John Morley's
assertion that, "Voltaire left France a poet, he returned to it a sage."

Bolingbroke, by the Doctor Goodnatured Wellwisher, Chaplain to Lord Chesterfield), two years after Bolingbroke's death.

There is no evidence that *An Important Study by Lord Bolingbroke*, billed as a précis of his *Works*[1] addressed to Lord Cornsbury, exists among the collected writings and publications of Bolingbroke, nor is there any evidence that he was in any way aware of it. The language and style of the *Important Study* bear no relation to Bolingbroke's philosophical and rather ponderous mode of expression in the five volumes of his *Works*, but are distinctly the language and style of Voltaire (who possessed a practically unused set of the *Works*). In the light of all the evidence, authorities agree that Voltaire was the author of the *Important Study*, written probably in his Cirey period and published in 1767, well after Bolingbroke's death, and not in 1736, as appears beneath the title. Why the date 1736? Why the use of his friend's name when Voltaire was so obviously the author? Did he wish to honor Bolingbroke? Was he deliberately perpetrating a fraud? Or was it simply an expedient for avoiding official censure? Was he so much of the theater that whatever he wrote must have a plot and a cast? Then again, it was and is an admitted practice of pamphleteers to be anonymous, or to adopt pseudonyms, or to put the names of others to their work rather than their own,

In answering these questions there exists a temptation to pass moral judgment on what appear to be devious and dishonest practices. But it cannot be forgotten that Voltaire was fighting to destroy fanaticism, superstition, and ignorance in the Christian religion as a part of his total campaign to crush infamy everywhere. In the course of battle, "he was always bitten and always biting," as Lanson says. "Bitten" by Church and State and personal enemies seeking every means to put an end to his "biting," Voltaire took heed of his own maxims: "never clash with the dominant superstition if you are not powerful enough to resist

---

[1] Published by David Mallett in 1754. Dr. Johnson said about the *Works* that it was the gun charged against Christianity.

it, or clever enough to escape the consequences," and persons who have desired "to stir up the populace without being sufficiently clever, either to arm such a populace, or to win for themselves powerful protectors . . . for the most part end up being hanged."

Voltaire died a natural death still a Catholic. His fame and reputation were international, his influence in France immense. A great many of the reforms that he advocated in French government and the judiciary were accomplished by the French Revolution, and in fact he may have exerted the greatest single force to bring on the Revolution or at least to pave the way for it. He hated war and revered freedom of thought; in his effort to improve the human condition, he was the greatest of the protesters of the status quo in eighteenth-century France and Europe. Voltaire would be among today's nonviolent protesters, blasting the Establishment with merciless satire, if he were well protected by friends in high places and invulnerable to consequences.

## iv

An important obligation rests upon the historian to produce sound and accurate statements based upon sources the validity of which he has established. Voltaire stunned his contemporaries, used to accepting as authority what had previously been written, with the enunciation of this principle developed in the course of his research for *Le Siècle de Louis XIV*. But he conveniently forgot his own rule if it got in the way of one primary objective in his writing of pamphlets—to make startling statements that hit the reader forcefully enough to leave a lasting impression. Let the scholarly pedants ferret out the errors; let a Larcher or an Abbé Guénée or an ex-Jesuit Nonotte gleefully expose the inaccuracies of his biblical citations and historical references. Theirs was a nitpicking operation that did not attack the major theses upon which Voltaire pounded away: the evils of fanaticism, superstition, ignorance—that is, *l'infâme*—and the absurd, irrational, and vicious practices and beliefs of Christianity and Judaism founded upon false history.

In the course of berating the Jews and Christians for their errors and inaccuracies, Voltaire committed a few of his own. Some of them occur repeatedly in these essays and elsewhere, since he seems to have drawn on a standard stock of topics and arguments that could be repeated under different titles.

Those familiar with the Bible will probably be irritated by these mistakes and by minor omissions from well-known passages. Quite evidently, Voltaire painted with a broad brush, seemingly impatient with the routine of quoting biblical text. Whatever the inclination to discount Voltaire because of his errors, it is a mistake not to read him carefully. In quoting Isaiah 7:14, he uses the word *"almah,"* which Beuchot, in a footnote, corrects to the usage of the Vulgate, *"vergo,"* virgin. The Hebrew *"almah"* signifies a young woman, not necessarily a virgin; another word, *"bethûlāh,"* means specifically a virgin. Voltaire here is rejecting *"vergo"* as an incorrect translation of the Hebrew *"almah,"* and in a footnote attacks the Christian notion that this passage in Isaiah foretells the virgin birth of Jesus.

Throughout his essays Voltaire displays a broad knowledge of history and its sources; for the most part, his statements are reliable. Infrequently, however, there are questions to be raised. He repeatedly ridicules Luke's statement that Augustus ordered a census of the empire. It has since been shown that Herod ordered a census in Palestine and acted with a Roman official, Sentius Saturninus, to carry it out at the time of the birth of Jesus. Herod's census was possibly the result of Augustus' order to take a census of the Empire's eastern provinces, which were near bankruptcy.[1]

In his discussion of the *Person of Moses*, Voltaire refers to a

[1] L. R. Taylor, *American Journal of Philology,* 1933, p. 120.

Phoenician historian, Sanchuniathon (c. 1000 B.C.), citing his silence on the subject of the book of Genesis and the Jewish Horde as evidence that Genesis and Moses are not nearly as ancient nor as authentic as the Jews claim. The credibility of such a thesis is impaired by the question of whether or not there was a Sanchuniathon, a name which means "the entire law of Chon," the deity of Tyre. Originally accepted as contemporary with the Trojan War, this name came to be regarded as mythological.

To Philon of Byblos (second century A.D.) is attributed a translation (his invention?) of Sanchuniathon's *Phoenician History*, used by Porphyry to prove that Genesis was not revealed to Moses, but was taken from the *Phoenician History*. Eusebius, in his *Demonstratio Evangelica*, cites Philon to combat Porphyry, thereby preserving the only known passages from the *History*. None of this makes for a strong support of the argument that Sanchuniathon's negative evidence possessed the significance attached to it by Voltaire.

Francesco Pazzi, with the support of Sixtus IV, the Archbishop of Florence, and the King of Naples, all enemies of the Medici family, plotted the murder of Giuliano and Lorenzo (the Magnificent) in, says Voltaire (p. 49), the Florentine church of La Reparada. Giuliano was killed April 26, 1478 (Lorenzo escaped) in Santa Maria del Fiore (Il Duomo), which had been built about two centuries before the murder, on the site of the old Santa Reparata. What purpose this bit of confusion served Voltaire is difficult to fathom.

Commentators have remarked his numerous errors and inaccuracies, of which the ones appearing in these translations are characteristic. Their significance in estimating the worth and reliability of Voltaire's arguments and conclusions will necessarily be an individual decision.

V

Voltaire appended extensive footnotes throughout the texts of his religious writings. Sometimes they are so extensive that it seems they are in reality a part of the text. For those who read principally only the text, neglecting the footnotes, Voltaire's practice will be somewhat disconcerting for the reason that therein are often contained the hardest-hitting passages of the work. Moreover, Voltaire seldom used footnotes to explain a fact or to refer to the source of a statement, as is the modern usage; quite often such matters are included in his text, leaving to the footnote an extension of his arguments on any given point. It is therefore advisable to regard a whole page of Voltaire as text without respect to the way in which it is divided; otherwise much of the caustic wit and outrageous statement that so angered his critics and so pleased his admirers will be overlooked.

There is evidence offered in a few of Voltaire's footnotes that, aided by Jacques Decroix, he reviewed the *Miscellany* toward the end of his life. The dates 1771, 1774, 1775, and 1776 appear principally in connection with the *Important Study* and a footnote signed "Decroix" (but undoubtedly written by Voltaire) must have been signed after 1774. Voltaire's footnotes are signed *Voltaire*.

The name of M. Beuchot occurs frequently in both the Hachette and Garnier (Moland) editions of the *Miscellany*. Adrian Jean Quentin Beuchot (1773–1851), military surgeon during the French Revolution, bibliographer, philologist, librarian, and author, appears to have played a significant part in the collecting, organizing, classifying, and editing of Voltaire's works. This is of particular interest with respect to the *Miscellany*.

He is acknowledged as the author of the preface, foreword, and notes of the Lefevre edition (also referred to as the *Édition Beu-*

*chot*) that came out 1829–1840 in about the same period, 1785–1834, as the Kehl, Gotka, Renouard, Baudoin, Sautelet, and Delangle editions of *The Complete Works of Voltaire* (Les Oeuvres Complètes de Voltaire) under various editors. (The introduction to the Garnier [Moland] edition lists fifty-one previous editions of Voltaire's *Complete Works* but does not include the Hachette.) Only Beuchot's notes and textual format, apparently unchanged after his death, survived in the Hachette and Garnier (Moland) editions. It must be concluded that in his own time Beuchot was considered a competent, even indispensable, editor of Voltaire with all the influence that such a person can exert on notation, format, and inclusion or exclusion of material. Beuchot's footnotes are signed *Beuchot*.

Because Voltaire and his editor Beuchot possibly assumed that it was unnecessary to explain to French readers many of the references to French, ancient, classical, medieval, and Renaissance history and persons, the present volume also contains footnotes by the translator, each indicated by an asterisk and initialed *kwa*. These relate to matters of fact and to the translation of the occasional quotations in Latin and Greek either from Voltaire's French version of the quote or directly from the quote when a French translation is lacking. In general, when translation of French sources was necessary about persons, places, or situations spoken of in the text, a footnote is appended. A number of French reference works were consulted for this purpose, particularly Larousse's *Grand Dictionnaire Universel,* Paris, 1865, and René Pomeau, *La Religion de Voltaire*, Paris, 1956.

Items about which information is readily available in standard reference works in English are not usually footnoted. Questions about classical history and mythology, English writers and statesmen, popes and cardinals, prominent French *philosophes* and kings, and references to the books of the Old and New Testaments may be resolved by consulting: *The British Dictionary of National Biography, The Oxford Classical Dictionary;* the King James

*Bible*; the Douay *Bible; The Oxford Companion to French Literature;* S. Baring Gould's *Lives of the Saints*; McGiffert's *Fathers of the Church; The Oxford Dictionary of the Christian Church,* and the *Jewish Encyclopedia.*

The latest treatments in English of the many aspects of Voltaire's complex life are available in Gustave Lanson, *Voltaire*, translated by Robert A. Wagoner, with an Introduction by Peter Gay and a Commentary by René Pomeau (Wiley and Sons, New York, 1966), and Theodore Besterman, *Voltaire* (Harcourt Brace and World Inc., New York, 1969).

# ZAPATA'S QUESTIONS

*Translated by the Sieur Tamponet, Doctor of the Sorbonne (1767)*

The Licentiate Zapata, appointed professor of theology at the University of Salamanca, presented these questions to the Council of Doctors in 1629. They were suppressed. The Spanish original is in the Brunswick Library.

*Wise Masters:*

(1) How may I undertake to prove that the Jews, whom we burn by the hundreds, were for four thousand years God's chosen people?

(2) Why did God, whom we cannot without blasphemy consider unjust, abandon the entire earth for a small group of Jews and then abandon this small group for another, which was for two hundred years much smaller and more despised?

(3) Why did he perform innumerable incomprehensible miracles in favor of this puny nation before the beginning of recorded history? Why has he not done more in the last few centuries? and why do we never see any, we who are the people of God?

(4) If God is the God of Abraham, why do you burn the children of Abraham? And since you do burn them, why do you recite their prayers, even while burning them? How can you, who adore their book of law, put them to death for having followed this law?

(5) How shall I reconcile the chronology of the Chinese, the Chaldeans, the Phoenicians, and the Egyptians with that of the Jews? and how shall I reconcile the forty different ways commentators have used to compute time? When I say that God dictated this book, I shall be told that God obviously doesn't know chronology.

(6) What arguments shall I use to prove that the books attributed to Moses were written by him in the desert? Could he say that he wrote on the other side of the Jordan when he had never crossed the Jordan? I will be told that God obviously doesn't know geography.

(7) The book entitled Joshua says that Joshua caused Deuteronomy to be graven upon stones coated with mortar: this passage from Joshua and those of earlier authors evidently prove that from the time of Moses and Joshua Oriental peoples inscribed their laws and their observations upon stone and brick. The Pentateuch tells us that in the desert the Jewish people lacked food and clothing; it therefore seems improbable that they would have had persons skillful enough to engrave a lengthy book when they had neither tailors nor shoemakers. In any case, how was a long work inscribed in mortar preserved?

(8) What is the best manner of refuting the objections of savants who find in the Pentateuch the names of cities that did not then exist, precepts for kings whom Jews regarded with horror and who did not govern until seven centuries after Moses, and finally some passages in which the author, who came long after Moses, betrays himself by stating: "The bed of Og [Deut. 3:11] that one still sees today at Rabbath . . . " " . . . and the Canaanite [Gen. 12:6] was then in the land." Etc. etc., etc?

These scholars, pointing to the difficulties and contradictions that they impute to the Jewish chronicles, can give licenciates a bit of trouble.

(9) Is the book of Genesis literal or allegorical? Did God really take a rib from Adam in order to make a woman? and why is it previously stated that he created them male and female? how did God create the light before the sun? how did he divide the light from

darkness since darkness is nothing other than the absence of light? how could he make the day before the sun was made? how was the firmament formed in the midst of the waters since there is no firmament, this false notion existing only in the imagination of the ancient Greeks? There are some who conjecture that Genesis was written only after the Jews had some knowledge of the erroneous philosophy of other peoples and I shall be subjected to the pain of hearing that God knows no more about physics than about chronology and geography.

(10) What shall I say of the Garden of Eden from which emanated a river that divided into four rivers: the Tigris, the Euphrates, the Phison—now believed to be the Phase—and the Gehon, which flows in Ethiopia and which in consequence can only be the Nile and whose source is a thousand leagues distant from the source of the Euphrates? I shall again be told that God is a bad geographer.

(11) I wholeheartedly long to eat of the fruit that hung from the tree of knowledge, and it seems to me that the prohibition against eating it is strange; having given man reason, God should have encouraged him to learn. Did he want to be served by a dunce? I should also like to speak to the serpent since he had so much sense; but I should like to know what language he spoke. The Emperor Julian, that great philosopher, asked this question of the great St. Cyril, who was unable to answer and told the wise emperor: "It is you who are the serpent." St. Cyril was not polite, but please note that he responded with this theological impertinence only after Julian was dead.

Genesis says that the serpent eats earth; you know that Genesis is mistaken and that earth alone nourishes no one. Given that God came every day at noon to stroll familiarly in the garden, and chat with Adam and Eve and the serpent, it would be very agreeable to make up a foursome. But since I believe you better suited to the company that Joseph and Mary had in the stable in Bethlehem, I shall not suggest a journey to Eden, especially since the door is guarded by a cherub armed to the teeth. It is true that, according to the rabbis, cherub means ox. Now there's a strange gatekeeper! Please, at least tell me what a cherub is.

(12) How shall I explain the story of the angels who became enamored of the daughters of men and who begat the giants? Will someone not object that this story is taken from pagan fables? But since the Jews invented everything in the desert, and since they were very ingenious, all other nations must clearly have taken their knowledge from the Jews. Homer, Plato, Cicero, Vergil knew nothing they did not learn from the Jews. Is that not demonstrated?

(13) How shall I explain the deluge, the cataracts from the sky that has no cataracts, all the animals brought from Japan, Africa, America, and southern lands, penned in a great coffer with their provisions for drinking and eating for a year, to say nothing of the time in which the earth, still too wet, was unable to produce their nourishment? How could Noah's small household have provided all these animals with the kind of food they needed? It was composed of only eight persons.

(14) How shall I make the history of the Tower of Babel sound plausible? This tower must have been higher than the pyramids of Egypt since God let the pyramids be built. Did it reach to Venus, or at least to the moon?

(15) By what artifices shall I justify the two falsehoods of Abraham, father of the faithful, who, if we count accurately, was one hundred and thirty-five when in Egypt and at Gerar he passed off the beautiful Sarah as his sister so that the kings of those lands might fall in love with her and make him presents? Shame! How base it is to sell one's wife!

(16) Give me the reasons that will explain to me why in spite of the fact that God commanded all Abraham's posterity to practice circumcision, it was not done under Moses?

(17) Can I figure out for myself whether the three angels to whom Sarah served a whole calf to eat, had bodies or if they borrowed them? And how can it be that when God sent two angels to Sodom the Sodomites desired to commit a certain sin with these angels? They must have been a nice lot. But why did Lot the Just offer his

two daughters to the Sodomites in place of the two angels? What girls! They even slept with their father from time to time. Ah! wise masters, that is not decent!

(18) Will people believe me when I tell them that Lot's wife was changed into a statue of salt? What shall I reply to those who tell me that this is perhaps a crude imitation of the ancient story of Eurydice, and that a statue of salt could not have stood up under rain?

(19) What shall I say when it becomes necessary to justify the blessings bestowed upon Jacob the Just who tricked his father, Isaac, and robbed Laban, his father-in-law? How shall I explain that God appeared to him at the top of a ladder? and how Jacob fought the whole night against an angel? etc., etc.

(20) How may I treat of the sojourn of the Jews in Egypt and of their escape? Exodus says that they stayed there four hundred years; a careful count shows only two hundred and five years [Ex. 12:40, says four hundred thirty years]. Why did Pharaoh's daughter bathe in the Nile, where no one ever bathes, because of the crocodiles? etc., etc.

(21) Moses having espoused the daughter of an idolator, how could God take him as his prophet without reproaching him for that marriage? How did Pharaoh's magicians do the same miracles as Moses, except those of covering the country with lice and vermin? How did they change into blood the water that had already been changed into blood by Moses? How was it that Moses, guided by God himself, and finding himself at the head of 630,000 troops, fled with his people, instead of conquering Egypt, whose first-born had already been put to death by God himself? Egypt has never assembled an army of 100,000 men since it was first mentioned in recorded history. Why did Moses fleeing with his troops from the land of Goshen, traverse half of Egypt and go back toward Memphis between Baalzephan and the Red Sea instead of following a direct route into Canaan? Finally, how could Pharaoh pursue with all his cavalry, since in the fifth plague visited on Egypt God caused

all horses and all animals to perish, and since furthermore Egypt, divided by waterways, had very little cavalry?

(22) How shall I reconcile what is said in Exodus with the discourse of St. Stephen in the Acts of the Apostles and with the passages from Jeremiah and Amos? Exodus says that sacrifices were made to Jehovah during forty years in the desert [Ex. 16:35]; Jeremiah, Amos [5:25], and St. Stephen [Acts 7:42] say that neither sacrifice nor host was offered during that time. Exodus [11:3] says they made the tabernacle in which was the ark of the covenant; and St. Stephen, in the Acts [7:43], says they carried the tabernacle of Moloch and Remphan.

(23) I am not enough of a chemist to explain away successfully the golden calf that Exodus says had been made in a single day, and that Moses reduced to cinders. Are these two miracles? Are they two deeds possible to human artifice?

(24) Is it also a miracle that the leader of a nation in a desert caused the slaughter of twenty-three thousand men of that nation by only one of the twelve tribes, and that twenty-three thousand men let themselves be massacred without defending themselves?

(25) Again, must I regard as a miracle, or as an act of ordinary justice, that twenty-four thousand Hebrews were slaughtered because one among them had lain with a Midianite woman, while Moses himself had taken a Midianite woman to wife? and those Hebrews who had been portrayed as so ferocious, were they not good fellows to permit themselves thus to be massacred for some girls? And apropos of girls, shall I be able to keep a straight face when I say that Moses found thirty-two thousand virgins in the Midianite camp, with sixty-one thousand asses? That's not two asses per maiden.

(26) How shall I explain the law that forbids the eating of hare because "they chew the cud, but divide not the hoof." [Deut. 14:7], whereas hares have a split hoof and are not ruminant? We have already seen that this good book has made of God a bad geographer, a bad chronologist, a bad physicist; it makes him no better a natu-

ralist. What reasons shall I give for the many no less wise laws, as that of the waters of enviousness, and the death punishment for a man who has lain with his wife during her menses? etc., etc., etc. How can I justify these barbarous and ridiculous laws that, it is said, emanated from God himself?

(27) What shall I reply to those who will be astonished that a miracle was necessary in order to cross the Jordan, which at its greatest width is no more than forty-five feet, which could easily be crossed with any sort of float, and which could be forded at so many places—witness the forty-two thousand Ephraimites slain at one ford of this river by their brethren?

(28) What shall I reply to those who ask how the walls of Jericho fell at a single blast of the trumpets, and why the other cities did not fall in the same manner?

(29) How shall I excuse the behavior of the courtesan Rahab, who betrayed Jericho, her fatherland? and why was this treason necessary since it sufficed only to sound a trumpet in order to take the city? and how shall I probe the profundity of the divine decrees which so ordered things that our divine Saviour, Jesus Christ, was born of this courtesan Rahab, as well as of the incest that Tamar committed with Judah, her father-in-law, and of the adultery of David and Bathsheba? so many of the ways of God are incomprehensible!

(30) How can I approve of Joshua, who hanged thirty-one petty kings whose small states, that is, villages, he usurped?

(31) How shall I talk about the battle between Joshua and the Amorites at Beth-horon on the Gibeon road? The Lord caused great stones to rain from the sky over the distance between Beth-horon to Azekah; five leagues separate Beth-horon from Azekah; so, the Amorites were exterminated by boulders that fell from the sky over a space of five leagues. The Scripture says that it was midday; why then did Joshua order the sun and the moon to stay themselves in the midst of the sky in order to give him time to achieve the defeat of a small force that was already exterminated? why did he order the moon to halt at midday? and how did the sun and the moon remain

in the same place an entire day? to what commentator shall I have recourse to explain this extraordinary verity?

(32) What shall I say of Jephtha, who sacrificed his daughter and caused to be massacred forty-two thousand Jews of the tribe of Ephraim who could not pronounce *shibboleth*?

(33) Must I affirm or deny that the law of the Jews make no mention anywhere of punishments or rewards after death? how can it be that neither Moses nor Joshua spoke of the immortality of the soul, known dogma of the ancient Egyptians, Chaldeans, Persians, and Greeks, dogma that had a little vogue among the Jews only after Alexander and that the Sadducees continued to reject because it is not in the Pentateuch?

(34) Just how shall I explain the story of the Levite who having come upon his ass to Gibeon, city of the Benjamites, became the object of the sodomitic passion of all the Gibeonites who wished to violate him? He abandoned his wife to them and the Gibeonites lay with her throughout the whole night. She died of it the next day. If the Sodomites had accepted the two daughters of Lot in place of the two angels, would the girls have died of it?

(35) I need your instruction in order to understand verse 19 of the first chapter of Judges: "The Lord accompanied Judah and made him master of the mountains; but he could not defeat the inhabitants of the valley because they had a great number of chariots armed with scythes." I cannot, with my feeble brain, comprehend how the God of heaven and of earth, who had changed the natural order so many times and suspended eternal laws in favor of his Jewish people, could not manage to vanquish the inhabitants of a valley because they had chariots. Could it be true, as many scholars claim, that at the time the Jews looked upon their god as a local, protective deity who sometimes was more powerful than the enemy gods, and sometimes less powerful? and is not that proven again by this response of Jephtha [Judges 11:24]: "You rightfully possess that which your God Chemoth has given you, therefore allow us to take what our God Adonai has promised us"?

(36) I shall add furthermore that it is difficult to believe that

there were so many chariots armed with scythes in a mountainous country, whereas the Scripture says in so many places, the greatest glory came from being mounted on an ass.

(37) The story of Ehud gives me even more trouble. I see the Jews nearly always enslaved, despite the aid of their god, who had promised upon oath to give them all the land between the Nile, the sea, and the Euphrates. For eighteen years they were subjects of a petty king named Eglon, when God, to help them, sent Ehud, son of Gera, who was able to use his left hand as well as his right hand. Ehud, son of Gera, having had a double-edged dagger made, hid it under his cloak, as did later Jacques Clement and Ravaillac.* He asks the petty king for a secret audience; he says he has a secret of the greatest importance to communicate to him on behalf of God. Eglon arises respectfully and Ehud with his left hand stabs him in the stomach. God completely approved of this act which, in the moral code of all nations of the earth, seems somewhat harsh. Tell me, which is the most divine assassination, that by St. Ehud, or by St. David, who caused the assassination of his cuckold Uriah, or by the blessed Solomon, who, having seven hundred wives and three hundred concubines, assassinated his brother Adonijah because he asked him for one of them, etc., etc., etc.

(38) Pray tell me by what cunning did Samson capture three hundred foxes, tie them together by their tails, and attach torches to their rumps in order to set fire to the crops of the Philistines. Foxes inhabit only wooded country. There was no forest in that area, and it seems difficult enough to take three hundred live foxes and attach them by their tails. Finally it is said that he slew a thousand Philistines with a large jawbone of an ass, and that from one of the teeth of this jawbone a fountain came forth. When it comes to asses' jawbones, you owe me an explanation.

(39) I ask you for the same instructions about the worthy Tobias, who slept with his eyes open and was blinded by a dropping from a swallow; about the angel who descended purposely from what is

* Assassins of Henry III and Henry IV of France, respectively.—*kwa.*

called the empyrean, to search with Tobias' son, for the money that the Jew Gabel owed to Tobias' father; about the wife of Tobias' son, who had seven husbands whose necks the Devil had wrung; and about the way sight was restored to the blind with fish gall. These stories are odd, and there is nothing more worthy of attention; only Spanish novels can compare with the stories of Judith and Esther. But shall I be able to interpret well the sacred text which says that the beautiful Judith descended from Simeon, son of Reuben, although Simeon may be the brother of Reuben, according to the same sacred text that cannot lie?

I like Esther very much, and I find the supposed king Ahasuerus very sensible in espousing a Jewess and lying with her six months without knowing who she is; and as all the rest is of this magnitude, perhaps you will aid me, you who are my wise masters.

(40) I need your aid almost as much in the story of the Kings as in that of the Judges, of Tobias, of his dog, of Esther, of Judith, and of Ruth, etc., etc. When Saul was declared king, the Jews were slaves of the Philistines. Their conquerors did not permit them to have either swords or spears; indeed, they were obliged to go to the Philistines to have their plowshares and axes sharpened. However Saul battled the Philistines, and gained victory over them. In this battle he is at the head of three hundred and thirty thousand troops, in a small country that could not even support thirty thousand souls; at the time he had at the most only a third of the Holy Land; even today this sterile land does not support twenty thousand inhabitants. The rest were forced to leave and make their living as moneylenders in Balk, Damascus, and Babylon.

(41) I do not know how I shall justify the action of Samuel, who cut King Agag to pieces, whom Saul had made prisoner, and whom he held for ransom.

I do not know if our King Phillip,* having taken a Moorish king prisoner and having reached an understanding with him, would have been well disposed toward butchering his royal prisoner.

* Phillip II of Spain.—*kwa.*

(42) We owe great respect to David, who was a man after God's heart; but I fear I lack the knowledge to justify, by ordinary laws, the conduct of David who associates himself with four hundred men of bad character, burdened with debts, as told in the Scripture [I Kings 22:2]; who goes forth to sack the house of Nabal, servant of the king, and who, eight days later, marries his wife; who offers his services to Achish, the enemy of his king, and who put to the torch and sword the lands of the allies of Achish without mercy for either sex or age; who, as soon as he is upon the throne, takes new concubines; and who, still not satisfied with his concubines, takes Bathsheba away from her husband, and has him killed whom he has dishonored. I still have some trouble imagining God to be born later in Judea of this adulterous and murderous woman who is among the ancestors of the Eternal Being. I have already forewarned you about this matter which makes devout souls extremely uneasy.

(43) The wealth of David and Solomon, amounting to more than five billion gold ducats, seems difficult to reconcile with the poverty of the country, and with the state to which the Jews were reduced under Saul, when they had nothing with which to sharpen their plowshares and their axes. Our cavalry colonels will simply shrug their shoulders if I tell them that Solomon had four hundred thousand horses in a small country where there had never been any and where they still have only asses, as I have already had the honor of informing you.

(44) If I must survey the history of the frightful cruelties of virtually all the kings of Judah and Israel, I fear I will offend rather than edify the sensitive. All those kings assassinated one another a little too often; it is a bad policy, if I am not mistaken.

(45) I see this small nation nearly always enslaved by the Phoenicians, the Babylonians, the Persians, the Syrians, and the Romans; and I shall have some trouble, perhaps, in reconciling so much misery with the magnificent promises of their prophets.

(46) I know that all the Oriental nations have had prophets, but I do not know how to interpret those of the Jews. What must I understand by the vision of Ezekiel, son of Buzi, near the river Chebar; or

by the four animals who each had four sides and four wings with the feet of calves, or a wheel that had four sides; or a firmament above the heads of the animals? How can I explain God's order to Ezekiel to eat a book of parchment, to have himself bound, to remain lying upon his left side for three hundred and ninety days, and upon his right side for forty days, and to eat his bread covered with his own excrement? I cannot penetrate the hidden meaning in what Ezekiel says in chapter 16: "when your breast was formed and when you had some hair I stretched myself out upon you, I covered your nudity, I gave you robes, shoes, belts, ornaments, earrings, but then you built yourself a brothel, and you prostituted yourself in public places"; and in chapter 23 the prophet says: "that Aholibah passionately desired to lie with those who have the male member as that of an ass, and who pour out their seed like horses." Wise masters, tell me if you are worthy of the favors of Aholibah.

(47) My duty will be to explain the great prophecy of Isaiah concerning Our Lord Jesus Christ; it is, as you know, in chapter 7. Rezin, king of Assyria and Pekah, petty king of Israel, besieged Jerusalem. Ahaz, petty king of Jerusalem, consults the prophet Isaiah about this siege; Isaiah replies "God will give you a sign; a girl or a woman shall conceive and bear a son who shall be called Emmanuel. He shall eat butter and honey before he is of an age to reject the bad and choose the good, the country will be rid of the two kings . . . , and the Lord shall whistle to the flies which are at the banks of the rivers of Egypt, and to the bees of the land of Assyria . . . , and in that day the Lord shall take a razor hired from those that are beyond the river, and shall shave the head, the pubic area, and the whole beard of the king of Assyria."*

Then in chapter 8, the prophet, in order to fulfill the prophecy, lies with the prophetess; she bears a son; and the Lord says to Isaiah: "You shall call this son Maher-Shalal-hash-bas, *Hasten to take the spoils, run quickly to the booty,* and before the child is old enough to

---

* This rendition of Isaiah disagrees with the Douay, King James, and Vulgate versions.—*kwa.*

name his father and mother, the power of Damascus shall be overturned."* I cannot, without your help, clearly explain this prophecy.

(48) How am I to understand the story of Jonah, sent to Nineveh to preach penitence? Nineveh was not Israelite, and it seems that Jonah had to teach the Judaic law there before leading the city to this penitence. Instead of obeying the Lord, the prophet flees to Tarsus; a tempest arises, the sailors throw Jonah into the sea to appease the storm. God sends a great fish who swallows Jonah. He lives three days and three nights in the stomach of the fish. God commands the fish to give up Jonah; the fish obeys; Jonah disembarks on the shore of Joppa. God orders him to go to Nineveh with the warning that in forty days it will be overthrown if it does not repent. It is more than four hundred miles from Joppa to Nineveh. Do not all these stories require a superior knowledge that I lack? I wish I could refute the scholars who claim that this fable is taken from the fable of Hercules. This Hercules was enclosed for three days in the stomach of a whale; but he lived very well because he roasted and ate its liver. Jonah was not so clever.

(49) Teach me the art of explaining the first verses of the prophet Hosea, whom God ordered expressly to take a prostitute [Hosea 1] and make her bear whore's sons.

The prophet obeys immediately; he addresses himself to Doña Gomer, daughter of Don Diblaim; he keeps her three years and has three children by her; that's one type. Then God wants another type. He orders him to lie with another *cantonera* who is married, and who has already cuckolded her husband [Hosea 3]. Always obedient, the worthy Hosea has no trouble finding a lady of this character, and it costs him only fifteen drachmas and a measure of barley. I pray you, tell me how much a drachma was then worth among the Jewish people, and what you give today to the girls by order of the Lord?

* This rendition of Isaiah disagrees with the Douay, King James, and Vulgate versions.—*kwa.*

(50) I have yet more need of your wise teachings concerning the New Testament; I fear that I will not know what to say when it is necessary to reconcile the two genealogies of Jesus. Because I will be told that Matthew makes Jacob the father of Joseph, and that Luke makes him the son of Heli, and this is impossible unless you change *he* into *ja*, and *li* into *cob*. They will ask: how is it that the one counts fifty-six generations and the other only forty-two, and why are these generations all different, and again, why, in the forty-two promised, one finds only forty-one; and, finally, why is this the genealogical tree of Joseph, who was not the father of Jesus. I am afraid to reply foolishly as have my predecessors. I hope that you will lead me out of this labyrinth. Do you share the opinion of St. Ambrose who says that the angel gave Mary a child through her ear, *Maria per aurem impraegnata est*;* or that of the Reverend Father Sanchez, who says that the Virgin grew big from the seed of her copulation with the Holy Spirit? It is a curious question; the wise Sanchez does not doubt that the Holy Spirit and the Holy Virgin may have simultaneously emitted seed; he thinks that this simultaneous encounter of the two seeds is necessary for procreation. It is quite clear that Sanchez knows his theology better than his physiology and that the making of babies is not a Jesuitic pursuit.

(51) If I announce, following Luke, that Augustus had ordered a census of the land when Mary was great with child and that Cyrenus or Quirinus, governor of Syria, published this census, and that Joseph and Mary went to Bethlehem in order to be counted there; and if they laugh in my face; and if the historians tell me that a census of the Roman Empire was never taken, that Cyrenus did not rule Syria until ten years after the birth of Jesus, that it was Quintilius Varus, not Cyrenus, who was the governor of Syria at the time, I shall be very embarrassed and doubtless you will clear away this small difficulty. Because if there were a single falsehood in a sacred book, would this book still be sacred?

(52) When I shall teach that the family went into Egypt ac-

* "Mary was impregnated through her ear."—*kwa*

cording to Matthew, they will reply that it is not true, and that it remained in Judea according to the other evangelists; and if I then agree that it stayed in Judea, they will insist that the family had been in Egypt. Would it not be briefer to state that it is possible to be in two places at the same time, as happened to St. Francis Xavier and many other saints?

(53) Astronomers may indeed laugh at the star that led the three Kings into a stable. But you are great astrologers; you will make sense of this phenomenon. Tell me above all, how much gold the kings offered: you are accustomed to take much of it from kings and the people. And with respect to the fourth king, who was Herod, why did he fear that Jesus, born in this stable, might become king of the Jews? Herod was king only by the grace of the Romans; it was the concern of Augustus. The massacre of the innocents is a little bizarre. I am vexed that no Roman historian spoke of these matters. An ancient martyrologist, quite veridical (as they all are), counts fourteen thousand infant martyrs. If you want me to add several thousand to that, just tell me.

(54) You will tell me how the Devil carried God and perched him on a hill of Galilee, from whence one could see all the kingdoms of the earth. The Devil, who promises all these realms to God, provided that God worship the Devil, will greatly scandalize many honest people, for whom I ask of you a word of recommendation.

(55) Pray tell me, when you go to a wedding party*, how God, who also went to a wedding party, changed water into wine for people who were already drunk.

(56) When you eat figs with your breakfast at the end of July, I implore you to tell me why God, being hungry, looked for figs at the beginning of March, when it was not yet time for figs?

(57) After having received your instructions on all the wonders of this kind, I should have to say that God had been condemned to be hanged for original sin. But if I am told that there never was a question of original sin either in the Old Testament or in the New; that it is only said that Adam was condemned to die the day he ate

---

* Voltaire uses the word *la noce*, which can also be a "spree."—*kwa*

from the tree of knowledge, but that he did not die of it; and that Augustine, Bishop of Hippo, and a one-time Manichean, was the first to establish the concept of original sin, I must say that since I will not be speaking to the people of Hippo, I could be mocked for speaking at length and saying nothing. For when certain disputers have shown me that it was impossible for God to be executed because of an apple eaten four thousand years before his death; impossible that in atoning for the human race he did not redeem it but left it in the clutches of the Devil; except for a few chosen ones, I would merely be spouting words, and I would have to hide myself in shame.

(58) Shed your light for me on the prediction of Our Lord in St. Luke, chapter 21. Jesus says here expressly, that he shall come in a cloud with great power and great glory, before the generation to which he speaks has passed. He has not done it, he has not come in the clouds; if he has come in some mists, we know nothing of it. Tell me what you know about it. Paul the Apostle also said to his Thessalonian disciples that they will go into the clouds with him to meet Jesus. [I. Thess. 4:17]. Why have they not made this trip? Does it cost more to go to the clouds than to the third heaven [II Cor., 12:2]? I beg your pardon, but I like the *Clouds* of Aristophanes better than those of Paul.

(59) Shall I say with Luke that Jesus ascended to heaven from the small village of Bethany? Shall I insinuate, with Matthew, that this happened in Galilee where the disciples saw him for the last time? Shall I believe a learned doctor who says that Jesus had one foot in Galilee and the other in Bethany? This opinion seems to me the most probable, but I shall await your decision on that.

(60) I shall be asked next if Peter had been in Rome; I shall doubtlessly reply that he was not pope there for twenty-five years; and the major reason I shall give for this is that we have an epistle from this worthy man, who knew neither how to read nor write, and that this letter is dated at Babylon; there is no reply to this, but I would like something more substantial.

(61) Will you advise me why the Credo, called the Symbol of the

Apostles, was not compiled until the time of Jerome and Rufinus, four hundred years after the Apostles? Tell me why the first Fathers of the Church cited only the Gospels now called the Apocrypha? Is it not an evident proof that the canonical four were not yet composed?

(62) Are you not as angry as I am that the first Christians forged so much bad verse which they attributed to the prophets; that they forged letters from St. Paul to Seneca, letters of Jesus, letters of Mary, letters of Pilate; that they thus established their sect by a hundred crimes of forgery that would be punished in every court on earth? These frauds are recognized today by all scholars. We are reduced to labeling them pious. But is it not sad that your truth may be founded only on falsehoods?

(63) Tell me why is it that though Jesus did not institute seven sacraments, we have seven sacraments? Why is it that though Jesus did not say that he is Triune, that he has two natures with two wills and one person, we make him Triune with one person and two natures? Why having two wills has he not had the will to instruct us in the dogma of the Christian religion.

And why, when he has said that among his disciples there would be neither first nor last, the Archbishop of Toledo has a revenue of a million ducats while I am reduced to a meager income?

(64) I know well that the Church is infallible; but is it the Greek Church, or the Latin Church, or the Church of England, or that of Denmark and Sweden, or that of the superb city of Neuchâtel, or that of the primitives called Quakers, or that of the Anabaptists, or that of the Moravians? The Turkish Church also has its good points, but it is said that the Chinese Church is much more ancient.

(65) Is the pope infallible when he lies with his mistress or with his own daughter, and when he brings to dinner a bottle of poisoned wine for the Cardinal Adriano de Corneto?*

When two councils anathematize each other, as has happened twenty times, which is the infallible council?

---

* Apparently an allusion to Pope Alexander VI and to Lucrezia Borgia, his "niece." The Cardinal reputedly played the role of chief executioner for Alexander.—*kwa*

(66) Finally, would it not be better not to sink into these labyrinths, and simply preach honesty? When God judges us, I strongly doubt that he will ask us whether grace is versatile or concomitant; whether marriage is the visible sign of an invisible thing; if we believe that there may be ten choirs of angels or nine; if the pope is above the council or the council above the pope. Will it be a crime in his eyes if we pray to him in Spanish when we do not know Latin? Shall we be the objects of his eternal anger for having eaten a dozen maravedis [a small Spanish coin] worth of bad meat on a certain day? And shall we be recompensed forever, sage masters, if we have dined with you for one hundred piastres, on turbot, sole, and sturgeon? You do not believe it in the depths of your hearts; you think that God will judge us according to our works, and not according to the ideas of Thomas or of Bonaventure.

Shall I not be of service to men in propounding only morality to them? This morality is so pure, so holy, so universal, so clear, so ancient that it seems to come from God himself, like the light that passes among us because of his first work. Has he not given men self-respect to look after their survival; goodwill, benevolence, virtue, to look after their self-respect; their mutal needs to form society; pleasure so we can enjoy it; anguish which warns us to enjoy ourselves with moderation; the passions which lead us to great deeds, and wisdom which places a check upon these passions.

Finally, has he not inspired the idea of a Supreme Being in all men united in society, in order that the adoration owed this Being may be the strongest bond of the society? The savages who roam the forests have no need of this awareness; for the duties of a society that they know nothing of do not concern them at all. But as soon as men are gathered together, God manifests himself in their reason: they need justice, they worship him as the source of all justice. God, who has no use for their vain adorations, receives them as necessary for men but not for himself. And just as he bestows on them the genuis for the arts, without which all society perishes, he gives them the sense of religion, the first of the sciences and the most natural one; a divine science whose principle is certain, although we always draw from it uncertain consequences. Will you permit me to announce these truths to the noble Spaniards?

(67) If you want me to hide this truth; if you absolutely order me to announce the miracles of St. James in Galicia, and of Our Lady of Atocha, and of Maria d'Agreda, who showed her bottom to little boys during her ecstacies, tell me how I must deal with the recalcitrants who will dare to doubt. Will it be necessary that with edification I have them put to the question—both ordinary and extraordinary? When I encounter Jewish girls, must I lie with them before burning them? And when they are put in the fire, have I not the right to take a thigh or a buttock for my supper with Catholic girls?

I await the honor of your reply.

Dominico Zapata

*y verdadero, y honrado, y caricativo*

Zapata, having had no reply, set himself to preaching God with simplicity. He announced to men the Father of men, remunerator, punisher, and pardoner. He disengaged truth from falsehood, and separated religion from fanaticism; he preached and practiced virtue. He was gentle, beneficent, and modest—and was roasted at Valladolid, in the year of grace 1631. Pray God for the soul of Brother Zapata.

# HOMILIES

*Delivered in London in 1765,*
*in a special assembly.*[1]

## FIRST HOMILY—On Atheism

My brothers, may my words have the power to pass from my heart
into yours! May I be able to shun vain declamation, and not be a
pulpit comedian who seeks applause for his voice, his gestures, and
his insincere eloquence! I do not have the insolence to instruct you;
with you I examine the truth. Neither the hope of riches and
honors, nor the allure of your esteem, nor an unbridled desire to
dominate minds animates my feeble voice. Having been chosen by
you to enlighten myself with you and not to lecture as a master, let
us seek together, in the sincerity of our hearts, that which reason,
in harmony with the interests of mankind, orders us to believe and
to practice. We must begin with the existence of a God. This subject has been treated by all nations—it is exhausted. It is for this
very reason that I speak of it to you, because you will anticipate all

[1] These four homilies that are stated as delivered in 1765, did not appear until
two years later. The "Secret Memoires," dated May 10, 1767, speak of them as
something new. The original edition, a small octavo of seventy-eight pages, carries
the data MDCCLXVII. A fifth homily was published in 1769. It will be found
under its date—*M. Beuchot*

39

that I shall say to you. We shall strengthen ourselves together by recognizing our first duty, we are children here assembled to talk about our father.

An admirable measure of the human spirit, a divine transport of our reason—if I may put it that way—is that ageless argument: *I exist; thus something exists from all eternity*, embraces all time from the very first step and the first glance. Nothing is greater, and nothing is more simple. This truth is as clearly demonstrated as the clearest propositions of arithmetic and geometry; for a moment it can astonish an inattentive mind; but a moment thereafter it subjugates that mind. It has been denied by no one, because at the moment of reflection, one sees as evident that if nothing existed from all eternity, all would be produced by nothingness. Our existence would have no cause: this is an absurd contradiction.

We are intelligent, therefore there is an eternal intelligence. Does not the universe attest to us that it is the work of such an intelligence? If a simple house built upon the ground, or a vessel that sails the seas of our small globe, proves invincibly the existence of a maker, the course of the stars and of all nature demonstrate the existence of their creator.

"No," replies a Strato or a Zeno, "movement is essential to matter; all combinations are possible with movement; therefore in an eternal movement it was absolutely necessary that the present universe come into existence. Throw a thousand dice during eternity, and at some time the same side is bound to turn up on all at the same time"; and it can be ascertained what ought to be wagered for or against that probability.

This sophism has often astonished the learned and confused the superficial; but let us see if it is not a fallacy.

Firstly, there is no proof that motion is necessary to matter; on the contrary, all scholars agree that it is indifferent to either movement or repose, and a single atom unremoved from its place destroys belief in this essential movement.

Secondly even if it is necessary that matter be in motion, as it is necessary that it be given configuration, it proves nothing against the intelligence that directs its movement and fashions its different shapes.

Thirdly, the example of a thousand dice that are arranged by chance is far less relevant to the question than is believed. It is not a question of knowing if movement will arrange dice in different sequences; it is doubtless quite possible that a thousand dice turn up a thousand sixes or a thousand aces, although this may be very difficult. In that case there is only an arrangement of matter without design, without organization and without usefulness. But that movement alone produces beings provided with organs, the interplay of which is incomprehensible; that these organs may always be in proportion to one another; that innumerable efforts produce innumerable results with a regularity that never contradicts itself; that all living beings produce their like; that the sense of sight, which, basically, has nothing in common with the eyes, functions whenever the eyes receive rays that issue from objects; that the sense of hearing, which is totally unconnected to the ear, may cause us all to hear the same sounds when the ear is struck by vibrations of the air—all of this is the real core of the question: that no system can operate without a maker. There is no connection between the movement of matter and emotion, still less with thought. The eternity of all possible motion will never give either a sensation or an idea; and—may I be pardoned—one must have lost sense or good faith to say that matter in motion creates sentient and thinking beings.

Spinoza, who reasoned methodically, also admitted that there is in the world a universal intelligence.

This intelligence, says he with several philosophers, exists necessarily with matter; it is its soul. One cannot exist without the other. The universal intelligence shines in the stars, floats in the elements, thinks in men, vegetates in plants.

*Mens agitat molem, et magno se corpore miscet.*[2]

[2] Virg., Aen., VI, 727—*Voltaire*
"Mind inspires shapeless mass and itself mingles with the vast body"—*kwa*

They are thus forced to recognize a supreme intelligence; but they make it blind and purely mechanical; they do not recognize it as a free, independent, and powerful principle.

According to them there is only one single substance, and one substance cannot of itself produce another. This substance is the universality of things that is all at one and the same time thinking, feeling, all inclusive, configurated.

But let us reason in good faith: do we not perceive a choice in all that exists? Why is there a certain number of species? Could there not evidently be a lesser number? Could there not be more of them? Why, asks the judicious Clarke, do the planets turn in one way rather than in another? I confess that, among other stronger arguments, this is the one that strikes me most forcibly: there is a choice, thus there is a master who acts according to his will.

This argument is still being waged by our adversaries; they are forever saying: "What you see is necessary since it exists"—"Very well," I shall reply to them, "all that can be deduced from your supposition is that, in order to give form to the world, it was necessary that the supreme intelligence make a choice. This choice was made: we feel and think by virtue of the rapport that God provided between our perception and our organs. Examine on the one hand the nerves and muscles, and on the other, sublime thoughts, and confess that only a Supreme Being is able to combine such dissimilar elements."

What is this Being? Does it exist in immensity? Is space one of its attributes? Is it in one place or all places or without place? May it preserve me from ever entering into these metaphysical subtleties! My feeble reasons would be much abused were I to seek to understand fully the Being, which, because of its nature and mine, must be incomprehensible to me. I should resemble a fool, who knowing that a house was built by an architect, would believe that this information alone suffices to know the person in depth.

Let us confine then our insatiable and useless curiosity; let us concentrate upon our true interest. Is the Supreme Maker, who has created the world and us, our master? Is He beneficent? Do we owe Him acknowledgment?

He is without doubt our master. Every moment we feel an invisible and irresistible power. He is our benefactor, seeing that we are alive. Our life is a boon since we love all of life, no matter how miserable it may become. Support for our life has been granted by this supreme and incomprehensible Being, since none of us can create the least of the plants from which we obtain the nourishment, and since none of us even knows how this vegetation takes form.

The ingrate can assert that it was absolutely necessary that God provide us with food, if he wanted us to exist for any length of time. It will say: "We are machines that succeed each other, and which for the most part break and shatter after the first steps of their lives. All the elements conspire to destroy us and after suffering we die." It is all only too true; but it also must be granted that if there were only one man who received from nature a sound and robust body, a sharp mind, an honest heart, that man would have to pay great tribute to his maker. There are many men whom nature has endowed with these gifts; at least they should look upon God as beneficent.

With regard to those whom the concourse of eternal laws, established by the Being of beings, has rendered unfortunate, what can we do but succor them? What can we say, but that we do not know why they suffer misfortune?

Misfortune floods the earth. What shall we infer from our weak rationalizations? That there is no God? But it has been demonstrated to us that He exists. Shall we say that God is wicked? But this idea is absurd and contradictory. Shall we suspect that God is powerless, and that He who has so well organized all the stars could not effectively organize mankind? This supposition is no less intolerable. Shall we say that there is a bad principle that alters the accomplishments of a beneficent principle, or that produces from it execrable works? But why does not this evil principle upset the order of the rest of nature? Why would it persist in tormenting some weak animals upon so puny a globe while it would respect the works of its enemy? Why would it not attack God in those millions of worlds that revolve regularly in space? Why would two gods, enemies of one another, each be equally necessary to the Being? How would they exist together?

Shall we take an optimistic view? This is basically only a hopeless fatalism. Lord Shaftesbury, one of the boldest of English philosophers, was the first to give recognition to this sad state of affairs. "The laws," he says, "of central power and of vegetation will not be changed for the love of an insignificant and powerless animal who, fully protected as he is by these same laws, will soon be reduced to powder by them."*

The illustrious Lord Bolingbroke has gone a great deal further; and the celebrated Pope has dared to reassert that the general good is composed of all particular evils.

A single examination of this paradox demonstrates its falsity. It would be as reasonable to say that life is the result of an infinite number of deaths, that pleasure is made up of all suffering, and that virtue is the sum of all crimes.

Physical evil and moral evil are without doubt the result of the makeup of this world, and it cannot be otherwise. When it is announced that *all is well*, nothing is meant but that everything follows physical laws. But surely all is not well for that innumerable multitude of beings who suffer, and for those who cause others to suffer. All moralists confess it in their discourses; all men cry it out when pointing to the evils of which they are the victims.

What execrable solace do you claim to give to persecuted and falsely accused wretches, expiring in torment, in assuring them: *All is well; you have nothing better to hope for*? This would be a statement to make to those whom one assumes are eternally guilty

* From Shaftesbury's *Characteristics of Men, Manners, Opinions and Times* (London, 1711–1773)—*kwa*

and who, it is said, are before time condemned of necessity to eternal tortures.

The Stoic Poseidonius is supposed to have said during a violent attack of gout: *No, gout is not an ill*. He possessed a less absurd pride than the sham philosophers who, amidst poverty, persecution, scorn, and all the horrors of a most miserable life, have the effrontery to cry out: *All is well*. Well and good that they are resigned, since they feign not to wish for compassion, but that while suffering and witnessing the suffering of nearly the whole earth they continue: *All is well, without any hope of betterment*; this is a pitiful delirium.

Shall we suppose finally that a necessarily good Supreme Being abandons the earth to some subordinate being who ravages it, to a jailer who tortures us? This is to make of God a tyrant who, not daring to do evil himself, continually causes it to be done by his slaves.

What position does there remain for us to take? Is it not the one taken by all the scholars of antiquity in India, Chaldea, Greece, Rome, that of believing that God will cause us to pass from this unhappy life to a better one, which will be the development of our nature? Because after all, it is clear that we have already met with different sorts of existence. We existed before a new assemblage of organs contained us in the womb; for nine months our being was very different from what it was before; infancy did not resemble the embryo; maturity has nothing of infancy: death can give us a different manner of existence.

"It is only a hope," proclaim those unfortunates who think and reason. "You are returning us to Pandora's box; evil is real, and hope can only be an illusion. Misfortune and crime lay siege to what life we have, and you speak to us of a life that we do not have, that we perhaps shall not have, and of which we have no idea. There is no connection between what we are today and what we were in the womb of our mothers. What tie would we have in the sepulcher with our present existence?"

"The Jews, whom you say had been led by God himself, never knew this other life. You say that God gave them laws but in these laws there is not a single word which announced the punishments and rewards after death. Cease then to present chimerical consolations for calamities that are all too real."

My brothers, as Christians let us not yet reply to these painful objections; it is not the right time. Let us begin by refuting them with the help of the scholars, before obscuring them with the aid of those who are beyond the scholars themselves.

We do not know what it is in us that thinks, consequently we cannot know if this unknown being will survive our body. It may be physically possible that there is in us an indestructible monad, a hidden flame, a particle of divine fire that exists eternally under various guises. I shall not say that this may be demonstrated, but with no wish to deceive, it can be said that we have as much reason to believe in as to deny the immortality of the thinking being. If the Jews have not known it formerly, they admit it today. All civilized nations agree on this point. This opinion, so ancient and so general, is perhaps the only one that can justify a Providence. A God of reward and vengeance must be recognized, or nothing recognized at all. It seems that there is no middle ground: either there is no God, or God is just. We have an idea of justice, we, whose intelligence is so confined. How would not this justice be in the Supreme Intelligence? We know how absurd it would be to say that God is ignorant, that he is weak, that he is false. Shall we dare to say that he is cruel? It would be better to believe in the fatality of things and to admit only one invincible destiny, than to admit a God who may have created one single creature in order to make it unhappy.

I have been told that the justice of God is not ours. I might just as well be told that the parity of two times two with four is not the same for God as for me. Truth is the same in my eyes as in His. All mathematical propositions are proven to the Infinite Being. There are not two different kinds of truth. The sole difference is probably that the Supreme Intelligence comprehends all truths at once while with slow steps we creep toward some. If there are not two kinds of truth in the same proposition, why would there be two kinds of justice in the same action? We can comprehend God's justice only because we have the idea of justice. It is as thinking beings that we know what is just and unjust. God who thinks infinitely, must be infinitely just.

Let us at least see, my brothers, how this belief is useful, how much we need to impress it upon all hearts.

No society can exist without compensation and without chastisement. This truth is so sensible and so well recognized, that the ancient Jews acknowledged at least temporal punishment. "If you lie," said their law [Deut. 28:20–30], "the Lord shall send upon you hunger and poverty, dust instead of rain . . . an incurable burning in the bowels . . . malignant ulcers on the knees . . . and on the legs . . . you shall betroth a wife, and another man shall lie with her, etc."

These curses constrained an unruly people to its duty; but it could also happen that a man guilty of the most heinous crimes did not have ulcers on his limbs, and did not languish in poverty and in famine. Solomon became idolatrous, and it is nowhere stated that he was punished with any one of these scourges. It is well known that the earth is infested with fortunate scoundrels and the oppressed innocent. It was therefore necessary to turn to the theology of the most populous and most civilized nations that long before had postulated penalties and rewards in the development of human nature—probably in the form of a new life—as the foundation of their religion.

It seems that this doctrine may be a cry of nature, that all ancient peoples heard and which was stifled only temporarily among the Jews before resounding in all its force.

Among all peoples who use their reason there are universal opinions that seem imprinted by the master of our hearts. Such is the persuasion of the existence of God, and of his merciful justice;

such are the first principles of morality common to the Chinese, the Indians, and the Romans, and which have never varied while our globe has been thrown into confusion a thousand times.

These principles are necessary to the preservation of the human species. Take away from men the concept of a vengeful and rewarding God, then Sulla and Marius bathe with delight in the blood of their fellow citizens; Augustus, Antony, and Lepidus surpass the furies of Sulla; Nero cold-bloodedly orders the death of his mother. It is certain that the doctrine of a vengeful God was extinct in Rome; atheism was dominant, and it would not be difficult to prove with history that atheism can sometimes cause as much evil as the most barbaric superstitions.

Do you really think that Alexander VI recognized a God, when, for the aggrandizement of the son of his incest, he employed one after another, treason, overt force, the stiletto, the cord and poison; and that abusing the superstitious weakness of those whom he assassinated, he gave them absolution and indulgences amidst their death throes? Surely, he insulted the Divinity, whom he ridiculed, at the same time that he practiced upon men these dreadful barbarities. Let us all confess, when we read the history of this monster and his abominable son, that we want them punished. The idea of an avenging God is thus necessary.

It can be—and it happens too often—that divine justice is no bridle upon a transport of passion. One is then intoxicated; remorse comes only when reason has regained its hold. In the end the guilty are tormented by remorse. The atheist can feel in place of remorse that secret and somber horror which accompanies these high crimes. The situation of his soul is irksome and cruel; a man soiled with blood is not sensitive to the niceties of society; his soul becomes atrocious, is incapable of life's consolation. He roars with fury, but he does not repent. He is not afraid of being asked to account for the prey he has torn to pieces; he will be always wicked, he will harden in his fierceness. On the other hand, the man who believes in God will become himself again. The first is a monster all his life, the second will have been barbaric only a moment. Why? Because one has a restraining force, while the other has nothing that stops him.

We do not read that the Archbishop Trolle* who caused all the magistrates of Stockholm to be slain in his presence, ever deigned to even pretend to expiate his crime by the least penance. The deceitful, ungrateful, slanderous, thieving, blood-thirsty atheist reasons and acts consistently, if he is sure of impunity among men. Because if there is no God, this beast is his own God; he sacrifices to himself whatever he desires, whatever stands in his way. The most tender prayers, the best arguments, can no more prevail upon him than upon a wolf hungry for carnage.

When Pope Sixtus IV instigated the assassination of the two Medici in the church of La Reparada, at the moment when the God whom the people adored was lifted on high, Sixtus IV, tranquil in his palace, had nothing to fear even if the conspiracy failed. He was sure that the Florentines would not dare take revenge, that he could freely excommunicate them, and that on their knees they would beseech his pardon for having dared to complain.

It is very probable that atheism has been the philosophy of all powerful men who have spent their lives in the environment of crimes that imbeciles call *politics, acts of state, art of governing.*

No one will ever persuade me that a cardinal,** a celebrated minister, believed that he was acting in the presence of God when he had twelve robed murderers, his obedient slaves, condemn to death one of the greats of state in his own country house, while he

---

* Gustave Trolle, in the course of a stormy political career, imprisoned Sten Sture who had nominated him to the See of Uppsala and initiated the famous "Blood Bath" to eliminate all opponents. Involved in Swedish, Danish and Norwegian politics and wars, Trolle died of a battle wound in Schleswig in 1535—*kwa*

** Richelieu, chief minister for Louis XIII, builder of a strong centralized administration, prosecuted the Duke of Montmorency for his part in a rebellion of the feudal nobility against the growing royal power. Defeated in battle and deserted by the head of the rebellion. the king's brother Gaston of Orleans, Montmorency was at the mercy of Richelieu. He was tried, condemned, and beheaded in 1632, an exemplary lesson to future feudal rebels—*kwa*

himself plunged into dissoluteness with his courtesans beside the apartment where his lackeys, posing as *judges*, menaced with torture a marshal of France whose death he was already savoring.

Some of you, my brothers, have asked me if a Jewish prince had a true idea of Divinity when at the point of death, instead of asking God's pardon for his adulteries, his homicides, and his innumerable cruelties, he persisted in his thirst for blood, and in the atrocious fury of vengeance; when with lips about to be forever closed, he advised his successor to assassinate Shimei, his minister, and his general Joab.

With you I admit that this action, for which St. Ambrose wished in vain to apologize, is perhaps the most horrible about which we can read in the history of nations. The moment of death is for all men the moment for repentance and for clemency: to want to avenge oneself, and not dare to; to charge another in his last words with an infamous murder is the height of cowardice and fury combined.

I shall neither examine if this revolting story is true, nor try to ascertain when it was written. I shall not discuss with you if we must view the chronicles of the Jews in the same light as we read the commandments of their law; if we have been wrong, in a time of superstition and of ignorance, to confuse what was sacred among the Jews with their profane lives. The laws of Numa were sacred among the Romans, but their historians were not. But if a Jew has been barbarous up to the last, what does it matter? Are we Jews? What tie have we with the absurdities and abominations of this little people? Crimes have been consecrated among nearly all peoples of the earth. What, then, are we to do? Detest these crimes and worship the God who condemns them.

It is recognized that the Jews believed in a corporeal God. Is that a reason for our having this idea of the Supreme Being?

If it is averred that the Jews believed God corporeal, it is no less clear that they acknowledged a God creator of the universe.

Long before they went into Palestine, the Phœnicians had their own God *Jaho*, whose name was sacred among them, and in time among the Egyptians and the Hebrews. They gave to the Supreme Being a more common name, *El*. This name was originally Chaldean. From this the city we call Babylon was named Babel, *the gate of God*. From it the Hebrew people, when they came in the course of time to establish themselves in Palestine, took the name of Israel, which means *seeing God* as Philo informs us in the *Treatise on Rewards and Punishments*, and as the historian Josephus tells us in his response to Apion.

The Egyptians recognized a supreme God despite all their superstitions; they named him *Knef*, and represented him by the figure of a globe.

The ancient Zerdust, whom we call Zoroaster, pointed to one God, to whom the bad principle was subordinated. The Indians, who boast of being the oldest society in the universe, still have their ancient books, which they claim were written four thousand eight hundred and sixty-six years ago. The angel Brama or Habrama, they say, the envoy of God, the ambassador of the Supreme Being, dictated this book in Sanskrit. This holy book is named *Shastabad*, and is far more ancient than the *Veda* itself, which has been for so long a time the sacred book on the banks of the Ganges.

The two volumes, the *Ezour-Vedas*,* which are the law of the Brahman sects and which are the beginning of the *Veda*, speak only of one God.

Heaven has willed that one of our compatriots who lived thirty years in Bengal—and who knows the language of the ancient Brahmans perfectly—should give us an extract from the *Shastabad* written a thousand years before the *Veda*. It is divided into five chapters. The first treats of God and his attributes, and commences thus: "God is one, he has given form to all that is; He is alike to a perfect sphere without end or beginning. He governs all

---

* Voltaire obtained his knowledge of these books from British East India Company officials Dow and Holwell and the French scholar Gentil. The true title is the *Yadjour-Veda*, unless as Peter Gay asserts the *Ezour-Vedas* are fraudulent.—*kwa*

with universal wisdom. Thou shalt not seek his essence and his nature; such an attempt would be vain and criminal. May it suffice thee to wonder day and night at his works, his wisdom, his power, his benevolence. Be happy in worshipping him."

The second chapter deals with the creation of heavenly intelligences; the third, with the fall of the secondary deities; the fourth, with their punishment; the fifth, with the clemency of God.

The Chinese, whose history and rites attest to a remote antiquity, but less so than that of the Indians, have always adored the *Tien*, the *Chang ti*, the Celestial Virtue. All their books of morality, all the edicts of the emperors advocate willing surrender to *Tien* or *Chang ti*, and the meriting of their benefactions.

Confucius did not establish religion among the Chinese, as the uninformed claim. Much before him the emperors went to the temple four times a year to present to *Chang ti* the fruits of the earth.

Thus you see that all civilized peoples—Indians, Chinese, Egyptians, Persians, Chaldeans, Phoenicians—recognized a supreme God. I shall not deny that among these ancient peoples there may have been atheists; I know that there were a great many in China; we see them in Turkey, they are in our country, and among all the nations of Europe. But why should our belief be shaken by their error? Do the erroneous theories of all the philosophers about light hinder us from firmly believing in the discoveries of Newton on this incomprehensible element? Will the erroneous physics and the ridiculous sophistries of the Greeks destroy in us an intuitive science provided by experimental physics?

All known peoples have had atheists; but I doubt very much that this atheism may have been a full persuasion, a luminous conviction in which the mind is fully satisfied, as in a geometrical demonstration. Is it not rather a half persuasion fortified by a storm of violent passion and pride rather than thorough conviction? The Phalarises, the Busirises (and they were at all levels) with reason made fun of the fables of Cerberus and the Eumenides; they clearly saw how ridiculous it was to imagine that Theseus was eternally seated upon a stool, and that a vulture forever tore at the perpetually regenerated liver of Prometheus. These fantasies, which dishonored the Divinity, destroyed him in their eyes. They said with confusion in their hearts: "We are always told only about the Divinity's absurdities; this Divinity is then only a chimera." They trampled underfoot a consoling and terrible truth, because it was surrounded with lies.

Oh! wretched scholastic theologians, may this example be a warning to you not to ridicule God! It is you who by your platitudes spread the atheism that you combat; it is you who create the atheists at court for whom a specious argument justifies all horrors. But if the torrent of disputes and fatal passions had left them time for introspection, they would have said: "The falsehoods of the priests of Isis, and of Cybele must incense me only against them, and not against the Divinity whom they outrage. If Phlegethon and Cocyte do not exist, that does not alter the existence of God. I wish to scorn mythology and to worship the truth. Though God is portrayed to me as a ridiculous tyrant, I shall nevertheless believe him wise and just. I shall not say with Orpheus that the shades of virtuous men walk in the Elysian fields; I shall not admit the metempsychosis of the Pharisees, nor the annihilation of the soul believed in by the Sadducees. I shall recognize an eternal providence without daring to guess what will be the means and effects of his mercy and of his justice. I shall not abuse the reason that God has given me; I shall believe that there are vice and virtue, just as there are health and sickness; and finally since an invisible power—the influences of which I sense continually—has made a thinking and acting being, I shall conclude that my thoughts and actions must be worthy of this power that has given me birth."

Let us not forget that there have been virtuous atheists. The Epicurean cult produced upright persons and it must be admitted that Epicurus himself was a virtuous man. The instinct for virtue, which consists of a mild temperament and abstention from all violence, can readily coexist with an erroneous philosophy. The Epicureans and the most famous atheists of our day—occupied with the pleasures of society, with study, and with the cares of maintaining their souls in peace—have strengthened that instinct which inclines them to never doing injury, by renouncing the worldly tumult that upsets the soul, and the ambition that perverts it. Some of society's laws are more rigorously observed than those of the state and of religion. The man who has repaid the services of his friends with base ingratitude, who has calumniated an honest man, who has conducted himself with revolting indecency, or who is known for his sordid and pitiless avarice, will not be punished by the laws, but by the society of honest men who will bring against him an irrevocable decree of banishment; he will never be received among them. Thus an atheist of gentle and agreeable manners—restrained furthermore by a curb that the society of men imposes—can very well lead a guiltless, happy, and honored life. There have been examples down the centuries; from the celebrated Atticus, a friend of both Caesar and Cicero, to the famous magistrate Des-Barreaux,* who having made a litigant who brought suit wait too long, paid him the amount of the action out of his own pocket.

The learned mathematician Spinoza, whose moderation, impartiality, and generosity were worthy of Epictetus, may also be cited as an example. I will be told that the celebrated atheist La Méttrie** was a mild and socially amiable man, honored during his life and after his death by the benevolence of a great king [Frederick II of Prussia], who, paying no attention to philosophical

---

* Des Barreaux, Jacques Vallée (1602–1673). Counselor in the *Parlement* of Paris but dismissed because of his atheism, hedonism, and scandalous behavior. (He burned one part of a court process in order to relieve his boredom.) Voltaire offered a defense against the charge of atheism in *Lettres à S.A. Le Prince de* ... (To His Highness The Prince of Brunswick-Luneburg) Letter VII, "Sur les Français" *Oeuvres Complètes*, Hachette, v. 20, p. 379.—*kwa*

** Julien Offroy de La Méttrie, a contemporary of Voltaire. A theologian turned doctor, he authored the then (1745) highly controversial *Natural History of the Soul*. Driven from France, he finally found refuge with Frederick the Great.—*kwa*

opinions reçompensed his virtue. But place these gentle and tranquil atheists in high places; break them up into factions, so that they would have to combat a Cesar Borgia, or a Cromwell, or even a Cardinal de Retz; do you think that they will not then become as corrupt as their adversaries? See what alternatives you give them; they would be imbeciles if they were not vicious. Their enemies attack them criminally; they must defend themselves with the same weapons or perish. Certainly their principles will not be opposed to assassinations, to whatever poisonings that seem necessary.

It is thus demonstrated that atheism can at most permit the existence of social virtue in the tranquil apathy of private life but that it must lead to all crimes in the turmoil of public life.

A given society of atheists who do not dispute among themselves, who peacefully while away their days in voluptuous amusements, can sometimes last without trouble; but if the world were governed by atheists, it would be just as well to be subject to the immediate control of those infernal beings who are portrayed to us as enraged against their victims. In a word, atheists who have power in their hands would be as vicious toward mankind as the superstitious would. Between these two monsters, reason holds out its arms to us: and that will be the object of my second discourse.

## SECOND HOMILY—On Superstition

My brothers, you are well aware that all well-known nations have established public worship. Men have always assembled to discuss their interests, and to communicate their needs to each other, and it was natural enough for their assemblies to begin with such testimony of respect and love as they owe the Author of life. This respect has been compared to that which children show to a father, and subjects to a sovereign. These examples are too weak to explain the worship of God. Man-to-man relationships cannot compare with the relationship of man to the Supreme Being: infinity separates them. It would even be blasphemous to render homage to God in the likeness of a monarch. A sovereign of the whole earth—if there could be one, if all men were so unfortunate as to be subjugated by one man—would only be an earthworm commanding other earthworms, and would be infinitely less in the presence of the Divinity. And then, in the republics that are incontestably anterior to any monarchy, how could God be conceived of in the likeness of a king? If there must be a perceptible image of God, that of a father, as defective as it is, would seem the one most suitable to our weakness.

But emblems of divinity were one of the first sources of superstition. From the time that we made God in our image, divine worship was perverted. Having dared to represent God in the shape of man, our miserable imagination, which never stops, attributed to him all man's vices. We looked upon him simply as a powerful master, and we charged him with every abuse of power; we celebrated him as a proud, jealous, angry, vindictive, capricious benefactor, and a pitiless destroyer who despoiled some to enrich others, without other reason than that he wanted to do so. We get our ideas by making comparisons, almost all our concepts stem from similarities: thus, when the earth was covered with tyrants, God was made the first of the tyrants. It was even worse when the Divinity was proclaimed by symbols taken from animals and plants. God became ox, serpent, crocodile, ape, cat, and lamb—browsing, hissing, bleating, devouring, and devoured.

Superstition has been so horrible among nearly all nations that if there were no monuments of it still in existence, it would be impossible to believe what we are told. The history of the world is one of fanaticism.

But among the monstrous superstitions that have covered the earth, have there been some innocent ones? Shall we be able to distinguish between poisons which act as remedies and those which preserve their murderous nature? Such an investigation merits, if I am not mistaken, the whole attention of rational minds.

One man does good among his fellow men, another destroys carnivorous animals, a third invents the arts through force of genius. As a consequence they appear more favored of God than ordinary men; it is imagined that they are children of God; they are made into demigods—secondary gods—after their deaths. They are set up not only as models for the rest of mankind, but as objects of its worship. He who adores Hercules and Perseus strives to imitate them. Altars become the prizes of genius and courage. I perceive in this only an error which results in good. In such cases, men are deceived only for their own advantage. If the ancient Romans had placed in the ranks of the secondary gods only the Scipios, Tituses, Trajans, and Marcus Aureliuses, who would have reproached them?

The infinite stretches between God and man; agreed: but if in the system of the ancients the human soul was regarded as a finite portion of the infinite intelligence, which plunges again into all creation without augmenting it; if it is supposed that God dwelt in the soul of Marcus Aurelius, and if this soul was superior to others because of its virtue during life, why not assume that it is still superior although it is withdrawn from its mortal body?

Our brothers, the Roman Catholics (because all men are our brothers), have populated heaven with demigods whom they call saints. If, in every instance they made a happy choice, let us admit without subterfuge, that their error might have been a service rendered to human nature. We lavish on them insults and scorn, when they celebrate an Ignatius, "Knight of the Virgin," a Dominic, "persecutor," a Francis, "fanatic and demented," who goes about naked, who speaks to the animals, who catechizes a wolf, who makes himself a woman of snow. We do not forgive Jerome, a learned but faulty translator of Jewish books, for having demanded, in his *History of the Desert Fathers*, our veneration of a St. Pachomius who made his rounds mounted on a crocodile. We are especially indignant to learn that Rome has canonized Gregory VII, "the incendiary of Europe."

But this is not true of the worship in France of King Louis IX, who was just and courageous. And if it is too much to invoke him, it is not too much to revere him; it is only a way of telling other princes: "Imitate his virtues."

Furthermore: I assume that someone may have placed in a basilica a statue of King Henry IV, who conquered his realm with the valor of an Alexander and the clemency of a Titus, who was good and compassionate, who knew how to choose the best ministers, and was himself his own prime minister. I suppose that, in spite of his weaknesses, we pay him homage beyond the respect that we render to the memory of great men; what ill can result? It certainly would be better to genuflect before him than before that multitude of unknown saints whose very names even have become the subject of opprobrium and ridicule. It would be a superstition, I grant, but a harmless superstition, a patriotic enthusiasm and not a pernicious fanaticism. If man is born to err, let us wish him virtuous errors.

The superstition that must be banished from the earth is that which makes God a tyrant and thus incites men to be tyrants. Whoever first said that we must hold reprobates in horror placed a dagger in the hands of those who considered themselves the faithful; whoever first prohibited all communication with those who were not of his persuasion sounded the tocsin of civil war throughout the land.

I believe what to my reason seems impossible; that is to say, I believe what I do not believe: I must then hate those who boast of believing an absurdity contrary to mine. Such is the logic of the superstitious, or rather such is their execrable derangement. To adore the Supreme Being, to love him, to serve him, to be useful to mankind, amounts to nothing: it is rather, according to some, a false virtue which they describe as a *splendid sin*. Thus, ever since we made it a sacred duty to dispute what we cannot understand;

ever since we made virtue reside in the pronunciation of some inexplicable words that each interpreted differently, Christendom has
been a theater of discord and carnage.

You will tell me that we must impute this universal pestilence to
raging ambition rather than to fanaticism. I shall reply that they
are beholden the one to the other. The thirst for power is slaked in
the blood of imbeciles. I do not aspire to healing powerful men of
this furious passion for enslaving souls; it is an incurable sickness.
Every man wants others to serve him eagerly, and in order to be
better served, he will persuade them to believe, if he can, that their
duty and their welfare consist in being his slaves. Go find a man
who possesses fifteen to sixteen millions in revenue and who has
throughout Europe four or five hundred thousand subjects, who
cost him nothing, if we do not count his guards and the militia.
Teach him that Christ, whose vicar and imitator he calls himself,
lived in poverty and with humility; he replies that times have
changed, and to prove it to you, he condemns you to perish in the
flames. You have corrected neither this man, nor a cardinal of
Lorraine, simultaneous possessor of seven bishoprics. What then is
one to do? We address ourselves to the people, we speak to them,
and brutalized as they are, they listen, they half open their eyes,
they shake off part of the most degrading yoke that was ever
borne; they rid themselves of some errors, they regain a little of
their freedom, that endowment, rather, that essence of man, of
which they had been despoiled. If we cannot cure the powerful of
ambition, at least we can cure the people of superstition; by
speaking and writing, we can make men better and more
enlightened.

It is quite easy to get them to see what they have endured for
fifteen centuries. Few people read, but all can understand. Listen
then, my dear brothers, and see the calamities that oppressed the
generations past.

Scarcely had the Christians—breathing liberty again under
Constantine—dipped their hands into the blood of the virtuous

Valeria, daughter, wife, and mother of the Caesars, and in the blood of her young son Candidian—the hope of the empire; scarcely had they murdered[1] the son of the emperor, Maximim, aged eight, and the daughter, aged seven; scarcely had these men, that have been portrayed to us as so patient for two centuries, thus signaled their fury in the beginning of the fourth century, than controversy gave birth to civil discords, which, succeeding one another without cessation, still agitate Europe. What are the subjects of these bloody quarrels? Subtleties, my brothers, of which not the least word is found in the Gospel. They wish to know whether the Son was begotten or created; if he was begotten in the confines of time or before time; if he was consubstantial or similar to the Father; if the *monad of God*, as Athanasius stated, is triune in three personalities; if the Holy Spirit is begotten or proceeding, or if it proceeds from the Father alone, or from the Father and the Son; if Jesus had two wills or one, one or two natures, one or two persons.

Finally, from *consubstantiality* to *transubstantiation*, terms as difficult to pronounce as to understand, all has been the subject of dispute, and all dispute has caused torrents of blood.

You know how much of it was spilled by our superstitious Mary, daughter of the tyrant Henry VIII, and worthy spouse of the Spanish tyrant, Philip II. The throne of Charles I was exchanged for the scaffold, and that king perished by execution, after more than two hundred thousand men had been slaughtered because of a liturgy.

You are aware of the civil wars in France. A group of fanatical theologians, called the Sorbonne, declares Henry III removed from the throne, and unexpectedly an apprentice theologian Jacques Clement assassinates him. It declares the great Henry IV, our ally, incapable of ruling, and twenty murderers succeed one another until one, a fanatic monk, a schoolmaster [Ravaillac], simply be-

[1] In 313.—*Voltaire*

cause he hears that this hero will protect his old allies against the adherents of the Pope, plunges a knife into the heart of the most valiant of kings and the best of men, in the midst of his capital city, before the eyes of his people and his friends. By an inconceivable contradiction, his memory is forever idolized, and the troupe of the Sorbonne who proscribed him, who excommunicated him and his faithful subjects, and who had no right to excommunicate anyone, still exists to the shame of France.

It is not the people, my brothers, it is not the peasant, nor the uneducated and peaceful artisan, who has started these ridiculous and fatal quarrels, source of so many abominations and so many parricides. Unfortunately, there is not one of which the theologians have not been the instigators. Men nourished by your labors, living in idleness, enriched by your sweat and misery, fought to see who would have the most partisans and the most slaves. They inspired you with a destructive fanaticism, in order to become your masters: they steeped you in superstition, not to instill in you a greater fear of God, but so that you might fear them.

The Gospel did not say to James, Peter, or Bartholomew: "Immerse yourselves in opulence; flaunt your honors; parade surrounded by guards." Furthermore it did not say: "Trouble the world with your incomprehensible questions." Jesus, my brothers, did not ask any of these questions. Should we wish to be better theologians than he whom you recognize as your only master? What! even though he told you: "All consists in loving God and your fellowman," you still strive for something else!

Is there someone among you—or rather—is there someone on earth who thinks that God will judge him on points of theology, and not upon his actions?

What is a theological opinion? It is an idea that may be true or false, but in which morality is not involved. It is quite evident that you must be virtuous whether the Holy Spirit proceeds out of the Father by spiration or proceeds from the Father and the Son. It is not less evident that you will never comprehend a proposition of this kind. You will never have the slightest notion of how Jesus had two natures and two wills in one person. If he had wanted you to know, he would have told you. I choose these examples from among a hundred others, and pass over in silence other disputes, in order not to open wounds that are still bleeding.

God has given you understanding; he cannot want you to pervert it. How can a proposition you cannot understand be useful to you? That God, who is all-giving, may have given more intelligence and talent to one man than to another, is to be seen every day. That he may have chosen a man to be closer to him than to other men; that he may have made of him a model of reason and of virtue, does not revolt our good sense. No one can deny that it may be possible for God to pour out his most beautiful gifts on one of his creations. We can then believe in Jesus, who taught virtue and practiced it; but let us fear that in desiring to go too far we overturn the whole structure.

He who is superstitious pours poison on the most healthful of foods; he is his own and other men's enemy. He believes himself the object of eternal vengeance, if he has eaten meat on a certain day; he thinks that a long gray robe, with a pointed cowl and a long beard, are much more agreeable to God than a shaven face and a full head of hair; he imagines that his salvation is dependent upon some Latin formulas that he does not understand. He educates his daughter in these principles; she buries herself in a prison from the time she is marriageable; she betrays posterity to please God; she feels guiltier than the Hindu woman who throws herself on the funeral pyre of her husband after she has borne him children.

Anchorites of southern Europe—self-condemned to a life as abject as it is hideous—do not compare yourselves with the penitents on the banks of the Ganges; your austerity does not approach their voluntary tortures; but do not think that God approves in you that which you affirm he condemns in them.

He who is superstitious is his own executioner, as he also is of whoever does not think as he does. He terms the most infamous accusation a *fraternal correction*; he accuses naive innocence that is not on its guard, and that, in the simplicity of its heart, has not placed a seal upon its lips. He denounces it to those tyrants of souls who simultaneously laugh at both the accuser and the accused.

Lastly, the superstitious man becomes fanatical, and it is then that his zeal is capable of every crime in the name of the Lord.

We no longer live, it is true, in those evil times when kinsmen and friends murdered each other, when a hundred pitched battles over some scholastic argument covered the earth with bodies. But sparks always spring out of the ashes of that immense holocaust: princes no longer march into battle at the behest of some priest or monk; but citizens still persecute each other in their own cities, and private life is often infected with the plague of superstition. What would you say of a family that would always be fighting over the manner in which it should salute the father? Look! my children the point is to love him; you address him as you think best. Are you brothers only to be divided? Must what ought to unite you always separate you?

I do not know of a single war among the Turks over religion. What did I say! a civil war? History has not recorded any sedition or trouble among them, that was provoked by such controversy. Is it because having less dogma, they have less pretext for dispute? Is it because they are born wiser and less troubled than we? They do not ask what your sect is, provided that you pay promptly a small tribute. Latin Christians, Greek Christians, Jacobites, Monothelites, Copts, Protestants, Reformed—all are welcome among them, but not even three nations among the Christians practice such humanity.

In short, my brothers, Jesus was not superstitious; he was not intolerant; he spoke with the Samaritans; he uttered not a single word against the cult of the Romans by whom his country was surrounded. Let us imitate his forbearance, and let us merit it from others.

Let us not be scared by this barbarous argument so often repeated. Here it is, I believe, in its full force.

"You believe that a virtuous man can find grace before the Being of beings, before the God of justice and mercy, at some time, in some place, in whatever religion he may have spent his short life. We, on the contrary, affirm that one can only please God by being born among us, or having been taught by us. It is proven to us that we are the only ones in the world who are right. We know that God having come upon earth, and having died for all men, wishes to have pity on our small group only, and even in this assembly there are only a few persons who will be able to escape eternal punishment. Take then the softest course, join our small group, and strive with us to be one of the elected."

Let us thank our brothers who hold this belief; let us congratulate them for being certain that the whole universe is damned, outside of a few of them, and let us believe that our sect is better than theirs, for this alone, that it is more reasonable and more compassionate. Whoever says to me: *Think as I do, or God will condemn thee*, will tell me shortly: *Think as I do, or I shall kill thee*. Let us pray God that He pacify these atrocious hearts and inspire brotherly love in all his children. Here we are in our island where the Episcopalian church rules from Dover to the little river Tweed. From there to the farthest of the Orkneys, Presbyterianism is accepted, and, under these two reigning religions there are ten or twelve other cults. Go to Italy, you will find papal despotism enthroned. It is no longer the same in France; she is treated by Rome as semi-heretical. Go to Switzerland, Germany, you go to bed today in a Calvinist city, tomorrow in a Papist one, the day after tomorrow in a Lutheran one. Go to Russia, you will see no more of all this. There is an altogether different sect. The court there is enlightened, truly, because of an imperial philosopher. August Catherine has placed reason upon the throne, as well as magnificence and generosity. But the people of her provinces detest equally Lutherans, Calvinists, and Papists. They wish neither to eat with one of them nor to drink from the same glass. Now, I ask you, my brothers, what would happen if in an assembly of all these sectarians, each would believe himself authorized by the Divine Spirit to cause his opinion to triumph? Do you not see swords drawn, gibbets readied, the fagots fired from one end of Europe to the other? Who then is right in this chaos of dispute? The tolerant, the beneficent. Do not say that in preaching tolerance we preach indifference. No, my brothers, he who worships God and does good unto men is not at all indifferent. This word far better suits the superstitious person who thinks that God will like him because he uttered unintelligible formulas, while in fact, he is very indifferent to the fate of his brother whom he allows to perish without succor, or whom he abandons in misfortune, or whom he flatters in prosperity, or whom he persecutes if he is of another creed, if he is without support and without protection. The more the superstitious man concentrates on absurd rituals and beliefs, the more indifferent he is to the true duties of humanity. Let us remember forever one of our charitable compatriots He founded a hospital for the old, in his province; he was asked if it was for Catholics, Lutherans, Presbyterians, Quakers, Socinians, Anabaptists, Methodists, Mennonites. He replied: "For mankind."

Please God! remove from us the error of atheism, which denies Thy existence; and deliver us from superstition, which outrages Thy existence and renders ours frightful.

### THIRD HOMILY—On the Interpretation of the Old Testament

My brothers, books govern the world, or at least all nations that know how to write; the others do not merit attention. The *Zend-Avesta*, attributed to the first Zoroaster, was the law of the Persians, the *Veda* and the *Shastabad* are still those of the Brahmans. The Egyptians were ruled by the books of Thoth, who was called the *First Mercury*. The *Alkoran* or *Koran* governs today, Africa, Egypt, Arabia, India, a part of Tartary, all of Persia, Scythia in the Chersonese, Asia Minor, Syria, Thrace, Thessaly, and all of Greece to the strait that separates Naples from Epirus. The Pentateuch governs the Jews and by a singular providence it is today our rule. Our duty is to read together this divine composition that is the foundation of our faith.

"In the beginning God created the heaven and the earth. And the earth was without form, and void; and darkness was upon the face of the deep. And the spirit of God moved upon the face of the waters. And God said: Let there be light, and there was light. And God saw the light, that it was good: and God divided the light from the darkness. And God called the light Day and the darkness he called Night. And the evening, and the morning were the first day. And God said, Let there be a firmament in the midst of the waters, and let it divide the waters from the waters. And God made the firmament and divided the waters which were under the firmament from the waters that were above the firmament: and it was so. And God called the firmament heaven. And the evening and the morning were the second day. And God said, Let the waters under the heaven be gathered together unto one place, and let the dry land appear; and it was so . . . ."

We know, my brothers, that God, in speaking thus to the Jews, condescended to adapt himself to their still coarse intelligence. No one is ignorant of the fact that our earth is only a dot in comparison with the space that we name improperly heaven, in which shines a prodigious number of suns, about which rotate planets that are far superior to ours. It is known that light was not made before the day and that our light comes from the sun. It is known that the solid space between the superior and inferior waters, space that literally means firmament, is an error of the ancient physical science adopted by the Greeks. But, since God was speaking to the Jews, he condescended to lower himself and speak in their language. Certainly no one would have understood him in the desert of Horeb had he said: "I have placed the sun at the center of your world; the small globe of earth rotates with the other planets around this great star, by which all the planets are illuminated; and the moon turns in one month around the earth. The other stars that you see are also suns that preside over the other worlds, etc."

If the Eternal Geometer had expressed himself thus, he would have expressed himself worthily, as a master who knew his subject; but no Jew would have understood a word of these sublime truths. This people was of a stock, stubborn and obdurate in understanding. So gross a people could only be nourished by such gross sustenance. It seems that this first chapter of Genesis was an allegory proposed by the Holy Spirit, to be explained one day by those whom God deemed worthy of his enlightenment. This was at least the idea that the leading Jews had, since they were forbidden to read the book before they were twenty-five, in order that the young people, guided by their masters, could read the work with more intelligence and respect.

The scholars claimed, then, that the Nile, the Euphrates, the Tigris, and the Araks did not literally have their sources in the terrestrial paradise, but that these four rivers that watered it signified evidently the four virtues necessary to man. It was evident, according to them, that the woman formed from the rib of man was a most striking allegory of the unalterable harmony that must pre-

vail in marriage; and that the souls of the espoused must be united,
just as their bodies are. It is the symbol of peace and of fidelity
which must reign in their society.

The serpent who captivated Eve and who *was more subtile than
any beast of the field*, is, if we believe Philo* himself and many
other Fathers, a figurative expression that portrays perceptibly our
corrupt desires. The use of words, that the Scriptures ascribe to
him, is the voice of our passions that speak to our hearts. God uses
the allegory of the serpent which was very common throughout the
Orient. He appeared cunning because he slips away quickly from
those who pursue him and strikes skillfully at those who attack
him. His change of skin was the symbol of immortality. The
Egyptians carried a silver snake in their processions. The Phoenicians, neighbors of the Hebrews' deserts, long before possessed
the allegorical fable of a serpent that had made war on man and
God. Finally, the serpent who tempted Eve had been recognized as
the Devil who wants always to tempt and corrupt us.

It is true that the doctrine of the Devil fallen from heaven and
become an enemy of mankind was not known to the Jews until
after several centuries; but the Divine Author who well knew that
one day this doctrine would be expounded deigned to plant the seed
in the first chapters of Genesis.

We know, in truth, the story of the fall of the bad angels only
through a few words in the Epistle of Jude: "Wandering stars, to
whom is reserved the blackness of darkness for ever. And Enoch
also, the seventh from Adam, prophesied of these . . . " It was
believed that these wandering stars were angels transformed into
malevolent demons and it was added to the prophesies of Enoch,
seventh man after Adam, which we no longer have. But whatever
the labyrinth in which the scholars lose themselves in explaining
these incomprehensible matters, it always ends up that we must
understand in an edifying sense all that can be taken literally.

The ancient Brahmans had theology, as we have said, many

* Philo Judaeus, a Jew, commented on the old Testament in Greek.—*kwa*

centuries before the Jewish nation existed. The ancient Persians had given several names to the Devil long before the Jews. And you know that the names of neither good nor bad angels are found in the Pentateuch. Neither Gabriel, nor Raphaël, nor Satan, nor Asmodeus were known in the Jewish books; and only a very long time after, when in slavery to Babylon, did this small nation learn these names. All of which proves at least that the doctrine of celestial and of infernal beings had been common to great nations. You will rediscover it in the book of Job, precious monument of antiquity. Job is an Arab personage; this allegory was written in Arabic. Entire Arabic phrases still remain in the Hebrew translation. Then there are Hindus, Persians, Arabs, and Jews who, one after another, admit to pretty much the same theology. Thus it is worthy of great attention.

But what is even more noteworthy is the morality that must result from all this ancient theology. Men, who are not born to be murderers, since God has not armed them as the lions and tigers; who are not born to be impostors, since they all necessarily love the truth; who are not born to be brigands and despoilers, since God has given equally to all the fruits of the earth and the fleece of sheep, but who nevertheless have become despoilers, perjurers, and murderers, are really angels transformed into demons.

Let us search forever in the Holy Scriptures, my brothers, for that which teaches us morality and not physicality.

Let the ingenious Calmet* employ his profound wisdom and his penetrating dialectic in finding the location of the terrestrial paradise; let us be content to merit, if we can, the celestial paradise by justice, tolerance, and good works.

"But for the tree of the knowledge of good and evil, thou shalt

---

* Dom Augustin Calmet (1672–1757), a Benedictine and Bishop of Senones, authored 120 volumes of *Commentaries* noted for their exact and critical treatment of the Old and New Testaments. The *Commentaries* were an invaluable source of ammunition for the philosophes, as Voltaire here attests. However Voltaire visited with Calmet in 1744 and again in 1756; during the first visit he wrote his *Essay on Customs* (Essai sur les Moeurs) in the Bishop's residence.—*kwa*

not eat of it; for in the day that thou eatest thereof thou shalt surely die."

Scholars acknowledge that there has never been a tree that gave knowledge. Adam did not die the day he ate of it; he lived for another nine hundred thirty years, says the Holy Scripture. Alas! what are nine centuries between two eternities? They are not even a minute in time and our days pass imperceptibly as a shadow. But does not this allegory tell us clearly that knowledge ill-understood is capable of destroying us? The tree of knowledge carries bitter fruit, since so many learned theologians have been persecuted or persecutors and so many have suffered a frightful death. Ah, my brothers, the Holy Spirit has desired to make us see how false knowledge is dangerous, how it puffs up the heart and at what point a scholar is often absurd.

It is from this passage that St. Augustine inferred the imputation made to all men from the disobedience of the first. It is he who developed the doctrine of original sin, both that the impurity of this sin may have corrupted our bodies, and that the souls that enter into our bodies may be steeped in it; a mystery in every way incomprehensible, but which warns us at least not to live in wickedness, although we are born in wickedness.

"And the Lord set a mark upon Cain, lest any finding him should kill him" [Gen. 4:15]. It is here above all, my brothers, that the Fathers are opposed to one another. Adam's family was not yet numerous; the Scripture gave him no other children than Abel and Cain at the time that the first was assassinated by his brother. How is God obliged to safeguard Cain against all those who will be able to punish him? Let us note only that God pardons Cain, a fratricide, after having doubtlessly caused him remorse. Let us profit by this lesson; let us not condemn our brothers to the most dreadful torments for trivial reasons. When God deigns to have indulgence for an abominable murder, let us imitate the God of mercy. Someone will raise the objection that God, while pardoning a cruel murderer, forever damns all men for the transgression of

Adam, who was only guilty of having eaten a forbidden fruit. To our feeble reason it seems that God may be unjust in branding for eternity all the descendants of the guilty one, not in order to atone for a fratricide but for a disobedience that seems excusable. It is, they say, an intolerable contradiction that cannot be conceded in the infinitely good Being; but this contradiction is only apparent. After delivering us, our fathers and our children, to the flames for the disobedience of Adam, God sends Jesus Christ, four hundred years later, to save us, and spares Cain's life in order to people the earth; thus he is everywhere the God of justice and mercy. St. Augustine calls Adam's fault a happy fault; but that of Cain was happier still, since God himself placed on him a sign which was a mark of his protection.

"Thou shalt make a roof on the ark of a cubit in height . . . "* We arrive here at the greatest of the miracles before which the heart is shattered and reason must be humbled. We know full well with what disdainful audacity the incredulous rise against the prodigy of a universal deluge.

In vain they object that in the rainiest years, not thirty inches of water a year falls on the earth; that moreover, this year there are as many areas that have not received rain as there are inundated areas; that the law of gravity prevents the ocean from exceeding its bounds; that should it cover the earth, it would leave its bed dry; that in covering the earth it could not rise above mountain peaks of fifteen cubits; that the animals that entered the ark could not have come from America or the southern lands; that seven pairs of clean animals and two pairs of unclean animals for each species could not have been contained even in twenty arks; that these twenty arks could not have held all the forage that they would need, not only for ten months, but during the following year, a year during which a too sodden earth could produce nothing; that animals that were the meat eaters would have perished for want of nourishment;

* Voltaire's version of Genesis 6:16.—*kwa*

that eight persons in the ark would not have been enough to distribute to the animals their daily provender. In a word, they are forever expatiating over difficulties; but all these difficulties are removed by showing them that this great event is a miracle; from then on, all dispute is ended.

"Go to, let us build us a city and a tower, whose top may reach unto heaven; and let us make us a name lest we be scattered abroad upon the face of the whole earth." [Gen. 11:4].

The incredulous maintain that a people can acquire fame and still be dispersed. They ask if mankind has ever been so senseless as to desire to build a tower that would reach to the sky. They say that this tower reaches only into the air, and that if by air one means the sky, it will necessarily be in the sky, even if it was only twenty feet high; and if at the time all men spoke the same language, the wisest thing they could have done was to congregate in the same city, and prevent the corruption of their language. They were apparently all in their own country, since they were all in accord about building it there. To drive them out of their own country is tyrannical; to force them to speak new languages all at once is absurd. Consequently, they say the story of the tower of Babel can only be regarded as an Oriental tale.

My reply to this blasphemy is that this miracle, having been written by an author who has reported so many other miracles, must be believed just as the others. The works of God are in no way bound to resemble the works of men. The centuries of the patriarchs and the prophets have nothing to do with the centuries of ordinary men. God, who no longer descends upon the earth, descended then often in order to see his works for himself. This is in the tradition of all the great nations of antiquity. The Greeks, who had no knowledge of the Jewish books until long after the translation done by Hellenistic Jews in Alexandria, had believed, before Homer and Hesiod, that the great Zeus and all the other Gods descended from the air to visit the earth. What fruit can we pluck from this generally established idea? That we are always in the presence of God, that we must not commit ourselves to any action or thought, which may not conform to his justice. In a word, the tower of Babel is no more extraordinary than all the rest. The book is equally authentic in all its parts: one cannot deny one case without denying all the others: we must conquer our proud reason whether we read this story as veracious or regard it as symbolic.

"And in the same day the Lord made a covenant with Abraham, saying: Unto thy seed have I given this land, from the river of Egypt unto the great river, the river Euphrates" [Gen. 15:18]. The unbelievers triumph in seeing that the Jews have never possessed more than a part of what God promised them. They find it even unjust that the Lord may have given them that portion. They say that the Jews had not the least right there; that a journey made formerly by a Chaldean, in a foreign country, could not constitute a legitimate pretext for invading this small land; that today a man who declares himself a descendant of St. Patrick would be badly received on coming to plunder Ireland, saying that he had received an order from God. But let us always consider how times have changed; let us respect the Jewish books, making sure to never imitate this nation. God no longer commands what he commanded in other days.

The question is asked who is this Abraham and why the Jewish people originated from a Chaldean, son of a heathen potter, who had no tie with the people of the country of Canaan and who could not understand their language? This Chaldean went to Memphis with his wife bowed under the burden of age but still beautiful. Why did this couple leave Memphis for the desert of Gerar? How was it that there was a king in that horrible desert? How is it that the king of Egypt and the king of Gerar were both in love with Abraham's aged spouse? These are only historical difficulties; what is essential is to give obedience to God. The Holy Scripture always represents Abraham to us as unreservedly submissive to the will of the Most High: let us aspire to emulate him rather than argue about him.

And there came two angels to Sodom at evening. . . . [Gen. 19

entire]. This is a bedrock of scandal for those critics who listen solely to their reason. Two angels, that is to say two spiritual creatures, two celestial ministers of God, who have corporeal bodies, who inspire infamous desires in a whole city, even in the old men; a father of a family who wishes to prostitute his two daughters in order to save the honor of these two angels; a city changed into a lake by fire; a woman metamorphosed into a statue of salt; two girls who deceive and inebriate their father in order to commit incest with him, for fear, they say, that his race may perish, while they have all the inhabitants of the city of Zoar among whom they could choose! All these events assembled form a revolting image; but if we are reasonable, we shall come to the same conclusion as St. Clement of Alexandria and all the Fathers who have followed him, that this is all allegory.

Let us remember that this was the manner of expression in the Orient. Parables were in use for such a long time, that when the Author of all truth came upon this earth, He spoke to the Jews only in parables.

The parables constitute all the profane theology of antiquity. Saturn who devours his children, is obviously, an example of time which destroys its own work. Minerva is wisdom; she was formed in the head of the master of the gods. The infant Cupid's arrows and blindfold are obviously only symbols. The fall of Phaeton is an admirable symbol of ambition. All is not allegory in pagan theology nor is it in the sacred history of the Jewish nation. The Church Fathers distinguish what is purely history or purely parable or what is a mixture of the two. It is difficult, I agree, to walk in these rugged paths; but provided that we learn to conduct ourselves in the path of virtue, what matters to us the path of knowledge?

The crime that God punishes is horrible; let that suffice us. Lot's wife was changed into a pillar of salt for having looked behind her. Let us moderate the passions of our curiosity; in a word, let all the stories of the Scripture serve to make us better persons, even if they do not render us more enlightened.

There are, it seems to me, my brothers, two ways of interpreting, figuratively and in a mystical sense, the Holy Scriptures. The first, which is incontestably the better, is to extract from all cases instructions for the conduct of life. If Jacob does a cruel injustice to his brother Esau, if he cheats his father-in-law Laban, let us keep peace in our families and act with justice toward our parents. If the patriarch Reuben dishonors the bed of his father Jacob, let us hold this incest in horror. If the patriarch Judah commits a still more odious incest with Tamar, his daughter-in-law, let us have only a greater aversion for these iniquities. When David ravishes the wife of Uriah and then murders her husband; when Solomon assassinates his brother; when nearly all the petty Jewish kings are barbarous murderers, let us change our morals in reading this frightful list of crimes. Let us, in short, read the whole Bible in this spirit; it disturbs him who wants to be a scholar, it consoles him who only wishes to be a good man.

The other way of developing the hidden meaning of the Scriptures is to consider each even as an historical and physical symbol. This is the method that St. Clement, the great Origen, the respectable St. Augustine, and so many other Fathers have employed. According to them, the bit of red cloth that the prostitute Rahab hangs in her window is the blood of Jesus Christ. Moses, extending his arms, foretells the sign of the Cross. Judah tying his ass's foal to a vine, portrays the entry of Jesus Christ into Jerusalem. St. Augustine compares Noah's ark to Jesus. St. Ambrose, in book seven of his *de Arca,* says that the small passage door contrived in the ark signifies the opening through which man ejects the coarse part of his food. If indeed all these explanations were true, what kernel could we extract from them? Will men be more just when they know the meaning of the little door in the ark? This method of explicating the Holy Scriptures is only a subtlety of the mind, and it can do injury to the simplicity of the heart.

Let us discard all subjects of dispute which divide nations, and discern the common bonds which may unite them. Submission to

God, resignation, justice, goodwill, compassion, tolerance, these are the great principles. May all the theologians of the earth live together like the merchants who, without questioning in what country they were born, in what tradition they have been schooled, follow among them the inviolable rules of equity, fidelity, and reciprocal confidence! Because of these principles they are the ties between all nations; but those who know only their own opinions and who condemn all others; those who believe that the light shines only upon them and that all others walk in darkness; those who would harbor a scruple against communing with foreign religions, do not all these merit the title of enemies of humanity?

I shall not conceal that the best-informed men assert that the Pentateuch is not by Moses. Newton, the great Newton, who alone has discovered the first principle of nature, who alone has known the light, this astonishing genius who has researched so profoundly in ancient history, attributes the Pentateuch to Samuel. Other men respected for their learning believe that it was written in the time of Hosea by the scribe Saphan; finally others claim that Ezra was the author on his return from captivity. All are in accord with modern Jews in disbelieving that this was the work of Moses. This concerted objection is not as terrible as it seems. We shall certainly revere the Decalogue no matter what hand wrote it. We are in dispute over the date of many laws that some attribute to Edward III and others to Edward II; but we adopt these laws, because we find them just and useful. If indeed, in the preamble, there are doubtful points that one revokes, if our fellow citizens reject these points, they do not reject the law, which continues to exist.

Let us always distinguish history from dogma and dogma from morality, from that eternal morality that all lawgivers have taught, and that all peoples have received.

O divine morality! O my God who art the creator of it! I shall not enclose You within the bounds of a province; You reign over all thinking and sensible beings. You are the God of Jacob, but You are the God of the universe.

I cannot finish this discourse, dear brothers, without speaking of
the prophets. Here is an important subject upon which our enemies
think to overwhelm us. They say that in antiquity all peoples had
their prophets, their divinators, their seers; but for example, if the
Egyptians formerly had false prophets, does it follow that the Jews
could not have had true ones? It is claimed that they had no
mission, no standing, no legal authorization, that is true, but could
they not have been authorized by God himself? They anathema-
tized each other; they treated each other as cheats and madmen;
and the prophet Zedekiah even dared to slap the prophet Micaiah
in the presence of King Jehosaphat. The *Paralipomenes** narrate
this instance; but is a ministry any less holy when its ministers dis-
honor it? And have not our priests done a hundred times worse
than slapping someone?

God orders Ezekiel to eat a book of parchment; to put human
excrement on his bread; then to divide his hair into three parts
and to throw one part into the fire; to tie himself up; to lie three
hundred ninety days on the left side and forty days upon the right
side. God expressly commands the prophet Hosea to take a "wife
of whoredoms" and to have "children of whoredoms." Finally
God wills that Hosea lie with an adulteress for fifteen drachmas
and a bushel and a half of barley All of these commandments
of God scandalize the souls who call themselves learned; but
will they not be more learned, if they see that these are allegories,
symbols, parables, suited to the customs of the Israelites; that one
must not hold a people to account for its usages, nor demand that
God account for orders that he has given in accordance with these
accepted usages?

Let us be edified by that which offends others; let us draw
salutary nourishment from what may be poison to them. When the
actual and literal sense of a passage seems conformable with our
reason, let us take it in this natural sense. When it seems contrary

---

* In the King James version, I Kings 22:24–27—*kwa*

to truth, to morality, let us search out the hidden meaning in which truth and morality are reconciled with the Holy Scripture. This is the way the Fathers of the Church have used it, and the way we act in the daily affairs of life; we always interpret favorably the discourse of our friends and partisans; shall we treat the holy books of the Jews—the object of our faith—more harshly? In the end let us read the Jewish books in order to be Christians; and if they do not render us wiser, they may serve at least to better us.

## FOURTH HOMILY—On the Interpretation of the New Testament

My brothers, in the New Testament as in the Old, there are profundities that we cannot fathom, and sublimities that feeble reason cannot attain. I shall claim here neither to reconcile the Gospels, which seem sometimes to contradict themselves, nor to explain the mysteries that, because they are mysteries, must be unexplained. Let men more learned than I investigate whether the Holy Family went into Egypt after the massacre of children in Bethlehem according to St. Matthew, or remained in Judea according to St. Luke. Let them determine whether Joseph's father was called Jacob, his grandfather Mathan, his great-grandfather Eleazar; or whether his great-grandfather was Levi, his grandfather Mathat, his father Heli: let them dispose of this genealogical tree according to their lights; it is a study that I respect. I do not know if it will clarify my mind, but I know full well that it cannot speak to my heart. Knowledge is not virtue. Paul the Apostle said himself, in his first Epistle to Timothy, that it is unnecessary to be preoccupied with genealogies. We shall be no better persons for knowing exactly who were Joseph's ancestors, the year in which Jesus was born, or if James was his brother or his first cousin. What shall it

have benefited us to have consulted all that remains to us of the
Roman annals in order to determine if in fact Augustus ordered
that there be made a census of the peoples of the earth when Mary
was pregnant with Jesus, when Quirinus was governor of Syria and
Herod still reigned in Judea? Quirinus, whom St. Luke calls
Cyrenus (say the scholars), was not governor of Syria until ten
years after: it was not in the time of Herod but that of Archelaus,
and never did Augustus order a census of the Roman Empire.*

We are told that the Epistle to the Hebrews, attributed to Paul,
was not Paul's; that neither Revelations nor the Gospel of John are
John's; that the first chapter of this Gospel is evidently by a Greek
Platonist; that this book could not possibly be by a Jew; that never
would a Jew have attributed these words to Jesus: "A new commandment I give unto you, that ye love one another." Certainly,
they say, this commandment was not new. It is stated expressly
and in most energetic terms in the laws of Leviticus: "Thou shalt
love thy Lord above all and thy neighbor as thyself." A man such
as Jesus Christ, they say, a man learned in the Scriptures and who
confounded the doctors at the age of twelve; a man who spoke always of the law, could not have been ignorant of the law; and his
beloved disciple could not have imputed to him so palpable an
error.

My brothers, let us not be troubled, let us consider that Jesus
spoke in a language little understood by the Greeks, composed of
Syriac and Phoenician; that we have the Gospel of St. John only in
Greek; that his Gospel was written more than fifty years after the
death of Jesus; that copyists could easily have altered the text; that
it is more probable that the text read: "I make a commandment to
you that is not new"; that it is not probable in fact that it carried
these words: "I make you a new commandment." Finally, let us

* The census mentioned in the Gospel of Luke was ordered by Herod who acted
with Sentius Saturninus to carry it out. [L. R. Taylor, *American Jour. Philol.*,
1933, p. 120]. Herod's census was possibly the result of Augustus' order to take a
census of the eastern provinces of the empire which were near bankruptcy.—*kwa*

return to our great principle: the precept is good; it is up to us to follow it if we can, be it Zoroaster who first announced it, or Moses who wrote it, or Jesus who reviewed it.

Should we penetrate the blackest depths of antiquity in order to determine if the darkness that covered the earth at the death of Jesus was an eclipse of the sun in full moon; if an astronomer named Phlegon, no longer alive had spoken of this phenomenon, or if anyone else has ever observed the star of the three Magi? These difficulties can preoccupy a student of the past; but in consuming precious time in disentangling this chaos he will not have employed it in good works; he will have more doubt than piety. My brothers, he who shares his bread with the poor is worth far more than he who has compared the Hebrew text with the Greek, and both with the Samaritan.

That which regards history gives birth to a thousand disputes; that which concerns our duty is not subject to them. You shall never understand how the Devil carried God into the desert; how he tempted him during forty days; how he transported him to the heights of a hill from where could be discovered all the kingdoms of the earth. The Devil who offers these realms to God, provided that God adores him, could revolt your soul; you shall seek out what mystery is hidden in these words and so many others. Your intellect will be exhausted in vain; each word will plunge you into uncertainty and the anguish of an uneasy curiosity that cannot be satisfied. But if you keep yourself within the bounds of morality, the tempest dissipates and you will repose in the bosom of virtue.

I dare to flatter myself, my brothers, that if the greatest of enemies of the Christian religion were to overhear us in this remote temple where the love of virtue brings us together; if the Lords Herbert, Shaftesbury, Bolingbroke, if the Tindals, Tolands, Collinses, Whistons, Trenchards, Gordons, and Swifts were witnesses of our gentle and innocent simplicity, they would have less contempt for and horror of us. They unceasingly accuse us of absurd fanaticism. We are not fanatics because we follow the religion

of Jesus; he adored God and we adore Him; he scorned vain ceremonial; and we despise it. No Gospel has stated that his mother
was the mother of God; nor that he was consubstantial with God,
nor that he had two natures and two wills in one person, nor that
the Holy Ghost proceeded from the Father and the Son. You will
find in no Gospel that the disciples of Jesus must arrogate to
themselves the title of *holy father*, or *lord*, or of *monseigneur*; that
twelve thousand pieces of gold must be the revenue of a priest who
lives in Lambeth, while so many useful farmers scarcely have
enough with which to sow the three or four acres they till—and
water with tears. The Gospel did not say to the bishops of Rome:
"Forge a Donation of Constantine in order to seize the city of the
Scipios and the Caesars, in order to dare to be suzerains of the
kingdom of Naples. German bishops, take advantage of a period
of anarchy to invade half of Germany." Jesus was a poor man who
preached to the poor. What should we say of the disciples of Penn
and Fox, enemies of ostentation, enemies of titles, lovers of
peace, if surrounded by soldiers they paraded with gold mitres on
their heads; if they despoiled the substance of the people; if they
wanted to govern kings, if their hangers-on followed by executioners would cry out in a loud voice: "Nation of fools, believe in
Fox and Penn or you shall be tortured to death"?

You know as well as I what a noxious contrast the centuries
have witnessed between the humility of Jesus and the pride of those
who have made a show of his name; between their avarice and his
poverty; between their debauchery and his chastity; between his
submission and their bloody tyranny.

Of all his words, my brothers, I confess that none have made a
greater impression than his response to those who had the brutality
to beat him before putting him to torture: "If I have spoken evil,
bear witness to the evil: but if well, why smitest thou me?" [John
18:23]. This is what must be said to all persecutors. If I have a different opinion than yours upon matters that are impossible to
understand; if I see the mercy of God where you wish only to see

his power; if I have said that all of the disciples of Jesus were equal when you have believed it your duty to trample them under foot; if I have adored only God, when you have given him associates; furthermore, if I have uttered evil in not being of your mind, testify to the evil; and if I have spoken what is good, why do you overwhelm me with abuse and opprobrium? Why do you pursue me, throw me in irons, deliver me to the torture, to the flames, revile me even after death? Alas! if I have spoken evil, you ought to pity me and instruct me. You are sure that you are infallible and that your opinion is divine; that the gates of hell shall never prevail against it; that one day all the earth will embrace your opinion; that the world will submit to you; that you will reign from the Atlas Mountains to the isles of Japan: in what way, then, can my opinion hurt you? You do not fear me, but you persecute me! you despise me, and you put me to death!

What to respond, my brothers, to these modest but powerful reproaches? That which the wolf replies to the lamb? "Thou has troubled the water that I drink." Thus have men treated one another, the Gospel and the sword in hand; preaching unselfishness while amassing treasure; proclaiming humility while treading upon the heads of prostrate princes; appealing for mercy even while they cause human blood to flow.

If these barbarians find some parable in the Gospel, the sense of which can be distorted in their favor by some fraudulent interpretation, they have seized it as an anvil upon which to forge their murderous weapons.

If two swords* suspended from a ceiling are spoken of, they arm themselves with a hundred swords in order to strike. If it is said that a king has slaughtered his fattened animals [Matt. 22:4], has forced the blind and the lame to come to his feast [Luke 14:23],

---

* Possibly an allusion to the "doctrine of the two swords" expounded by Boniface VIII in the famous bull *Unam Sanctam*, 1302, wherein it is asserted that the Papacy, the spiritual sword, is supreme over kings who wield the temporal sword.— *kwa*

and has him who does not have his nuptial robe cast into the outer darkness [Matt. 22:13], does this my brothers, give them the right to shut you in a dungeon like that guest, to dismember you by torture, to pluck out your eyes and render you blind like those who have been dragged to that feast; to kill you, as that king butchered his fatted animals? It is however such misunderstandings that are used to justify the desolation of a great part of the world. These terrible words [Matt. 10:34]: "I came not to send peace, but a sword," have caused more Christians to die than ambition ever did.

The Jews, dispersed and unhappy, console themselves in their humiliation when they see us always opposed to one another since the first days of Christianity, always at war whether openly or secretly, the persecuted and the persecutors, the oppressors and the oppressed; they are united among themselves and they laugh at our eternal quarrels. It seems that we have been possessed solely with the notion of wreaking vengeance upon them.

Wretches that we are! We insult the pagans, and they have never known our theological quarrels; they have never spilled a drop of blood in explaining a dogma; and we have inundated the earth with it. I would say to you above all, in the bitterness of my heart: Jesus has been persecuted; whosoever will think like him will like him be persecuted. Because, after all, what was Jesus to the eyes of men, who could not with certainty surmise his divinity? He was a good man who, born in poverty, denounced to the poor the superstition of the wealthy Pharisees and insolent priests; he was the Socrates of Galilee. You are aware that he said to the Pharisees [Matt. 23:24, 25]: "Ye blind guides, which strain at a gnat, and swallow a camel: Woe unto you, [Scribes and Pharisees, hypocrites!] for ye make clean the outside of the cup and of the platter, but within they are full of extortion and excess."

He often called them [Matt. 23:27, 33] *whited sepulchers, generation of vipers*. They were, however, men constituted in dignity. They avenged themselves by torturing him to death. Arnold of

Brescia, John Hus, Jerome of Prague said a great deal less about the pontiffs of their day, and they were tortured just the same. Never clash with the dominant superstition, if you are not powerful enough to resist it, or clever enough to escape the consequences. The story of Our Lady Of Loreto* is more extravagant than all the *Metamorphoses* of Ovid, it is true; the miracle of San Gennaro** at Naples is more ridiculous than that of Ignatia, of whom Horace speaks, I agree; but stating forthrightly in Naples, in Loreto, what you think of these absurdities will cost you your life. It is not thus among some more enlightened nations: the peoples there have their errors, but they are less gross; and the least superstitious people is always the most tolerant.

Let us reject then all superstition in order to become more human: but in speaking against fanaticism, let us not irritate the fanatics; they are sick persons in delirium who wish to beat up their doctors. Let us alleviate their ills, let us never exasperate them, but let us pour drop by drop into their souls the divine balm of tolerance, which they would reject in horror were it presented to them in one dose.


## FIFTH HOMILY—On the Communion Delivered in London in a Special Assembly Easter Day, 1769[1]

We are here assembled, my brethren, for the most august and holiest ceremony of the year: the communion.

What is the communion? It is to share one's obligation in com-

---

* Angels transported the house of the Virgin Mary from Nazareth to a site south of Ancona in Italy to protect it from the Jews and Muslims. Many miracles are said to have occurred there attributed to the Virgin (Our Lady).—*kwa*

** San Gennaro (Sanctus Janurius), about A.D. 305, was cast into a fiery furnace and came out unscathed. He was not, however, able to survive ultimate martyrdom. He was beheaded. The approach of his head causes blood to boil.—*kwa*

[1] The first four Homilies were of 1767.—*Beuchot*

mon; to communicate the fraternal spirit that ought to animate mankind. Here we commemorate a supper that Christ—whom we recognize as our lawgiver—had with his disciples. He ordained that we do something "in remembrance" of him [Luke 22:19]. We obey. It is true that we do not eat lamb cooked with lettuce, such as he ate, in accordance with the ritual of the Jewish law, which he observed from the moment of his birth until the last moment of his life; it is true that our light repast is no longer a supper as it was in other times; it is true that we do not send to the house of an unknown person to tell him [Matt. 26:18]: "The master saith, My time is at hand; I will keep the Passover at thy house with my disciples." In the morning we gather together in contemplation, we eat the same consecrated bread, we drink the same wine.

But why should we serve this communal nourishment, if we should not have a community of charity, beneficence, tolerance of all the social virtues?

I will not argue here about spiritual mastication, different from the real one, I shall enter into none of the scholastic distinctions, they are too far above our happy simplicity. Let Pope Innocent III, in his fourth book of *Mysteries*, expend his great genius on what would happen to the mystical or real body of Jesus if a communicant got diarrhea, and what form his excrement would take; these concerns are too sublime for me.

Let Durand, in his *Rational* (Book IV, chap. xli), decide what matters are begotten by accident; let Tolet,* in his *Priestly Instruction*, vow that a priest could consecrate and transubstantiate all of a baker's bread and all of a tavernkeeper's wine; let the Council of Trent add that this transformation does not occur unless the priest may expressly intend it; let many doctors say that in the Eucharist there is quantity without *quantum*, and accident without substance;

* David Durand, a Protestant minister, lived in England appointed by the government as minister of the French Church in Savoy. He was principally known for his *Religion of the Mahometans*, a work that Voltaire must have known as a contemporary. Francois, Cardinal Tolet, a Jesuit, attained remark as the one who brought the Protestant Henry IV of France into the Roman Church.—*kwa*

let them declare that someone can be snubnosed without having a
nose and lame without havings legs, *simitas sine naso, claudicatio
sine crure*: I do not believe that a knowledge of these sublime
issues will serve to make us better men or that we acquire greater
virtue for having investigated how one can be snubnosed without a
nose.

What is deplorable, gentlemen, what is horrible, is that blood
has flowed during two centuries over these theological matters,
and that our Queen Mary, daughter of Henry VIII, caused to burn
more than eight hundred citizens who did not wish to agree that
roundness might exist without a round body, and that there might
be whiteness without a white substance. We can only dip the little
bread that we shall eat together in our tears while we recall the
memory of the calamities and horrors that flooded nearly all of
Europe over matters that would make the Kaffir and the Hottentot
blush and feel as much indignation as scorn for us.

The holy ceremony that we are going to perform is called a
sacrament; very well: I did not come here to dispute about words.
Neither you nor I know what a sacrament is; it is a Latin word
that meant an oath among the Romans. I do not see that we take
any oath here. We are told today that sacrament is the same thing
as saying *mystery*; I agree to that, without having the least idea of
what a mystery is. Among the Greeks this word signified something hidden. But why is it necessary that there be hidden things in
religion? Ought not everything be public? Ought it not be common
to all men to whom the same God gave birth, and upon whom the
sun shines equally?

If someone made a point of telling us that the adoration of God,
the love of our neighbor, justice, moderation, compassion, alms,
are mysteries, none of us would believe him. Men never hide their
projects, their feelings, their conduct, unless in doing evil or from
fear of being recognized. Why then should we put into a religion
what we abhor in civil life? What should we say of a hidden law, of
a law that could be understood with difficulty only by a small

number of lawyers? How should we follow this law, especially if in-
terpretations of it were never in accord? All law that is not clear,
precise, intelligible to all minds, is only a snare set by the cheat for
simple souls. A mysterious decree by a sovereign would be something so absurd and so intolerable that I do not believe there is a
single example of it on earth. Shall we accuse God of having done
what the most senseless of tyrants were never so insane as to do?
Would God speak only in enigmas to humanity? What am I
saying! To the smallest part of humanity, in order to hide himself
entirely from all the rest, and to show himself only in part to this
small number of favorites who with many crimes have contended
among themselves for the good graces of their master?

God said to all men: "Love me and be just." There is a clear
law, and one about which it is impossible to dispute. When we find
in our codes of law equivocal passages—a great plague afflicting
humans—we attempt to interpret them in the most reasonable
sense; we abide by that part of the law which is most clearly enun-
ciated. Now then, I ask you, what is more reasonable and more
luminous than these words: "Do this in memory of me"? It is by
virtue of these words that we are assembled. We perform a ceremony that we believe necessary, because it is ordained, because it
inspires harmony among us, because it renders us more dear to one
another.

But in uniting ourselves more closely, we do not regard as our
enemies the Christians called Quakers, or Anabaptists, or Mennonites, who do not take communion; the Presbyterians who com-
mune by consuming Jesus Christ spiritually; the Lutherans and the
Anglicans who consume at the same time the body and the bread
and drink at the same time the blood and the wine; and even the
Papists who claim to eat the body and drink the blood, while
touching neither bread nor wine. We comprehend nothing of the
ideas or rather the words of ones or the others, but we look upon
them as brothers whose language we do not understand. We pray
for them without understanding them; we unite ourselves with them

in spite of themselves, in that spirit of charity which makes one great dispersed family of the whole world: *Caritas humani generis,\** said Cicero, if I may here quote from a heathen who was a virtuous man.

Woe to every sect that says: "I alone am upon the earth; the light shines only for me; a dark night covers the eyes of all other men; only for me have the vast heavens been created; there is my home; all others are condemned to an existence of eternal horror and desolation!"

Such inhuman language is less that of a heart grateful for the mercy of God which has distinguished it from the mass of beings than an expression of insensate pride delighting in its own rash illusions. Callousness necessarily accompanies such a pride. How could a man unfortunately permeated with so abominable a belief have feelings of compassion for those whom he thinks God holds in horror, from all eternity and for all eternity? He can only see them with the same eyes with which he professes to see demons that have been pictured to him as his enemies in different forms. If sometimes he shows toward them a little humanity, it is because nature, stronger in him than his prejudices, has in spite of himself mollified the heart that his sect hardened; the natural virtue that God has given him outweighs the religion that he has received from men.

Gentlemen, the chief of the Papist sect is not alone in calling himself infallible; all those who belong to his intolerant church think they are as infallible as he; and it could not be otherwise; they have adopted all his dogma. According to them, their leader cannot err: therefore they cannot err in believing what their master teaches, and in doing everything that he commands. This excess of madness is perpetuated particularly in the cloisters. There rules conviction, enemy of inquiry, and fanaticism, fierce offspring of conviction. It is there that blind obedience crawls, burning with a desire to command others; there are forged the shackles that have enchained so many nations one after another. The small number

---

\* "The love of humanity."—*kwa*

which has discovered the fraud, and laments it in secret, is only the more eager to spread it around; it derives a fiendish pleasure from enforcing belief in what it does not believe, and its hypocrisy is sometimes more of a persecution than fanaticism itself.

This is the yoke under which a part of Europe still bows its head, a yoke that we detest, but that we ourselves carried for a long time, when a legate came to our island to open and close heaven for a price in gold; to sell indulgences and collect a tithe; to terrify people or incite them to wars that he called holy. I believe, my brothers, that those times will never return; but to insure that they will not return, we must often recall them to memory.

Let us profit from this sacred ceremony that inspires charity in us, so that we will never allow religion to inspire tyranny and discord in us. Here we are all equals; here we all partake of the same bread and of the same wine; here we render unto the Being of beings the same acts of grace. We should never allow foreigners to have the insolence to prescribe laws as if they were our masters nor to dictate the manner in which we ought to adore the universal Master, nor to tell us how we ought to behave or what we ought to think. A stranger has no more right to our consciences than to our purses. However, in one of our three realms there is a foreigner who still secretly dominates.[2] Into that place are sent unknown ministers who spy upon consciences. In that place are in fact mysteries and a hidden religion. Secretly it insinuates discord, while we openly proclaim peace; its communion is nothing but the rejection of other men; in its eyes all are either heretic or infidel. From the time that it usurped the throne of the Caesars, it has not changed its line; and although the eyes of nearly all nations may be opened finally to its absurd pretensions and to its depredations, it preserves, in its decadence, the same pride that it possessed when it saw so many kings on their knees before it. In vain our first legislator said: "There shall be neither first nor last among you";[3]

[2] Ireland.
[3] This is not textually in the Gospel; what it says is that "The first shall be last"; see Matthew 19:30; 20:16, Mark 10:31: Luke 13:30.—*M. Beuchot*

the Bishop of Rome still proclaims himself the first among men because his see is in a city that formerly was the first in the Occident.

What would you think, my dear brothers, of a surveyor from London who believed himself king of all surveyors of our territory, under the pretext that he practiced surveying in the capital? Would we not lock him up as insane if he dared to order that no one should believe in the properties of triangles, without an edict emanating from his office? However that is what the Roman Church has done: except that the opinions which it teaches are hardly geometrical truths.

Yet, let us pray for it, provided that it is not engaged in persecution; and let us regard the Papists as our brothers, although they do not wish to be our brothers. Judge which of us comes closest to the greatest law of nature. They say to us: "You are in error and we condemn you." We reply to them: "You appear to be in slavery, in ignorance, of demented mind: we pity you and cherish you."

May the fruit of our communion then always be, my brothers, to behold human frailty and misery without aversion and without anger, and to love, if it is possible, those we consider devoid of reason as much as those who seem to us to be on the road of truth, when they think like ourselves.

After our being strengthened in this first duty of all men—of whatever religion they might be—to adore God and love one's neighbor, how would it be useful to us to determine on what day Jesus partook of the Paschal Supper, if he lay upon a couch while eating, in the manner of the Roman aristocracy, or if he ate standing, staff in hand, as the Jewish law ordained [Ex. 12: 11]. Will the morality that ought to direct all our conduct be more pure if we discuss whether Jesus was crucified on the eve, or the day before the eve of the Jewish Passover? If this is not clear in the Gospels, it is very clear that we ought to be good people every day of the year preceding and following this ceremony.

Many scholars are disturbed because the Gospel of St. John says nothing about the institution of the Eucharist, about the blessing of the bread, and about those mysterious words that have caused so much misery: "This is my body; this is the chalice of my blood." They are astounded because the well-loved disciple keeps silence upon the principal point of the mission of his master.

They dispute about the hour of his death, and about the women who gave assistance in his torment—St. Matthew saying that they were far away and St. John affirming to the contrary that they were near the Cross, and that Jesus spoke to them.

There is argument about his Resurrection, about his apparitions, about his ascent into the air. The very words that we find in St. John [20:17]: "I ascend unto my father and your Father, and to my God, and your God," have furnished to the church of those who are called Socinians a pretext, which they have believed plausible, to maintain that Jesus was not God but only sent by God.

They cannot decide upon the place from which he ascended into heaven. St. Luke says that it was in Bethany; St. Mark does not state in which place. St. John and St. Matthew do not speak of it. St. Luke in his Gospel [24:51], gives us to understand that Jesus ascended into heaven the day after his resurrection: In the Acts of the Apostles [1:3], it is said that it was forty days after. All these contradictions exasperate the spirit of scholars but do not render them more modest, nor more gentle, nor more compassionate.

The birth, the life, and the death of Jesus are eternal subjects of interminable disputes. St. Luke tells us that Augustus ordered a census of all the land and that Joseph and Mary came to Bethlehem to be counted, although Joseph was not a native of Bethlehem, but of Galilee. However no other Roman author, nor Flavius Josephus himself makes mention of this census. Luke says that Joseph and Mary were enumerated under Cyrenus or Quirinus, governor of Syria; but it is asserted by Tacitus that this Cyrenus or Quirinus did not govern Syria until ten years after, and that Quintilius Varus was then governor. Luke names Heli as the father of Joseph and grandfather of Jesus; Matthew lists Jacob as Joseph's father; and both, while giving an absolutely different genealogy for Joseph, tell us that Jesus was not his son. Luke assures us that Joseph and Mary took Jesus into Galilee; Matthew says that they took him into Egypt.

Should an angel, my brothers, descend from the Milky Way in order to resolve these conflicts, and were he to tell us the true name of Joseph's father, of what good would it be to us? What would it profit us? Would we be better persons? Is it not evident that we ought to be good fathers, good spouses, good sons, good citizens, whether the father of Joseph called himself Heli or Jacob, or whether they took the infant Jesus into Galilee or Egypt? Whether Luke agrees or does not agree with Matthew, the wealthy beneficed clergy of Germany will not be less rich, and we shall not envy them their wealth.

There is not a page in the Scripture that has not been the subject of controversy and of hatred as a consequence. What must be done then, my very dear brothers, in the darkness in which we walk? I have already said to you, and you think the same as I: we ought to search for justice more than for enlightenment, and to tolerate everyone, in order that we may be tolerated.

# AN IMPORTANT STUDY BY LORD BOLINGBROKE

OR *The Fall of Fanaticism*

*Written at the end of 1736*

## Foreword by the EDITORS\*

We publish a new edition of the most eloquent, profound and forceful book that has yet been written against fanaticism. We have made it our obligation before God to help in the fight against this monster that devours the substance of a part of humanity. This précis of Lord Bolingbroke's doctrine collected in its entirety in six volumes of his posthumous *Works*, was addressed by him a few

\* None is listed. It is quite clear that Voltaire is "the Editors" and here is translating the supposed précis by Bolingbroke into French. Beuchot states that this Foreword had already appeared in the 1767 editions of Voltaire's *Works*. The last footnote at the end of the *Study* bears the date, March 18, 1767, at London. Since the date 1736 cannot be verified, it would seem from the above evidence that the *Study* made its first appearance in print in 1767 regardless of when it was written and thus fits well into the period in which Voltaire was doing most of his works on religion.

For a discussion of Henry St. John, Viscount Bolingbroke, and his relation to the *Study* and to Voltaire, please refer to the Introduction.—*kwa*

years before his death, to Lord Cornsbury. This edition is greatly
expanded over the first; we have collated it with the manuscript.

We beg the scholars, to whose attention we bring this very useful
work, to have as much discretion as wisdom, and to spread the
light without telling from what hand it has come. O Lord! protect
the learned; confound the informers and the persecutors.


## PREFACE

The ambition to dominate minds is one of the strongest of passions. A theologian, a factional man, wishes to conquer like a
prince; and there are many more sects in the world than kingdoms.
To whom should I submit my soul? Shall I be a Christian, just because I come from London or Madrid? Shall I be a Muslim simply
because I was born in Turkey? I ought to think only for myself; the
choice of a religion is my greatest interest. You adore God through
Muhammed; or through the Grand Lama; or through the Pope.
How unfortunate! Adore God for your own reasons.

The stupid indolence in which most men stagnate with respect to
their most important goal would seem to prove that they are
miserable animal machines whose thoughts are occupied only with
the present moment. We treat our intelligence like our body; for
money we often abandon both to charlatans. In Spain the people
die at the hands of a vile monk, and of a quack; and our people are
nearly as badly off[1]. A vicar, a dissenter, lay siege to their last moments.

[1] No: milord Bolingbroke goes too far; here we live and die as we please. Only
the cowardly and the superstitious send for a priest. And the priest makes mock of
them. He knows that he is not God's ambassador to the dying.

But in Papist countries, at the third attack of fever someone comes to frighten
you with ceremony, to spread before you all the paraphernalia of extreme unction
and the banners of death. The God of Catholics escorted by six candlesticks is
brought to you. All sorts of scoundrels have the right to enter your chamber; the
more this lugubrious pomp is put on display, the more the priest profits. He
pronounces your sentence and goes to a public house to drink up the fees of the

A very small number of men search; but factional spirit, the desire to impress preoccupies them. A great man among us [Samuel Clarke] has been Christian only because of his enmity to Collins; our Whiston was Christian only because he was Arian. Grotius wished only to confound the Gomarists. Bossuet upheld Papism against Claude, who battled for the Calvinists. In the early centuries Arians fought the Athanasians. The Emperor Julian and his followers combatted both factions and the rest of the world fought against the Christians, who carried on against the Jews. Whom to believe? We must investigate; it is a duty that no one calls in question. A man who accepts his religion without question is no different than an ox that one yokes.

The prodigious number of sects in Christianity in itself leads to the presumption that all of them are in error. The thinking man says to himself: If God had wished to make his cult known to me, it would be because this cult was necessary to our species. If it were necessary he would have bestowed it on all alike, just as He has given everyone two eyes and a mouth. He would be consistent in everything since the two things necessary to all men are consistent. The principles of universal reason are common to all civilized peoples, all recognize a God; they can then flatter themselves that such knowledge is truth. But each of them has a different religion; they can thus conclude that being right in adoring a God, they are wrong in all that they have imagined in excess of this.

If the principle universally agreed upon seems likely, the diametrically opposed consequences that we draw seem false; it is natural to mistrust them. Defiance increases when it is seen that the goal of all those who are the heads of the sects is to rule and enrich themselves as much as they are able and that, from the

---

process. The weaker spirits are so stricken with horror at this ceremony that many of them die of it. I know that M. Falconnet, a physician to the king of France, having seen one of his patients turn toward death solely because of the spectacle of his extreme unction, declared to the king that he would never again have the sacraments administered to any one.—*Note of 1771 by Voltaire*

Daïris of Japan to the bishops of Rome, they were only occupied with building for a pontiff a throne founded on the misery of the people, and often cemented with their blood.

Let the Japanese investigate how the Daïris have so long subjugated them; let the Tartars make use of their reason in judging whether or not the Grand Lama is immortal; let the Turks judge their Koran; but we Christians must examine our Gospel.

Since I wish to examine sincerely, it is my duty to swear that I shall not deceive: I find suspect those who have written only to prove their conviction.

Pascal begins by stirring up his readers, in his amorphous, collected *pensées*; says he, "Let those who combat the Christian religion learn to know it, etc." I see in these words a factional man who wishes to subjugate.

I am informed that a vicar in France by the name of Jean Meslier, who recently died[2], upon his deathbed asked pardon of God for having taught Christianity. This attitude of a priest at the point of death has more effect upon me than the enthusiasm of Pascal. I have seen a vicar in Dorsetshire, diocese of Bristol, renounce a living of two hundred pounds sterling, avowing to his parishioners that his conscience would not permit him to preach to them the absurd horrors of the Christian church. But neither the testament of Jean Meslier, nor the declaration of the worthy vicar, are decisive proofs for me. The Jew Uriel Acosta publicly disowned the Old Testament in Amsterdam; but I shall not believe the Jew Acosta more than the priest Meslier. I ought to read the legal documents with concentrated attention, not permitting myself to be swayed by any of the advocates, weighing before God the assertions of the two parties and deciding according to my own conscience. I may discuss the arguments of Wollaston and of Clarke, but I can only believe my reason.

[2] This is very true; he was vicar of Etrepigni, near Rocroi, on the borders of the Champagne. Many interested persons have extracts from his testament.—*Note in 1776 by Voltaire*

Let me begin by saying that I do not wish to touch upon our Anglican Church inasmuch as it was established by acts of Parliament. I regard it furthermore as the most learned and orderly in Europe. I am not of a mind with the *Independent Whig*\* which seems to wish to abolish the priesthood entirely, putting it again in the hands of the father of the family, as in the time of the patriarchs. In its present stage, our society does not permit such a change. I think that it is necessary to preserve the clergy to be the masters of morals and to offer our prayers to God. We shall see if they ought to be jugglers, trumpets of discord, and bloody persecutors. The first thing to do is to see to my own education.

## CHAPTER I—On the Books of Moses

Christianity is founded on Judaism[1] let us see then if Judaism is the work of God. Someone gives me the books of Moses to read. First of all, I have a duty to ascertain if these books are by him.

1. Is it probable that Moses may have had engraved upon a rock the Pentateuch, or at least the books of the law, and that he

\* *The Independent Whig*, published by Thomas Gordon and Jean Trenchard, commented on current political and religious affairs in Britain. Trenchard stirred up much controversy with a polemic, *The History of Superstition*, 1709, and four volumes of *Essays on Civil and Religious Liberty and Other Important Subjects*, 4th ed., 1737.—*kwa*

[1] Suppose, by some impossibility, that a sect as absurd and frightful as Judaism might have been the work of God; it would be demonstrated in this case, and by this sole supposition, that the sect of the Galileans was founded only upon imposture. That is demonstrated rigorously.

When one assumes whatever truth, announced by God himself, authenticated by the most tremendous prodigies, sealed with human blood; when God, according to you, has said a hundred times that this truth, this law, will be eternal; when He has said in this law that you must mercilessly kill him who would lessen the law or add to it; when He has commanded that every prophet [Deut. 13:1, 5, 6] who performs miracles in order to substitute something new in this ancient law be put to death by

may have had engravers and polishers of stone in a horrible desert,
where it is said that his people had neither tailors, nor makers of
sandals, nor materials to clothe themselves, nor bread to eat, and
where for forty years God was obliged to perform a continuous
miracle [Deut. 29:5] in order to nourish them and conserve their
vestments?

2. It is stated in the book of Joshua [8:32] that Deuteronomy
was inscribed upon an altar of rude stones encased in mortar. How
was an entire book written upon mortar? Why were these letters
not erased by the blood that flowed continuously on this altar?
How did this altar, this monument of Deuteronomy, exist in a
country where for such a long time the Jews were reduced to a
slavery that their brigandage had so well merited?

3. The innumerable faults in geography and chronology and the
contradictions that are found in the Pentateuch have forced many
Jews and Christians to maintain that it could not be the work of
Moses. The scholar Leclerc, a multitude of theologians, even our
great Newton, have embraced this opinion; so it is at least a very
probable one.

4. Does not simple common sense suffice to judge that a book
which begins with these words: "Here [Deut. 1:1] are the words
that Moses pronounced on the other side of the Jordan,"* can only

---

his best friend, by his brother, it is clear as day that Christianity, which does away
with Judaism in all its rites, is a false religion and directly the enemy of God
himself.

It is alleged the Christian sect is founded upon the Jewish sect. It is as though it
were said that Islam was founded on the ancient religion of the Sabaeans: it was
born in their land; but far from being born of Sabaenism, it has destroyed it.

Add to these a very much stronger argument which is that it is not possible that
an immutable Being, having given a law to the supposed Noah, unknown to all peoples except the Jews, afterward gave another law in Pharaonic times, and a final
third law in the time of Tiberius. This shameful story of a God who grants three different and universal religions to a miserable, small, unknown nation, would be the
most absurd that the human mind has ever invented, if all the events following were
not more so.—*Voltaire*

* This line does not agree with Deut. 1:1 in the King James version, which reads

be the work of an unskillful forger, since the same book assures us that Moses never went beyond Jordan? Is not Abbadie's response that "this side of" can be understood for "the other side of," ridiculous? Ought we to accept a preacher from Ireland who died insane rather than Newton, the greatest man there ever was?

Furthermore, I ask all reasoning men if there is some likelihood that Moses in the desert gave precepts to the Jewish kings, who came so many centuries after him and if it is possible that in the same desert, he [Deut. 14] assigned forty-eight cities with their suburbs solely to the Levite tribe, independently of the tithe that the other tribes must pay them [Numb. 35:7]? Without doubt it is quite natural that the priests attempted to gobble up everything; but it is not natural that they were given forty-eight cities in a small district where there were scarcely two villages; at least as many cities would have been necessary for each of the other Jewish tribes; the total would have amounted to four hundred and eighty cities with their suburbs. The Jews have not written their history otherwise. Each episode is a ridiculous exaggeration, a coarse lie, an absurd fable.[2]

---

"on this side." However, *The New English Bible* with the Apocrypha (Oxford and Cambridge, 1970) has "Transjordan."—*kwa*

[2] Lord Bolingbroke was satisfied with a small number of proofs. If he had wished, he could have reported more than two hundred. One of the strongest, in our opinion, that makes us see that the books claimed to have been written in Moses' and Joshua's time were in fact written in the time of the Kings, is that the same book is cited in the book of Joshua and in that of the Jewish kings. We call this book *The Just* and the Papists call it *The History of the Just*, or *The Book of the King* (Jasher or the Upright).

When the author of the book of Joshua speaks of the sun stopping upon Gibeon, and the moon over Ajalon at high noon, he cites the *Book of the Just* [Jos. 10:13].

When the author of the Chronicles or the Books of the Kings speaks of the song composed by David on the death of Saul and his son Jonathan, he cites again the *Book of the Just* [Kings II, 1:18].

Now, if you please, how can the same book have been written in the time of Moses, and in the time of David? This horrible blunder did not escape Lord Bolingbroke; he speaks of it elsewhere. It is a pleasure to witness the embarrassment of that innocent Dom Calmet, who searches vainly for a palliative to this absurdity.—*Note of 1771 by Voltaire*

## CHAPTER II—On the Person of Moses

Was there ever a Moses? Everything about him from his birth to his death was so stupendous that he appears as fantastic a personage as our wizard Merlin. If he did exist, if he brought about the tremendous miracles that he is supposed to have done in Egypt, could it be possible that no Egyptian author would have spoken of these miracles, that the Greeks, those admirers of the marvelous, would not have said a single word of them? Flavius Josephus who, in order to make his despised nation appear worthy, researched the works of the Egyptian authors who spoke of the Jews, has not the effrontery to cite a single passage that mentions the prodigies of Moses. Does not this universal silence lead to the presumption that Moses is a legendary person?

Even those who have little studied antiquity know that the ancient Arabs were the inventors of many stories that in time were diffused among other nations. They are the source of the story of the ancient Bacchus, assumed to be of far greater antiquity than the time when the Jews said their Moses appeared. Bacchus or Back, born in Arabia, had inscribed his laws upon two tablets of stone; he was called Misem, a name that strongly resembles Moses; he had been saved from the waters in a chest and his name signified *saved from the waters*. He had a wand with which he worked miracles; this rod changed into a serpent when he wished. This same Misem passed through the Red Sea "on dry foot" at the head of his army; he divided the waters of the Orontes and the Hydaspis and held them off to the right and the left; a column of fire illuminated his army during the night. The ancient Orphic verses, chanted in the orgies of Bacchus, celebrated a part of this madness. This myth was so ancient that the Fathers of the Church believed that this Misem, this Bacchus, was their Noah.[3]

Is there not the greatest probability that the Jews adopted this myth, then wrote it down when they began to have some knowledge of literature under their kings? The marvelous was as necessary to them as to other peoples, but they were not inventors; never was so small a nation more crude; all their illusions were plagiarisms, as all their ceremonial was patently imitative of the Phoenicians, the Syrians, and the Egyptians.

What they have added of themselves seems of so revolting a crudeness and absurdity that it provokes indignation and pity. In what ridiculous novel would we put up with a man who with a wave of the wand, changes all waters into blood, in the name of an unknown god, and with magicians who do as much in the names of the gods of the country? The only advantage that Moses may have had over the king's sorcerers was that he gave birth to lice, something the sorcerers could not do. About this feat a great prince[4] has

---

[3] It must be observed that Bacchus was known in Egypt, in Syria, in Asia Minor, in Greece, among the Etruscans, long before any people had heard of Moses and above all of Noah and all his genealogy. What is found only in Jewish writings was absolutely unknown to the Oriental and Occidental peoples, from the name of Adam up to that of David.

The wretched Jewish nation had its own chronology and myths, the latter resembling only distantly those of other peoples. Its writers, who worked only very slowly, plundered what they found among their neighbors, and disguised their larcenies badly: witness the fable of Moses that they borrowed from Bacchus; witness their ridiculous Samson, taken from Hercules; the daughter of Japtha, from Iphigenia; the wife of Lot, imitation of Eurydice, etc. Eusebius preserved for us precious fragments of Sanchuniathon who indisputably lived before the time in which the Jews place their Moses. Sanchuniathon says nothing of the Jewish horde. If it had existed, if there had been any truth in Genesis, surely he would have written a few words about it. Eusebius would not have failed to praise them. The Phoenician Sanchuniathon did not say a thing; therefore the Jews did not exist then as a nation and the myths of Genesis had not yet been invented by anyone.—*Note of 1771 and 1776 by Voltaire*

[4] Frederick II, who probably derived the idea from the *Sermon of the Fifty.*—*Beuchot.*

The Sermon of the Fifty (le Sermon des Cinquante), written about 1749 and delivered in the Prussian court in 1751–1752, was Voltaire's first overt attack on Christianity. It was so violent that not daring to acknowledge it for fear of the Bastille or worse, he attributed its authorship to the atheist La Méttrie who had died in 1751 in Berlin.—*kwa*

said that the Jews probably knew more about lice than all the magicians of the world.

Why does an angel of the Lord come to kill all the animals of
Egypt? and why, after that, does the king of Egypt have an army of
cavalry? And why does this cavalry enter into the depths of the
Red Sea?

Why does the same angel of the Lord come during the night to
kill all the first-born of Egyptian families? It was then surely that
the supposed Moses ought to have seized that beautiful country
instead of fleeing like a coward and a knave with two or three
million men among whom, it is said, were six hundred and thirty
thousand fighting men. It was with this huge number that he fled
before the younger brothers of those whom the angels had killed.
He went out to wander in the desert, where not a drop of water
was to be found; and to make this fine expedition easy for him, his
God divides the waters of the sea, making two mountains of it to
the right and the left, so that his favorite people may die of hunger
and thirst.

All the rest of the story of Moses is equally absurd and barbarous. His quail, his manna, his conversations with God;
twenty-three thousand men of his people murdered by the priests
at his order; twenty-four thousand massacred at another time; six
hundred and thirty thousand troops in a desert where there never
have been more than two thousand men; all this surely seems the
height of extravagance; and someone has said that *Orlando
Furioso* and *Don Quixote* are books of geometry in comparison
with the Hebrew books. If there only were some honest and
natural deeds in the myth of Moses, one could believe fully that
such a personage did exist.

They have the effrontery to tell us that the feast of the Passover
among the Jews is proof of the passage of the Red Sea. They
thanked the God of the Jews, at this feast, for the goodness with
which he had all the first-born of Egypt murdered; nothing, they
say, was more true than this holy and divine butchery.

"Is it conceivable," asks the orator and bad reasoner Abbadie,* "that Moses could have established tangible evidence of an event recognized as fake by six hundred thousand witnesses?" Poor man! thou ought to have said in excess of two million witnesses; because six hundred and thirty thousand fighting men, fugitives or not, certainly imply more than two million persons. You say then that Moses read his Pentateuch to two or three million Jews! You believe then that these two or three million men would have written against Moses, if they had discovered some error in his Pentateuch, and that they might have had their remarks printed in the periodicals of the land! All that is left for you to say is that three million men signed as witnesses and, that you have seen their signatures.

You believe then that the temples and rites established in honor of Bacchus, Hercules, and Perseus prove that Perseus, Hercules, and Bacchus were sons of Jupiter and that, among the Romans, the temple of Castor and Pollux was a demonstration that Castor and Pollux had fought for the Romans! Thus assumptions are made about matters still in question; and the participants in controversy utter upon a matter most important to the human race arguments that Lady Blackacre[5] would not dare to mention in the hall of *common plays*. This is what fools have written, what imbeciles comment, what rogues teach and what young children are made to learn by heart; and the scholar, who is filled with indignation and who is irritated by the most abominable absurdities that have ever disgraced human nature, is called blasphemer!

---

* Author of *Treatise on the Truth of the Christian Religion.—kwa*

[5] An extremely amusing personage in the comedy *The Plain Dealer* by Wycherley.—*Beuchot*

## CHAPTER III—On the Divinity Attributed to the Jewish Books

How has anyone dared suppose that God singled out a band of Arab robbers to be his chosen people, and to arm this band against all other peoples? And why, while fighting at its head, has he suffered his people to be so often vanquished and enslaved?

How is it that in giving laws to these brigands he forgot to curb this small nation of robbers with a belief in the immortality of the soul and punishment after death[1], while all the great neighboring nations—Chaldeans, Egyptians, Syrians, Phoenicians—had long before embraced this useful belief?

Is it possible that God might have prescribed for the Jews the manner of riding in the saddle on the desert[2], and hidden from

[1] Here is the strongest argument against the Jewish law, and one which the great Bolingbroke has not carried far enough. Indian, Egyptian, Babylonian, Greek, Roman lawgivers all taught the immortality of the soul; in Homer himself are found twenty passages; and the assumed Moses says nothing about it! There is not one single word about it in either the Jewish Decalogue, or in the whole of the Pentateuch! It must have been that commentators, either very ignorant or rascals as well as foolish, may have twisted some passages of Job, who is not a Jew, to persuade men more ignorant than themselves that Job had spoken of a life to come, because he says [19:25, 26]: "I shall rise from my dungheap at some time; my redeemer is alive; I shall recover my skin, in my flesh I shall see him; beware of denouncing and persecuting me."

What tie, I beg you, does a sick person who hopes for healing have with the immortality of the soul, with hell and paradise? If our Warburton had set himself to demonstrating that the Jewish law never taught another life, he would have rendered a very great service. But, because of a most incomprehensible wrongheadedness he has chosen to convince us that the crudeness of the Pentateuch was a proof of its divinity; and in the excess of his pride, he has maintained this chimera with the extremest insolence.—*Voltaire, 1771*

[2] Dean Swift says that, judging by the Pentateuch, God had far more concern for the backsides of the Jews than for their souls. See Deuteronomy, 23: 12, 13; you will conclude that the Dean was quite right.—*Voltaire 1771 and 1776*

About this, Beuchot remarks that it was Collins not Swift who made the quip.—*kwa*

them the dogma of a future life? Herodotus tells us that the famous temple of Tyre was built two thousand three hundred years before him. It is said that Moses led his group into the desert about sixteen hundred years before our era. Herodotus wrote five hundred years before this common era; thus the temple of the Phoenicians existed a dozen centuries before Moses; hence the Phoenician religion had been established for a much longer time. This religion proclaimed the immortality of the soul as did the Chaldean and the Egyptian. The Jewish rabble never possessed this dogma as a foundation of its religion. It was, it is said, a coarse nation to whom God adapted himself. God adapt himself! And to whom? To some Jewish thieves! How could God be more coarse than they! Is that not a blasphemy?

## CHAPTER IV — Who Is the Author of the Pentateuch?

I am asked, who is the author of the Pentateuch: I would as lief be asked who wrote *The Four Brothers Aymon, Robert the Devil*, and the story of the enchanter *Merlin*

Newton, who so far demeaned himself as to examine this question seriously, claims that it was Samuel who wrote such ravings, apparently to make the kings odious to the Jewish tribes whom this detestable priest desired to govern. As for myself, I think that the Jews learned to read and write only during their Babylonian captivity, since their characters were at first Chaldaic and then Syriac; we have never known a purely Hebrew alphabet.

I conjecture that Ezra forged all these *Tales of a Tub* on his return from captivity. He wrote them in cuneiform, in the jargon of the country just as today's northern Ireland peasants would write in English characters.

The Cutheans, who inhabited the land of Samaria, wrote the

same Pentateuch in Phoenician letters which were current among them, and we still have this Pentateuch.

I believe that Jeremiah was able to contribute a great deal to the composition of this novel. Jeremiah, as is well known, was strongly attached to the kings of Babylon; it is evident in his rhapsodies that he was in the pay of the Babylonians and that he betrayed his own country; he consistently desired that it surrender to the king of Babylon. At that time the Egyptians were the enemies of Babylon. It was in order to pay court to the great king, master of Hershalaïm Kedusha, now called Jerusalem[1], that Jeremiah and then Ezra inspired in the Jews so much horror of the Egyptians. They made sure not to say anything against the peoples of the Euphrates. They were slaves who humored their masters. They fully admitted that the Jewish people had nearly always been enslaved; but they respected those whom they then served.

What the other Jews may have written of the acts and deeds of their petty kings, impresses me as little as the story of the knights of the round table and Charlemagne's dozen peers; and I regard as the most futile of all researches that of discovering the name of the author of a ridiculous book.

Who has written the first story of Jupiter, of Neptune, and of Pluto? I do not know, and I do not care to know.

There is a very old *Life of Moses* written in Hebrew,[2] but which has not been inserted in the Judaic canon. Its author is unknown, as the authors of the other Jewish books; it is written in the style of the *Thousand and One Nights*, which is that of all Asiatic antiquity. Here are a few examples.

In the 130th year after the migration of the Jews into Egypt, sixty years after the death of Joseph, the pharaoh, during his sleep

[1] Hershalaïm was the name of Jerusalem, and Kedusha was its secret name. All the cities had a secret name which was carefully kept from enemies, for fear they might join the name to enchantments and thereby make themselves master of the city. All things considered, the Jews were probably no more superstitious than their neighbors; they were only more cruel, more usurious, and more ignorant.—*Voltaire*

[2] The *Life of Moses* has been printed at Hamburg, in Hebrew and Latin.—*Voltaire*

saw in a dream an old man who held a balance in his hand. In one of the scales were all the Egyptians with their children and wives, in the other a lone infant at his mother's breast, who weighed more than the whole of Egypt. The king immediately called all his magicians who were all seized with astonishment and fear. One of the counselors divined that it meant that a Hebrew child would be the ruin of Egypt. He advised the king to kill all the small boys of the Jewish nation.

The adventure of Moses saved from the waters is nearly the same as that in Exodus. At first he was called Moses Schabar and his mother, Jechotiel. At the age of three, Moses, playing with the pharaoh, took his crown and put it on his own head. The king wished to have him killed, but the angel Gabriel descended from heaven and begged the king to do him no harm. "He is a child," said he to him, "he intended no malice. In order to prove to yourself how ingenuous he is, show him a ruby and a burning coal, you will see that he will choose the coal." The king tried the experiment. The young Moses did not fail to choose the ruby, but Gabriel juggled it and put the burning coal in its place; the little Moses burned his hand to the bone. The king pardoned him, believing him a dolt. Thus Moses, having been saved by water, was yet again saved by fire.

The remainder of the account is in the same vein. It is difficult to decide which is the more admirable, this myth about Moses or that of the Pentateuch. I leave this question to those who have more time to waste than I. But I admire above all the pedants, like Grotius, Abbadic and even the Abbott Houteville, longtime go-between in Paris for a farmer general,* then secretary to the famous Cardinal Dubois whom I have heard say that he defied all cardinals to be more atheist than he. All these people rack their brains to persuade—what they do not believe—that the Pentateuch is by Moses. So! my friends, what would be proved? That Moses

* One who purchased a concession from the French government to collect from the public taxes of various kinds. Fortunes were made by the farmers-general who imposed very high levies. The French Revolution ended the practice.—*kwa*

was a fool. One thing is sure, that today I would have a man who wrote similar extravagances committed to Bedlam.[3]

## CHAPTER V—That the Jews Have Taken Everything from Other Nations

It has often been said that it is the small people in servitude that attempt to imitate their masters; it is the small, weak, and untutored nation that crudely conforms to the customs of the great nation. It is Cornwall that apes London and not London that apes Cornwall.* Is anything more natural than that the Jews may have taken what they could of religion, laws, and customs from their neighbors?

We are now certain that their god, pronounced by us Jehovah, and by them Jaho, was the ineffable name of the god of the Phoenicians and the Egyptians; it was well-known in antiquity. Clement of Alexandria, in the first book of his *Stromateis,* reports that those entering the temples of Egypt were obliged to carry on them a kind of talisman composed of this word Jaho; and when a person knew how to pronounce this word in a certain fashion, whoever heard him fell stone dead, or at least vanished. It was by such means that the temple charlatans strove to convince the superstitious.

It is well enough known that the figure of the serpent, the cherubs, the ceremony of the red cow, the ablutions since known as baptism, the robes of linen reserved to the priests, the fasting, the abstinence from pork and other meats, circumcision, the scapegoat were all borrowed from Egypt.

The Jews admit that they had a temple only very late in time and more than five hundred years after their Moses, according to

[3] Bedlam, insane asylum in London.—*Voltaire*

* A reference probably to the county of Cornwall to emphasize the idea that country districts are not cultural leaders.—*kwa*

their always erroneous chronology. They finally invaded a small city in which they built a temple in imitation of the great peoples. What had they had before? A chest. This was the usage of nomads and of the Canaanites of the interior whose lands were poor. There was an ancient tradition among the Jewish horde that when it was nomadic, that is to say, when it was wandering in the deserts of Arabia Petraea, it carried a chest wherein was a crude image of a god named Remphan, or a kind of star carved in wood.[1] You see traces of this cult in some prophets and above all in the supposed discourses that the Acts of the Apostles [7] puts in the mouth of Stephen.

According to the Jews themselves, the Phoenicians (whom they call Philistines) had the temple of Dagon before the Judaic troop had a house. If that's the way it was, if their whole religion in the desert existed in a chest in honor of the god Remphan, who was only a star revered by the Arabs, it is clear that the Jews were nothing else originally than a band of vagabond Arabs, who established themselves by brigandage in Palestine, and who finally made up for themselves a religion after their own fancy, and a history full of myths. They took part of the myth of the ancient Back or Bacchus of whom they made their Moses. But, that these myths are revered by us, that we have made them the basis of our religion, and that these same myths still have a certain influence in the century of philosophy, is what above all infuriates the informed. The Christian church sings Jewish prayers, and puts to the stake whoever follows the Jewish law. How pitiful, how contradictory, and how awful!

[1] "Have ye offered unto me sacrifices and offerings in the wilderness forty years? Ye carried the tabernacle of Moloch and the star of your god Remphan?" [Acts, 7:43; Amos, 5:26; Jeremiah 32:35.] Here are singular contradictions. Add to them the story of the idol of Micah adored by all the tribe of Dan and removed by a grandson of Moses himself, as the reader may verify in the book of Judges, 7 and 8. It is, however, this mass of absurdities that provides an income of twelve thousand guineas to milord of Canterbury, and a realm to a priest who claims to be the successor of Peter, and who unceremoniously established himself in Rome in place of the emperor.— *Voltaire*

## CHAPTER VI—On Genesis

All peoples by whom the Jews were surrounded had a Genesis, a
Theogony, a Cosmogony, long before the Jews existed. Is it not
evident that the Genesis of the Jews had been taken from the
ancient myths of their neighbors?

Jaho, the ancient god of the Phoenicians, unraveled chaos, the
Khaütereb; he arranged Muth, matter; he formed a man with his
breath, Calpi; he caused him to live in a garden, Aden or Eden; he
defended him against the great serpent Ophionea, as the old
fragment of Pherecydes* says. What agreement with the Jewish
Genesis! Is it not natural that through the ages a small, rude
people may have borrowed tales from a great people who were inventors of the arts?

There was a belief, disseminated in Asia, that God created the
world in six time periods called by the Chaldeans, long before the
Jews, the six *gahambârs*.

This was also an idea of the early Indians. The Jews who wrote
Genesis were then only imitators; they mixed their own absurdities
with these myths and it must be confessed that we cannot help but
laugh when we see a serpent speaking familiarly with Eve, God
speaking to the serpent, God promenading every day at midday in
the Garden of Eden, God making breeches for Adam and a cotton
loincloth for Eve. Everything else seems as senseless; many of the
Jews themselves blushed at it. Eventually they treated these
fantasies as allegorical stories. How could we take literally what
the Jews have considered as simply stories?

Neither the story of Judges, nor that of Kings, nor any prophet
cites a single passage from Genesis. None has spoken either of

* Pherecydes of Syros, c. 540 B.C., authored an account of the origin of the
world, the probable title of which is the *Heptamikos.—kwa*

Adam's rib, taken from his chest in order to form a woman, nor of the tree of knowledge of good and evil, nor of the serpent who seduced Eve, nor of original sin, nor of any one of these vagaries. Once more, is it up to us to believe them?

, Their rhapsodies demonstrate that they have pilfered all their ideas from the Phoenicians, Chaldeans, and Egyptians, just as they pillaged their goods whenever they could. They took the very name of Israel from the Chaldeans, as Philo acknowledges in the first page of the account of his deputation to Caligula[1], and we in the Occident would be foolish to believe that all of what these barbarians of the Orient had stolen really belonged to them!

## CHAPTER VII—On the Mores of the Jews

If we pass from the myths of the Jews to their mores, are they not as abominable as their stories are absurd? By their own admission they were a people of brigands who carried into the desert what they robbed from the Egyptians. Their leader, Joshua, crosses the Jordan by a miracle similar to the miracle of the Red Sea; why? To put to fire and sword a city that he did not know, a city whose walls his God caused to fall at the sound of a trumpet.

The Greek legends were more humane. Amphion built cities with the sound of his flute, Joshua destroyed them; he delivered to the sword and to the flames old men, women, children, and animals. Was there ever a more senseless horror? He exempted only a prostitute who had betrayed her native land; what need had he of

---

[1] Here are the words of Philo: "The Chaldeans give to the just the name of Israel, 'seeing God'."—*Voltaire*, 1776

Philo Judaeus, although a Jew, commented on the Old Testament in Greek. He went with a deputation from Alexandria to Caligula to argue for the equality of Jews with Greeks in that city. His definition of Israel seems to have been uniquely his own and does not conform to the concept of "striving with God."—*kwa*

the perfidy of this wretched woman, since his trumpet caused walls
to fall, as that of Astolphus put everyone to flight? And let us
remark in passing that this woman, nicknamed Rahab the Lewd, is
one of the grandmothers of the Jew whom we have since made a
god, a god who also counts the incestuous Tamar, the impudent
Ruth, and the adulterous Bathsheba among those of whom he was
born.

Then we are told that this same Joshua [12:24] had thirty-one
kings of the land hanged; which is to say thirty-one village captains
who had fought for their homes against this troop of assassins. If
the author of that history had set out purposely to render the Jews
detestable to other nations, could he have done better? In order to
add blasphemy to lawlessness and barbarity, the author dares to
assert that all these abominations were done in the name of God by
the express order of God, and were as well blood sacrifices offered
to God.

That's a holy people for you! Compared to the children of Israel, the Hurons, the Canadians, and the Iroquois have been hu-
manitarian philosophers; and it is in favor of these monsters that
the sun and the moon were made to stand still at full noon [Jos.
10:11–13]! And why? To give them time to pursue and massacre
the poor Amorites already crushed by a rain of stones that God
threw upon them from on high along five long leagues of road. Is
this the story of Gargantua? Is it that of the people of God? And
what is the more intolerable about this story—the excess of horror
or the excess of the ridiculous? Would it not add more of the ridiculous to entertain oneself by combatting this odious mass of fables
which outrage equally good sense, virtue, nature, and Divinity? If,
unfortunately, a single adventure of this people were true, all peoples would have united to exterminate it; if they are false, one cannot tell sillier lies.

What shall we say of Jephtha who sacrificed his own daughter to
his bloodthirsty God, and of the ambidextrous Ehud who assassinated Eglon, his king, in the name of the Lord, and of the divine

Jael who assassinated the general Sisera by driving a nail into his head; and of the debauched Samson, whom God favors with so many miracles? A crude imitation of the fable of Hercules.

Shall we speak of a Levite who comes on his ass with his concubine, and some straw and hay, to Gaba, of the tribe of Benjamin? And then there are the Benjamites who wish to commit the sin of sodomy with that wretched priest, as the Sodomites had wished to do with the angels[2]. The Levite reaches an agreement with them, and he abandons to them his mistress or wife whom they enjoy the whole night, and who dies of it the next morning. The Levite cuts his concubine in a dozen pieces with his knife, an act not so easy to perform, and there ensues a civil war.

The eleven tribes arm four hundred thousand soldiers against the tribe of Benjamin [Jud. 20:2]. Four hundred thousand soldiers, good God! In a territory that was not then fifteen by five or six leagues. The Grand Turk never had half such an army. The Israelites exterminate the tribe of Benjamin, old men, young people, women, young girls, according to their laudable custom. Six hundred youths escape. The tribe could not be allowed to perish; the six hundred boys must be given at least six hundred girls. What did the Israelites do? There was in the vicinity a small city named Jabesh; they surprise it, kill all, massacre all, even the animals, and reserve four hundred girls for four hundred Benjamites. Two

---

[2] The illustrious author has forgotten to speak of the angels of Sodom. However the point is worth some trouble. If ever there were extravagant abominations in the history of the Jewish people, that of the angels whom officials, porters, even small boys of the city desired to violate is of a frightfulness that no pagan legend can approach and makes your hair stand on end. And they dare to write about these loathsome acts! And youth is brought to honor them! And they have the insolence to pity the Brahmans of India and the Magi of Persia, to whom God had not revealed these things and who were not God's people! And there are still found among us vile souls so altogether debased and impudent as to command us:

"Believe these infamies, believe or the wrath of a vengeful God will fall upon you; believe or we shall persecute you, be it in the consistory, conclave, episcopal court, bar of justice, or tavern." How long will these rascals make wise men tremble? Where is the man of goodwill who does not feel aghast at such horrors? And they are tolerated! What do I say? They are adored! What imbeciles! What monsters!—
*Voltaire*

hundred boys remain to be provided for; it is agreed with them that they shall ravish two hundred girls of Shiloh, when they will dance at the gates of Shiloh. All right, Abbadie, Sherlock, Houteville and companions, create explanations to justify this race of cannibals; prove that all this is a type, a symbol which proclaims Jesus Christ to us.

## CHAPTER VIII—On the Mores of the Jews Under Their Melchim or Petty Kings, and Under Their High Priests, up to the Destruction of Jerusalem by the Romans

The Jews have a king, in spite of the priest Samuel, who does what he can to retain his usurped authority [I Kings, 8]; and he has the audacity to assert that *to have a king is to renounce God*. Finally, a shepherd who looked for she-asses is elected by lot. The Jews were then under the yoke of the Canaanites; they had never had a temple; their sanctuary, as we have seen, was a chest that was carried in a cart; the Canaanites had taken their chest from them. God, who was very irritated, had, however, permitted the act; but in order to avenge himself on the victors he punished them with hemorrhoids, and he sent rats into their fields. The victors appeased him by returning the chest together with five rats of gold and five anal openings also in gold [I Sam. 6:5]. No vengeance or offering could be more worthy of the king of the Jews. He pardons the Canaanites, but he causes the death of fifty thousand and seventy of his own men for having looked upon his chest.

It was under these auspicious circumstances that Saul was elected king of the Jews. There was neither sword nor lance in their small country; the Canaanites or Philistines did not permit the Jews, their slaves, to sharpen their plowshares and their axes; they were forced to go to Philistine workers for these minor aids: however we are told that King Saul [I Sam. 11:8] had at the outset an army of three hundred thousand men, with whom he won a battle [ibid., 15]. Our Gulliver has similar stories, but not such contradictions.

In another battle, this same Saul receives the pretended King Agag for a conference. The prophet Samuel arrives on behalf of the Lord and says to him [ibid., 15:19]: *Why have you not killed everyone?* And he takes a holy cleaver and hacks King Agag to pieces. If this actually happened, what kind of people were the Jews, and what kind of priests were their priests!

Saul, reproved by the Lord for not having himself cut to pieces his prisoner King Agag, finally goes to fight the Philistines after the death of the gentle prophet Samuel. He then consults about the outcome of the battle a woman who has the spirit of Python; it is known that women who have the spirit of Python can invoke shades. The witch of Endor shows Saul the ghost of Samuel which rises from the earth. But this concerns only the precious philosophy of the Jewish nation; let us examine its morality.

A harp player, for whom the Eternal had conceived a tender affection, succeeded in being consecrated king while Samuel was still alive; he rebels against his sovereign; he gathers four hundred malcontents: and as the Holy Scripture says [ibid., 22:2]: "And all that were in distress, and oppressed with debt, and discontented came to him."

This was a man *after God's own liking* [ibid., 25]; also the first thing he wishes to do is to assassinate a tenant named Nabal, who refuses contributions to him; he marries his wife; he marries eighteen women, not counting the concubines [ibid., 27]; he flees to King Achish, enemy of his country; he is well received; and as a reward he goes out to sack the villages of the allies of Achish; he slaughters all, without sparing infants at the breast, as is always ordained by the Jewish rite; and he leads King Achish to believe that he has sacked Jewish villages. It must be confessed that our highway robbers have been less culpable in the eyes of men; but the ways of the God of the Jews are not ours.

Good King David took the throne away from Ishbosheth, son of

Saul. He caused Miphiboseth, son of his protector Jonathan, to be assassinated. He delivered to the Gibeonites for hanging two of Saul's children and five of his grandchildren. To cover up his adultery with Bathsheba he killed Uriah; and again it is this disreputable Bathsheba, mother of Solomon, who is a grandmother of Jesus Christ.

The rest of Jewish history is only a tissue of consecrated crimes. Solomon begins with the murder of his brother Adonijah. If God granted Solomon the gift of wisdom, it appears that he refused him those of humanity, justice, continence, and faith. He has seven hundred wives and three hundred concubines. The Song that is imputed to him is of the nature of those erotic books that cause the modest to blush. It speaks only of women's breasts, of mouth kissing, of a belly similar to a heap of wheat, of voluptuous postures, of fingers in the opening, of thrills; and finally it finishes by saying: "What shall we do with our small sister? She does not yet have breasts; if she is a wall let us build on it, if she is a door let us close it." Such are the morals of the wisest of the Jews, or at least the morals that miserable rabbis and even more absurd Christian theologians ascribe to him.

Finally, to add the excess of the ridiculous to this excess of impurity, the Papists have decided that the stomach of the Shulamite and her opening, her breasts and her mouth kissing, are the symbol of the marriage of Jesus Christ with his Church.[1]

Of all the kings of Judah and Samaria, very few were not assassins or assassinated. The result was that this batch of criminals who slaughtered each other in public places and in the temple, even as Titus besieged them, fell by the sword and into the chains

[1] We know that the Christian theologians pass this lewd book off as a prediction of the marriage of Jesus Christ with his Church. As though Jesus fondled the breasts of his Church and put his hand to her opening; and upon what is this lovely explanation founded? On the fact that *Christus* is masculine and *Ecclesia* feminine. But if in place of the feminine *Ecclesia*, one were to use the masculine word *coetus, conventus*, what would be the result? What notary would draw up such a marriage contract?—*Voltaire*

of the Romans along with the rest of this small nation of God (of whom ten-twelfths had so long been dispersed in Asia) and were sold in the markets of the Roman cities, each Jew being evaluated at the price of one pig, an animal less impure than that nation itself, if it was the way its historians and prophets describe it.

No one can deny that the Jews wrote these dreadful things. When they are thus assembled before our eyes we are revolted. These are the heralds of Providence, the precursors of the reign of Jesus! All Jewish history, you say, O Abbadie! is the prediction of the Church; all prophets have predicted Jesus; let us then examine the prophets.

## CHAPTER IX—On the Prophets

Prophet, nabi, roëh, seer, soothsayer, it is all the same thing. All ancient authors agree that the Egyptians, Chaldeans, all the Asiatic nations, had their prophets, their soothsayers. These civilizations were much older than the small Jewish nation, that, when it was a horde in a corner of the earth, had no other language than that of its neighbors, and that, as has been said elsewhere, borrowed from the Phoenicians even the name of God: *Eloha, Jehova, Adonai, Sadai*; finally, it took all the rites and the customs of the people who surrounded it, while constantly denouncing these very people.

Someone has said* that the first soothsayer, the first prophet, was the first rascal who encountered a fool; thus prophecy dates from remote antiquity. But let us add fanaticism to fraud; these two monsters live together comfortably in the human brain. We have seen arrive in London, from the depths of Languedoc and

---

* Beuchot notes that it was Voltaire himself, but gives no reference.—*kwa*

Vivarais, herds of prophets, very similar to those of the Jews, who combined the most horrid enthusiasm with the most disgusting lies. We have seen Jurieu prophesy in Holland. Such imposters have existed from time immemorial; not only wretched creatures who made predictions but others who dreamed up prophecies made by the ancients.

The world has been full of sibyls and Nostradamuses. The Koran counts two hundred and twenty-four thousand prophets. The bishop Epiphanius, in his notes on the supposed *Canon of the Apostles*, counts seventy-three Jewish prophets and ten prophetesses. The calling of prophet among the Jews was neither a dignity, nor a rank, nor a position in the state; one did not become a prophet as one becomes a doctor at Oxford or Cambridge; whoever wished to prophesy did so; it sufficed to have, or to believe to have, or to feign to possess, the will and the spirit of God. The future was announced by dancing and playing the psaltery. Saul, although a reprobate, dared to be a prophet. Each faction in the civil wars had its prophets, just as we have our writers in Grub Street[1]. The two sides treated each other as fools, liars, visionaries, rascals, and in that alone they spoke the truth. *Scitote Israel stultum prophetam, insanum virum spiritualem** said Hosea, according to the Vulgate [Hos. 9:7].

"Her prophets are light and treacherous persons," said Zephaniah, prophet of Jerusalem. "They are like our apothecary Moore who advertises in the papers: 'Take my pills, beware of counterfeits.'"

The prophet Micah foretold misfortunes to the kings of Samaria and Judah, and the prophet Zedekiah gave him an enormous box on the ear, saying to him: "Which way went the spirit of the Lord from me to speak unto thee?" [II Chron. 18:23].

---

[1] Grub Street is where most of the bad pamphlets that are authored daily in London are printed.—*Voltaire*

* "Israel shall know it: the prophet is a fool, the spiritual man is mad." King James, Hosea, 9:7.—*kwa*

Jeremiah, who prophesied in favor of Nebuchadnezzar, tyrant of the Jews, placed chains about his neck [Jer. 27:2] and a saddle or a yoke upon his back, because it was a symbol; he must send this symbol to the petty neighboring kings as an invitation to submit themselves to Nebuchadnezzar. The prophet Hananiah, who regarded Jeremiah as a traitor, tore the bonds from him, broke them, and threw his yoke upon the ground [Jer. 28:10].

Here is Hosea whom God orders to take a prostitute and have whoresons [Hosea, chap. 1]. *Vade, sume tibi uxorem fornicationum, et fac tibi filios fornicationum,* says the Vulgate. Hosea promptly obeys. He takes Gomer, daughter of Diblaim; he has three children by her; thus this prophecy and this whoring lasted at least three years. That is not enough for the god of the Jews; he wishes Hosea [chap. 3] to lie with a woman who has already cuckolded her husband. It costs the prophet only fifteen drachmas, and a bushel and a half of barley; little enough for adultery[2]. It cost the patriarch Judah still less for the incest with his daughter-in-law Tamar.

There is Ezekiel who, after receiving from God an order to sleep three hundred and ninety days on his left side, and forty days on his right side, to swallow a book of parchment, to eat a *sir reverend*[3] on his bread, introduces God himself, the creator of the world, speaking thus to the young Aholah: "Thou hast grown up, thy breasts have appeared, thy pubic hair has begun to grow; I have covered thee, but thou hast set thyself up in a bad place; thou hast opened thy thighs to all who pass . . . thy sister Aholibah has prostituted herself with more passion [Ezek. 23]; she has searched

[2] Notice that the prophet makes use of a proper word *fodi eam*; I f . . . her. Oh abomination! And they put these infamous books in the hands of young boys and girls, and seducers lead these young victims to the convents!—*Voltaire*

[3] A "sir reverend" in English, is a turd. What in the world! Out of his own mouth God would have ordered a prophet to eat feces for three hundred and ninety days, lying upon his left side! What madman in Bedlam, lying in the midst of his own excretions, could imagine such disgusting horrors? And they are spread among a people who has calculated gravity and the aberration of light from fixed stars!—*Voltaire*

out those who have the member of an ass and who discharge like horses."*

Our friend, General Withers, to whom someone once read these prophecies, asked in what brothel the Holy Scriptures had been written.

The prophecies are rarely read. It is difficult to sustain reader interest in their long and tedious nonsense. Cultured people who have read *Gulliver* and *Atlantis* know neither Hosea nor Ezekiel.

When we bring to the attention of sensible persons these execrable passages, drowned in the trash of the prophesies, they are wholly astonished. They can not conceive that an Isaiah [20:2] walks completely nude in the midst of Jerusalem, that an Ezekiel [5:2] cuts his beard in three parts, that a Jonah [2:1] may be three days in the stomach of a whale, etc. If they read of such outlandish conduct and lewdness in one of the books that are called profane, they would throw the book away with loathing. It is the Bible: they remain confused; they hesitate, they condemn these awful deeds, but dare not forthwith condemn the book that contains them. It is only with the passage of time that they dare make use of their common sense; they end up by detesting that which rascals and imbeciles have made them worship.

When were these books, lacking in reason and modesty, written? No one knows. The greatest probability is that the most of the books attributed to Solomon, Daniel, and others were composed in Alexandria; but once more, what matters the time and place? Is it not enough to recognize clearly that these are monuments of the most outrageous folly and infamous debauchery?

How then have the Jews been able to venerate them? It is because they were Jews. We must further consider that these monuments to excess were preserved alone among the priests and scribes. We know how rare books were in all countries where printing, invented by the Chinese, arrived only much later. We

---

* This is Voltaire's rather free paraphrase of passages in Ezekiel 23.—*kwa*

shall be yet more astonished when we shall see the Fathers of the Church adopt these repulsive fantasies, or offer them as proof of their church.

Let us go from the Old Testament into the New. Let us proceed to Jesus and the establishment of Christianity; and in order to make the transition, let us bypass the assassinations of so many kings, and children thrown into the midst of flames in the valley of Tophet, or crushed in streams under rocks. Let us pass quickly over this frightful and uninterrupted series of sacrilegious enormities. Wretched Jews! it was among you that a man who carried the very common name of Jesus was born of the dregs of the people. Let us see who this man Jesus was.

## CHAPTER X—On the Person of Jesus

Jesus was born in an era when fanaticism still was dominant, but when a little more decency prevailed. The long dealings of the Jews with the Greeks and the Romans had acquainted the masters of the nation with some less crude and unreasonable customs. But the populace, always incorrigible, retained its demented spirit. Some Jews oppressed under the kings of Syria, and under the Romans, had imagined at that time that God would someday send them a liberator, a messiah. This expectation ought naturally to have been fulfilled by Herod. He was their king, he was an ally of the Romans, he had rebuilt their temple, the architecture of which far surpassed that of the temple of Solomon. The nation no longer suffered under foreign domination; it paid taxes only to its own monarch; the Jewish religion flourished, the ancient laws were respected; Jerusalem, we must confess, was in the period of its greatest splendor.

Idleness and superstition gave birth to many factions or religious societies, Sadducees, Pharisees, Essenes, Judaites, Therapeutics, Johannines or disciples of John; much as the Papists have Molinists, Jansenists, Jacobins, and Cordeliers. But no one then spoke of waiting for a messiah. Neither Flavius Josephus, nor Philo, who have entered into Jewish history in such great detail, say that people then deluded themselves with the idea that there would be a Christ, an anointed one, a liberator, a redeemer, of whom they had less need than ever; and if there was one, it was Herod. In fact, there was a party, a sect, the Herodians, who recognized Herod as the envoy of God.[1]

These people had always given the name of the anointed one, messiah, christ, to whoever had done them a little good: sometimes to their pontiffs, sometimes to foreign princes. The Jew who compiled the fantasies of Isaiah has him say [45:1] with base flattery quite worthy of a Jewish slave: "Thus saith the Lord to his anointed Cyrus, whose right hand I have holden, to subdue nations before him. . . ." The Fourth Book of the Kings calls the wicked Jehu, anointed, messiah. A prophet announces to Hazael [IV Kings (II Kings, KJ) 8:13], king of Damascus, that he is messiah and anointed by the Almighty. Ezekiel says to the king of Tyre [28:12, 14, 16]: "Thou art the anointed cherub, a messiah, the seal of the resemblance of God."* If the king of Tyre knew that they gave him these titles in Judea, he could have made himself some

[1] The sect of Herodians did not last long. The title of envoy of God was a name that they gave indifferently to whoever had done them a good turn, be it Herod the Arab, or Judas Maccabeus, or the Persian kings, or the Babylonians. The Jews of Rome celebrated the feast of Herod until Nero's time. Persius states it expressly (*Satire V*, verse 180):

> "*Herodis venere dies, unctaque fenestra*
> *Dispositae pinguem nebulam vomuere lucernae*
> *Tumet alba fidelia vino.*"—*Voltaire*

Voltaire's French translation of Aulus Persius Flaccus is to be found in *The History of the Origin of Christianity*, (Oeuvres Complètes de Voltaire,) Hachette edition, 1859, vol. 23, p. 506. The English of his translation is:

"Here are the days of the feast of Herod, filthy lamps are disposed against windows blackened with oil, . . . they refill their wine from white jugs."— *kwa*

* Again, Voltaire's free interpretation.—*kwa*

kind of god; he had an apparent enough right, if we suppose that Ezekiel had been inspired. The evangelists have not said as much about Jesus.

Be that as it may, it is certain that no Jew hoped, nor desired, nor announced an anointed one, a messiah in the time of Herod the Great, under whom it is said that Jesus was born. When, after the death of Herod the Great, Judea was governed as a Roman province, and another Herod was made tetrarch of the small, un-civilized district of Galilee, many fanatics meddled by preaching to the masses, particularly in Galilee, where the Jews were cruder than elsewhere. It is thus that Fox, a wretched peasant, established in our day the sect of the Quakers among the peasants of one of our counties. The first one to found a Calvinist church in France was a carder of wool, named Jean Leclerc. It was thus that Münzer, John of Leyden and others, founded Anabaptism among the peasants of some of the cantons of Germany.

I have seen fanatics in France found a small sect among the rab-ble of a faubourg of Paris. All sectarians begin in this manner throughout the world. They are for the most part the poor who cry out against the government, and who might end up as party heads or on the gallows. Jesus was hanged at Jerusalem without having been anointed. John the Baptist had already been condemned there to be executed. Both left some disciples among the riffraff. Those of John turned toward Arabia where they still are.[2] Those of Jesus were very obscure at first; but when they associated with some Greeks, they began to be known.

Under Tiberius, the Jews having perpetrated more than their usual dishonest tricks, having above all seduced and robbed Fulvia, wife of Saturninus, they were driven from Rome and were rees-tablished there only after paying out a great sum of money. They were again punished severely under Caligula and under Claudius.

Their disasters encouraged the few Galileans who composed the

---

[2] The Christians of St. John are principally located at Mosul and around Basra.— *Voltaire*

new sect to separate themselves from the Jewish communion. They
finally found some persons with a little education who became their
leaders, and who wrote in their favor against the Jews. This was
what produced the enormous quantity of *Evangels*, a Greek word
which means *good news*. Each produced a *Life of Jesus*: none were
in agreement, but all resembled one another in the quantity of incredible prodigies that in vying with one another they attributed to
their founder.

The synagogue, for its part, seeing that a new sect born among
its own people spread a *Life of Jesus* very injurious to the Sanhe-
drin and to the nation, sought to find out who was this man to
whom, up until then, it had paid no attention. There still remains a
bad work of that time entitled *Sepher Toldos Jeschut*. It seems to
have been done many years after the execution of Jesus, in the period when the Gospels were compiled. This small book is full of
miracles like all of the books of the Jews and the Christians; but as
extravagant as it is, one is forced to grant that there are things in it
which are much more probable than those in our Gospels.

In the *Toldos Jeschut* it is related that Jesus was the son of one
named Mirja, married in Bethlehem to a poor man named
Jocanam. There was in the vicinity a soldier whose name was
Joseph Panther [or Pantera], a well-fashioned man and rather
good-looking; he became enamored of Mirja or Maria (Hebrews
did not express vowels, and so often took an A for an I).

Mirja became pregnant by Panther; Jocanam, confused and for-
lorn, left Bethlehem and went into hiding in Babylon, where there
were still a great many Jews. The conduct of Mirja dishonored her;
her son Sesu or Jeschut was declared illegitimate by the city's
judges. When he had become of age to attend public school, he
seated himself among the legitimate children; he was made to leave
this rank; from there stemmed his animosity toward priests which
he manifested on reaching the age of maturity. He showered upon
them the most atrocious abuse, calling them a *generation of vipers*
[Matt. 12:34], *whited sepulchers* [Mark 23:27]. At last, having

picked a quarrel with the Jew Judas upon some matter of interest, as upon points of religion, he was denounced by Judas to the San- hedrin [Matt. 23]; he was arrested, he began to cry, he asked pardon, but in vain; he was scourged, then stoned, and in the end hanged.

Such is the substance of the story. There were added afterward insipid fables, impertinent miracles, that did great harm to its essence; but the book was known in the second century; Celsus cited it, Origen refuted it; it has come down to us much disfigured.

The essence I have cited is certainly more credible, more natural, more conformable to what goes on every day in the world, than any of the fifty Gospels of the *christicoles*. It is more probable that Joseph Panther had gotten Mary with child than that an angel came through the air to pay a compliment on behalf of God to a carpenter's wife, just as Jupiter sent Mercury to Alcmene.

All that is told to us of this Jesus is worthy of the Old Testament, and of Bedlam. There is caused to come I don't know what *agion pneuma*, a holy breath, a Holy Spirit of whom we never heard before and who is made a third part of God, God himself, God the creator of the world; he impregnates Mary, which has occasioned the Jesuit Sanchez, in his *Summa Theologica*, to examine whether God had much pleasure of Mary, if he expended seed and if Mary also issued seed.

Jesus becomes the son of God and a Jewess, not yet God himself, but a superior creature. He performs miracles. The first is to have himself carried by the Devil [Matt. 4:8; Luke 4:5] to the peak of a mountain in Judea from where all the kingdoms of the world could be seen. His vestments appear all white [Matt. 17:2]; and what wonders! he changes water into wine [John 2:9] at a repast where the guests were already drunk.[3] He causes a fig tree

---

[3] It is difficult to say which is the more ridiculous of the claimed miracles. A good many people hold out for the wine of the marriage feast of Cana. That God says to his Jewish mother [John 2:4]: *Woman, what is there between thee and me?* is certainly a strange remark; but that God eats and drinks with drunkards, and changes six

to dry up [Matt. 11:19; Mark 11:13] that gave him no figs for his breakfast at the end of February; but the author of this account had at least the honesty to remark that it was not the season for figs.

He goes to sup with women [John 12:2] and then with tax collectors; but yet they claim in his biography that he regards tax collectors, those publicans, as a loathsome class [Matt. 9:10 and 11]. He enters the temple [John 2:15, 18], that is to say, into the great enclosure where the priests lived, in that court where merchants were authorized by law to sell hens, pigeons, lambs to those who came to make a sacrifice. He takes a large whip and beats the merchants about the shoulders, pursues them with blows from leather thongs—them, their hens, their pigeons, their sheep, and their cattle—throws all their money on the ground, and they let him get away with it! And if we are to believe that book attributed to John, they are content to ask him for a miracle to prove that he has the right to create such an uproar in so respectable a place.

It already was a great miracle that thirty or forty merchants let themselves be flogged by a lone man and lose their money without a murmur. There is nothing in *Don Quixote* that approaches such exaggeration. But instead of performing the miracle that they request of him, he is content with saying: *Destroy this temple and I shall rebuild it in three days.* The Jews rejoin, according to John: *It has taken forty-six years to build this temple, how canst thou rebuild it in three days?*

It was indeed untrue that Herod had spent forty-six years in the building of the temple at Jerusalem. The Jews could not have replied with such a falsehood. And let us observe, in passing, that the

---

vessels of water into six vessels of wine for the drunks who had too much to drink already, is a blasphemy as detestable as it is absurd! the Hebrew makes use of a word that corresponds to the word *tipsy*; the Vulgate [John 2:10] *inebriati*, inebriated.

Saint Chrysostom, mouth of gold, assures us that this was the best wine that anyone had ever drunk; and many Fathers of the Church have claimed that the wine signified the blood of Jesus Christ in the Eucharist; Oh, folly of superstition! into what an abyss of extravagance have you plunged us! —*Voltaire*

incident makes it clear to us that the Gospels were written by persons who were completely uninformed.

All these miracles seem to be done by our charlatans of Smithfields. Our Toland and our Woolston have treated them as they deserve. The most beautiful of all, in my estimation, is that in which Jesus sends the Devil into the bodies of two thousand pigs in a country where there were no pigs [Matt. 8; Mark 5; Luke 8].

After this delightful trick, Jesus is represented as teaching in the villages. What is the tenor of his discourse? He compares the Kingdom of Heaven to a mustard seed, to a bit of leaven mixed with three measures of flour, to a net with which one fishes for good and bad fish, to a king who has killed his poultry for his son's wedding feast, and who sends his servants to invite the neighbors to the wedding. The neighbors kill those who came to invite them to dinner; the king kills those who killed his servants, and burns their cities; he orders beggars that are encountered on the highways to be brought in to have dinner with him. He notices that a poor guest has no robe, and instead of giving him one, has him thrown into a dungeon. Such is the Kingdom of Heaven according to Matthew.

In other sermons the Kingdom of Heaven is always compared to a usurer who insists on a hundred percent in profit. I will be told that our Archbishop Tillotson preaches in another vein.

How does the story of Jesus end? It ends as happens here and elsewhere in the world to those not quite clever enough who tried to stir up the populace so as to arm it or to win for themselves powerful protectors; for the most part they end up by being hanged. In fact, Jesus was such a one for having called his superiors generation of vipers and whited sepulchers. He was publicly executed but secretly resuscitated. Finally, he ascended into heaven [Acts 1:9, 10] in the presence of eighty of his disciples,[4] though no

---

[4] To ascend to heaven in a perpendicular line; why not in a horizontal line? To ascend is against the laws of gravitation. He could have skimmed over the horizon and gone to Mercury or Venus, or Mars, or Jupiter, or Saturn, or any stars, or to the moon, if one of these stars was setting at the time. What foolishness is in the words,

other person in Judea saw him mount into the clouds, something
that would have been easy to see and that would have created a
stir.

Our creed, which the Papists call the *Credo*, a creed attributed
to the Apostles and evidently invented more than four centuries
after the Apostles, tells us that before going up to heaven, Jesus
had made a trip to hell. You will note that there is not a single
word about it in the Gospels; yet it is one of the principal articles
of faith of the *christicoles*; you are not Christian if you do not
believe that Jesus went to hell.

Who was the first to imagine this journey? It was Athanasius,
about three hundred and fifty years later. It is in a treatise against
Apollinaris upon the Incarnation of the Lord that he said that the
soul of Jesus descended into hell, while his body was in the
sepulcher. These words are worthy of attention and reveal with
what sagacity and wisdom Athanasius reasoned. Here are his own
words: "It was necessary that after his death his essentially diverse
parts had diverse functions; that his body reposed in the sepulcher
in order to destroy corruption, and that his soul descended into hell
to conquer death."

The African Augustine is of the same mind as Athanasius in a
letter that he wrote to Evodius: *Quis ergo nisi infidelis negaverit
fuisse apud infernos Christum?** Jerome, his contemporary, was
nearly in agreement; and it was in the time of Augustine and Jerome that this creed, the *Credo*, was composed and which is taken
as the creed of the Apostles among the ignorant.[5]

---

*to go to heaven, descend from heaven!* As though we were the center of all the
spheres, as though our earth were not one of the planets that revolve in space about so
many suns and that enter into the composition of this universe, which we so inappropriately call heaven.—*Voltaire*

  * "Who therefore unless an infidel will deny that Christ has been in hell."—*kwa*

  [5] Reader, you evidently see that they did not dare at the outset to imagine so many
revolting fictions. Some adherents of the Jewish Jesus were content in the beginning
to say that he was a man of good who was unjustly crucified, just as we and other
Christians have assassinated so many virtuous men. Then they become bolder;

Thus do opinions, beliefs, churches, establish themselves. But how has this detestable nonsense been able to gain credit? How did it outstrip the other nonsense of the Greeks and Romans, and in the end the Empire itself? How has it caused so much evil, so many civil wars, lighted so many pyres, and caused so much bloodshed? Of this we shall render an exact account.

## CHAPTER XI—What Concept Must Be Formed of Jesus and His Disciples

Jesus is evidently a humble peasant of Judea, without doubt more alert than most of the inhabitants of his district. Without knowing—it seems—how to read or write, he wished to form a small sect to oppose the Recabites, Judaites, Healers, Essenes, Pharisees, Sadduccees, Herodians; because sect was all among the unfortunate Jews since their establishment in Alexandria. I have already compared Jesus to our Fox, who like him, was an uneducated man from the dregs of the population, sometimes like him preaching a morality of good and above all preaching an equality that so much flatters the mob. Like him Fox established a society that within a short time deviated from his principles, supposing that he had any. The same thing happened to Jesus' sect. Both spoke openly against the priests of their time; but the laws being more humane in England than in Judea, all that the clergy could

---

someone dares to write that God has resurrected him. Soon thereafter his legend grows. This one supposes that he has gone to heaven and into hell; another says that he will come to judge the living and the dead in the valley of Jehosaphat; finally he is made a god. Three gods are made. Sophistry is pushed to the point of asserting that the three gods constitute only one. We eat one of these three gods, and drink another, and render them in our urine and feces. We persecute, burn, and break on the wheel those who deny these loathsome acts; and all this, in order that Mr. So-and-so in England might enjoy ten thousand pieces of gold in revenue and that in other countries they may even have more money.—*Voltaire*

obtain from the judges was to place Fox in a pillory. But the Jewish priests forced the presiding Pilate to order Jesus scourged, then hanged on a gibbet in the form of a cross, like a felonious slave. This is inhuman but every nation has its customs. To know whether they nailed his feet and hands need cause us little concern. It seems to me difficult enough to find a nail sufficiently long to pierce two feet, one upon the other, as is claimed; but the Jews were certainly capable of such an abominable atrocity.

The disciples remained as attached to their hanged patriarch as the Quakers have been to their pilloried patriarch. After some time had elapsed they decided to noise it about that their master had been secretly resurrected. This fantasy was the more readily received among the confrères, since it was precisely the time of the great quarrel raised among the Jewish sects about whether or not the resurrection was possible. Platonism, which was very much in vogue in Alexandria and which many Jews studied, very soon came to the support of the nascent sect, and from it came all the mysteries, all the absurd dogma with which the sect was stuffed. This is what we shall now unfold.

## CHAPTER XII—On the Establishment of the Christian Sect and Particularly about Paul

When the first Galileans spread among the populace of the Greeks and the Romans, they found them infected with all the absurd traditions that can enter the ignorant mind in love with myths; gods disguised as bulls, as horses, as swans, as serpents, in order to seduce women and girls. The magistrates and the principal citizens did not approve of these excesses; but the populace fed upon them, and it was the Jewish rabble that spoke to the pagan rabble. To my mind it resembles among us the disciples of Fox disputing with the disciples of Brown, bishop of Cork. It was not difficult for some fanatical Jews to win acceptance of their fantasies among the dolts who believed in fantasies no less silly. The attraction of novelty lured weak minds wearied of their ancient foolishness and so ready to embrace new errors—just as people at Bartholomew Fair[1] become disgusted with an old farce they have heard too often, and so demand a new one.

If we can believe the books of the *christicoles*, Peter, son of Jonas, lived in Joppa with Simon the tanner, in a hovel where he resurrected Dorcas the dressmaker.

See the chapter of Lucian, entitled *Philopatris*, in which he speaks of the *Galilean with the bald head and big nose, who was raised up to the third heaven.*[2] See how he treats an assembly of Christians in which he found himself. Our Presbyterians of Scotland and the beggars of Saint Médard in Paris are precisely the same. Ragged men nearly naked, of maniacal manner, heaving sighs, making contortions, swearing by the *son who is come out of the father*, predicting a thousand misfortunes to the empire, blaspheming against the emperor. Such were the first Christians.

The one who had done the most to bring the sect into repute was Paul, he of the bald head and big nose, whom Lucian ridicules. It seems to me that the writings of Paul suffice to show how right Lucian was to do so. What nonsense when he writes to the society

[1] Bartholomew Fair, where there still are charlatans and astrologers.—*Voltaire*

[2] It is very doubtful that Lucian had seen Paul, and even that he was the author of the *Philopatris*. However, it could well be that Paul, who lived in Nero's time, was still alive in Trajan's time, when it is said that Lucian began to write.

One asks how this Paul could succeed in formulating a faith with his detestable nonsense, for which the Cardinal Bembo had so much contempt. We reply that without this nonsense he never would have succeeded over the demoniacs whom he governed. Is is possible that our Fox, who has founded among us a sect of primitives called Quakers, may have had more good sense than Paul? Long ago, someone said that fools found religions, but the prudent govern them.—*Voltaire*

As long as Voltaire was on the attack Cardinal Bembo was an appropriate reference. The Cardinal's way of life (1470–1547), which included several children and an affair with Lucrezia Borgia, occasioned raised eyebrows even in his time. But he was learned in Greek and Latin and author of *A History of Venice.—kwa*

of Christians which was being formed in the Jewish slime at Rome!
"For circumcision verily profiteth, if thou keep the law: but if thou
be a breaker of the law, thy circumcision is made uncircumcision,
etc. [Rom. 2:25]. . . . Do we then make void the law through faith?
God forbid: yea, we establish the law [Rom 3:31]. . . . For if
Abraham were justified by works, he hath whereof to glory; but
not before God" [Rom. 4:2]. In expressing himself thus, Paul
spoke evidently as a Jew and not as a Christian; but he speaks even
more like a senseless madman who is unable to put together two
ideas coherently.

What a discourse to the Corinthians! "[Our fathers] . . . were all
baptized unto Moses in the cloud and in the sea" [I. Cor. 10:2]. Is
not Cardinal Bembo right in labeling these letters *epistolaccie* and in
advising that they not be read?

What should we think of a man who says to the Thessalonians:[3]
"Let your women keep silence in the churches. . . ." and who in the
same epistle [I Cor. 14:34] announces that they must speak and
prophesy wearing a veil?

Is his quarrel with the Apostles that of a wise and moderate
man? Does he not reveal himself a partisan in everything? He
converts into a Christian, he teaches Christianity and for seven
days in a row he makes sacrifices in the temple in Jerusalem on the
advice of James so that he won't be thought a Christian. He writes
to the Galatians [5:2]: "Behold, I Paul, say unto you, that if ye be
circumcised, Christ shall profit you nothing." And then he cir-
cumcises his disciple Timothy, whom the Jews claim was the son of
a Greek and a prostitute. He is an intruder among the Apostles
and he brags to the Corinthians [I. 9:1–7] of being as much an
Apostle as the others: "Am I not an Apostle? have I not seen Jesus
Christ our Lord? are not ye my work in the Lord? If I be not an
apostle unto others, yet doubtless I am to you . . . . Have we not
the right to be nourished at your expense? Have we not the right to

---

[3] It is not in the Epistle to the Thessalonians, but in the First Epistle to the Corinthians 14:34.—*Beuchot*

take with us a wife who may be our sister (or if you wish, a sister who may be our wife), as do the other apostles and brethren [frères] of the Lord? Who goes to war always at his own expense? etc."*

How many things there are in this passage! The right to live at the expense of those whom he has subjugated, the right to make them pay the expenses of his wife or of his sister, finally the proof that Jesus had brothers and the presumption that Mary or Mirja delivered more than once.

I would very much wish to know of whom he speaks again in the second letter to the Corinthians [11:13] "For such *are* false apostles . . . . However whereinsoever any is bold [11: 21-25] . . . I am bold also. Are they Hebrews? so am I. Are they the seed of Abraham? so am I. Are they ministers of Christ? . . . I am more; in labors more abundant, in stripes above measure, in prisons frequent, in deaths oft. Of the Jews five times received I forty stripes save one. Thrice was I beaten with rods, once was I stoned, thrice I suffered shipwreck, a night and a day I have been in the deep."**

Behold then Paul who has been twenty-four hours in the depths of the sea without being drowned; it is one-third of Jonah's adventure. But is it not clear that he manifests here his base jealousy of Peter and the other apostles and that he wishes to excel them by having been an offender of the law and having been whipped more often than they?

Does not the madness for power appear in all its insolence, when he says to the same Corinthians: "This is the third time I come to you. In the mouth of two or three witnesses shall every word be es-

---

* The above quotes are not a faithful rendition of the biblical text. "At your expense" is Voltaire's, possibly derived from Paul's later question about going to war. The reading "a woman who may be our sister" and its parenthetical reverse are also Voltaire. See *Zapata's Questions*, No. 48.—*kwa*

** The passage is quoted here as it appears in the King James translation. In the French text Voltaire quotes the Bible freely, with many additions and omissions.—*kwa*

tablished. I shall spare none. . . . [those who] heretofore have sinned, and to all others, . . . if I come again, I will not spare."

To what imbeciles and what brutish hearts of the vile populace did he write as a tyrannical master? To those to whom he dared to say that he had been overjoyed in the third heaven. Low and impudent imposter! Where is this third heaven in which thou hast traveled? Is it on Venus or on Mars? We laugh at Muhammad when his commentators claim that he visited all the seven heavens in one night. But at least Muhammad does not talk in his Koran of such a fantasy as was ascribed to him; yet Paul dares to assert that he has done nearly half of this trip!

Who then was this Paul who is still so much talked about and who is cited every day every which way? He says that he was a Roman citizen [Acts 16:37]. I dare to affirm that he lies impudently. No Jew was a Roman citizen until Phillip and Decius.* If he was from Tarsus,* Tarsus was not a Roman colony or Roman city until more than a hundred years after Paul. If he was from Giscala, as says Jerome, this village was in Galilee, and the Galileans assuredly never had the honor of being Roman citizens.

"He was . . . brought up . . . at the feet of Gamaliel"; that is to say that he was Gamaliel's domestic. In fact it is remarked that he watched over the cloaks of those who stoned Joseph, which is the work of a valet, a hangman's valet. The Jews claimed that he wanted to marry the daughter of Gamaliel. Some trace of this adventure is seen in the ancient book which contains the history of Thecla. It is not astounding that the daughter of Gamaliel did not desire a small, bald valet, whose eyebrows joined above his misshapen nose, and who had crooked legs: it is thus that the Acts of Thecla depict him. Disdained by Gamaliel and his daughter, as he deserved to be, he attached himself to the newborn sect of Cephas, James, Matthew, and Barnabas, in order to foment trouble among the Jews.

---

* Phillip and Decius were Roman emperors—244–249 A.D. and 249–251 A.D., respectively. The *Constitutie Antoniniana* had already granted, 212,213, citizenship to all of the free population of the Empire.—*kwa*

With only a little spark of reason, we can see that this cause of the unfortunate Jew's apostasy is more natural than the cause attributed to him. How shall we be persuaded that a celestial light caused him to fall from his horse at noonday, that a celestial voice made itself audible to him, that God said to him [Acts 9:4]: "Saul, Saul, why persecutest thou me?" Should we not blush at such foolishness?

If God had wished to oppose the persecution of the disciples of Jesus, would not he have spoken to the princes of the nation rather than to Gamaliel's valet? Have they been less chastised since Saul fell off his horse? Was not Saul-Paul himself chastised? What good is this ridiculous miracle? I call upon heaven and earth to witness (if I may use these improper words, heaven and earth) that there has never been a legend more insane, more fanatic, more disgusting, more worthy of revulsion and scorn.[4]

## CHAPTER XIII—On the Gospels

From the time that the half-Jewish, half-Christian societies had gradually established themselves among the lower classes in Jerusalem, Antioch, Ephesus, Corinth, and Alexandria, sometime after Vespasian, each of the small groups wanted to create its own Gospel. We know of fifty-four, but there were many more. All

[4] What is necessary, it seems to me, is to remark carefully about this Jewish Paul that he never says that Jesus is God. He gives him all the honors possible, but the word God is never meant for him. He has been predestined in the Epistle to the Romans, Chapter 1. He wishes that they may have the peace of God through Jesus, Chapter 5. He counts upon the grace of God through one man only, Jesus. There is one single verse in all the writings of Paul where the word God could fall upon Jesus; it is in the Epistle to the Romans, Chapter 9. But Erasmus and Grotius have proven that this passage is falsified and badly interpreted. In fact it would be very strange that Paul, recognizing Jesus as God, should have given him this name only a single time. It might have then been a blasphemy. As for the word Trinity, it is neve found in Paul, who, however, is considered as the founder of Christianity.—
*Voltaire*

contradict themselves, as is well known, and it could not be
otherwise, since they were all contrived in different places. All
agree on one point only—that their Jesus was the son of Mary
(Maria) or Mirja, and that he was hanged; and all attribute to him
as many wonders as are found in the *Metamorphoses* of Ovid.

Luke furnishes him with a genealogy absolutely different from
that compiled by Matthew; and none of them think of drawing up
a genealogy of Mary, sole source of his birth. Doubtless each wrote
fantasies from his imagination for his little society. It stems from
this that one evangelist claims that Jesus was born in Egypt,
another holds that he was brought up entirely in Bethlehem; this
one has him go once to Jerusalem, that one three times. The one
stages the arrival of Three Magi, whom we call the Three Kings,
guided by a new star, and has the first Herod massacre all the little
children of the land when he was near death.[1] The other passes
over in silence the star, the Magi, and the massacre of the innocents.

In order to explain this mass of contradictions, we have been
obliged to compile a concordance; and this concordance is even
less concordant than that which they desired to concord. Nearly all
the Gospels that the Christians communicated to their small flocks
were obviously forged after the capture of Jerusalem: there is
evident proof of it in that which is attributed to Matthew. This
book [23:35] puts in the mouth of Jesus these words to the Jews:
"That upon you may come all the righteous blood shed upon the
earth, from the blood of the righteous Abel unto the blood of
Zacharias, son of Barachias, whom ye slew between the temple and
the altar."

[1] The massacre of the innocents is assuredly the height of absurdity, just as much
as the tale of the Three Magi led by a star. How could Herod who was dying at that
time, fear that a carpenter's son born in a village might dethrone him? Herod held
his realm from the Romans. It would have been necessary that this child would
make war on the empire. Can such a fear enter into the head of a man who is not
absolutely insane? Is it possible that someone may have imposed on human
credulity such absurdities so beneath *Robert the Devil* and *John of Paris*. Man is
then a contemptible species, since he is thus controlled.—*Voltaire*

A forger always betrays himself by some trait. During the siege of Jerusalem there was a Zacharias son of Barachias [*ibid.*], murdered between the temple and the altar, by the zealot faction. From that the imposture is easily discovered; however, in order to uncover it, it might be necessary to read all of the Bible. The Greeks and the Romans never read it: these stupidities and the Gospels were entirely unknown to them; anyone could falsify with impunity.

An evident proof that the Gospel attributed to Matthew was written a considerable time after him, by some wretched half–Jewish, half–Christian Hellenist, is in this famous passage: "If he neglects to hear the Church [Matt. 18:17], let him be unto thee as an heathen man and a publican." In the time of Jesus and of Matthew there was no church. The world *église* [church] is of Greek origin. The assembly of the people of Athens was called the *ecclesia*. This expression was adopted by the Christians only in the course of time when they had some form of government. It is thus clear that a forger took the name of Matthew in order to write this Gospel in very bad Greek. I admit that it would be comical enough that Matthew, who had been a publican, might compare the heathens to publicans. But whoever the author of this ridiculous comparison, he could only have been a harebrain from the dregs of the people who consider a Roman knight, charged with collecting the taxes set by the government, as a dreadful person. Such a notion is in itself destructive of all administration and is not only unworthy of a man inspired by God but unworthy of an honest citizen's lackey.

There are two *Gospels of the Infancy*: the first relates how a young rascal slapped the behind of the small Jesus, his playmate, and that little Jesus caused him to die on the spot, *kai parachrēma pesoẁn àpéthanen.** Another time he fashioned small clay birds, and they flew away. The manner in which he learned his alphabet was thoroughly divine. Such stories are no more ridiculous than

---

* "and on the spot he fell down dead."—*kwa*

those of the abduction of Jesus by the Devil, of the Transfiguration on Tabor, of the water changed to wine, of the devils sent into a herd of swine. This Gospel of the Infancy was also venerated for a long time.

The second book of the infancy is no less curious. Mary, carrying her son into Egypt, encounters some girls grieving because their brother had been changed into a mule. Mary and her little one did not hesitate to return the mule to his human form, and it is not known whether the unfortunate one gained in the trade. On the way, the wandering family encounters two robbers, one named Dumachus and the other Titus.[2] Dumachus wanted to rob the Holy Virgin and do her even worse harm. Titus took Mary's part, and gave forty drachmas to Dumachus in order to persuade him to let the family pass without injury. Jesus declared to the Holy Virgin that Dumachus would be the bad thief, and Titus the good thief; that they would one day hang with him, that Titus would go to paradise and Dumachus, to the Devil.

The Gospel According to St. James, who was Jesus' older brother, or *According to Peter Barjona*, a Gospel recognized and lauded by Tertullian and Origen, was held in the greatest esteem. It was called *Protevangelion*, First Gospel. It is perhaps the first to have spoken of the new star, of the arrival of the Magi, and of the infants whom Herod ordered massacred.

There is still another kind of Gospel, or Acts of John, in which Jesus is represented as dancing with his Apostles on the eve of his death; and the thing is the more likely because the Therapeutae were in fact accustomed to dancing in a circle, which ought to please the Heavenly Father very much.[3]

---

[2] Such fitting names for Egyptians.—*Voltaire*

[3] It is not said in St. Matthew that Jesus danced with his Apostles, but it is said (26:30): "They sang a hymn, and went to the Mount of Olives."

It is true that in the hymn this couplet is found: "I wish to sing, dance all for joy." Which leads us to see that in fact they mixed dancing with singing, as in all religious ceremonies of that time. St. Augustine reports this song in his letter to Ceretius.

Why does today's most scrupulous Christian laugh without a qualm at all these Gospels, and Acts, which are no longer in the canon, and yet dare not laugh at those which the Church has adopted? They have nearly the same stories; but the fanatic adores under one name what appears to him the height of the ridiculous under another.

Four Gospels were finally chosen; for the principal reason, according to St. Irenaeus, that there are only four cardinal winds; and that God is seated on the cherubim and that the cherubim have four forms. St. Jerome or Hieronymous, in his preface to the Gospel of Mark, adds to the four winds and the four animals, the four rings that held the four poles upon which the chest called the ark was carried.

Theophilus of Antioch proves that Lazarus having been dead for four days, only four Gospels could be accepted. St. Cyprian proves the same thing by the four rivers that flowed through the terrestrial paradise. It would be indeed impious not to yield to such reasons.

But before preference had been given to these four Gospels, the

---

It makes little difference to know if in fact this song reported by Augustine was sung or not; here it is:

I wish to liberate, I wish to be liberated.
I wish to save and I wish to be saved.
I wish to beget and I wish to be begotten.
I wish to sing, dance all for joy.
I wish to cry, strike yourselves all for sorrow.
I wish to adorn and I wish to be adorned.
I am the light for you who see me.
I am the door for you who knock on it.
You who see what I do, do not say what I do.
I have acted it all in this discourse, but I have not been fooled.

What an extraordinary song! It is little worthy of the Supreme Being. This little canticle is nothing other than what is called *persiflage* in France, and nonsense among ourselves. It is not at all proven that Jesus sang after having celebrated the Passover; but it is proven by all the Gospels that he celebrated the Passover after the Jewish rite, and not according to the Christian one, and we shall say here in passing what Lord Bolingbroke insinuated elsewhere, that there can be found in the life of Jesus Christ no action, no dogma, no rite, no discourse which may have the least tie with the Christianity of today, and still less with the Christianity of Rome than with all the others.—*Voltaire*

fathers of the first two centuries nearly always cited only the Gospels today called the Apocrypha. It is incontestable proof that our four Gospels are not the work of those to whom they have been attributed.

I wish that they were; I wish, for example, that Luke had written that which is under his name. I would say to Luke: "How dare you assert that Jesus was born under the government of Cyrenus or Quirinus, when it has been established that Quirinus was not governor of Syria until more than ten years later? How can you have the impudence to say that Augustus ordered a *census of the whole world*,* and that Mary went to Bethlehem to be counted? Census of the whole world! What an expression! You have heard that Augustus had an account book that contained details of the forces of the empire and of its finances; but a census of all the subjects of the empire! That is something that he never thought of; much less a census of the entire world, no Roman or Greek or barbarian document has ever contained such a fantasy. You therefore stand self-convicted of the greatest falsehood; and yet we must adore your book!"

But who invented these four Gospels? Is it not very probable that they were Hellenistic Christians, since the Old Testament is nearly always cited following only the version of the Septuagint, a version unknown in Judea. The Apostles knew Greek no more than Jesus had known it. How could they then have cited the Septuagint? Only the miracle of the Pentecost could have taught Greek to the unlearned Jews.

What a mass of contradictions and impostures has remained in these four Gospels! Had there been only one, it would have sufficed to demonstrate that it is the work of darkness. Had there been only the account that is found in Luke, that Jesus was born under the government of Cyrenus, when Augustus ordered the census of the whole empire, would not this untruth alone be sufficient cause to reject the book with scorn? First, there never was

* See for discussion of this point, the Introduction.—*kwa*

such a census, and no author speaks of it. Second, Cyrenus was not the governor of Syria until ten years after the time of the birth of Jesus. So many words, so many errors in the Gospels. And it is thus that one succeeds with the people.

## CHAPTER XIV—How the First Christians Conducted Themselves with the Romans and How They Forged Verses Attributed to the Sibyls, etc.

People of good sense ask how this tissue of myths that so flatly outrages reason, of blasphemies that impute so many horrors to the Divinity, could gain any credence. In fact, they would have been very astonished if the first Christian sectarians had converted the court of the emperors and the Senate of Rome, but an abject rabble addressed itself to a no less contemptible populace. This is so true that in his discourse to the *christicoles* Emperor Julian said: "At first it was enough for you to seduce some servants, some beggars like Cornelius and Sergius. May I be considered as the most shameless of imposters, if amongst those who embraced your religion under Tiberius and Claudius, there was even one man of noble birth or merit."[1]

---

[1] It is strange that the Emperor Julian called Sergius a nobody, a beggar. It could be that he read the Gospels with little attention or that his memory failed him at this moment, which is common enough among those who, being preoccupied with important matters, still want to take upon themselves the burden of controversy. He is mistaken, and the Acts of the Apostles which he refutes are also evidently mistaken. Sergius was neither a nobody, as Julian said, nor a proconsul, nor governor of Cyprus as say the Acts [8:7].

There was only one proconsul in Syria, of which the island of Cyprus was a dependency, and it was the proconsul of Syria who appointed the propraetor of Cyprus. But this propraetor was always an eminent person.

Perhaps the emperor wanted to speak of another Sergius whom the Acts of the Apostles may have clumsily changed into a proconsul or propraetor. The Acts are a crude rhapsody, full of contradictions, as is all that the Jews and Galileans have written.

At the crossroads and in the taverns the first Christian apologists therefore said to the pagans who raised objections: "Be not frightened by our mysteries: you have recourse to expiation to purge you of your crimes: we have a most salutary expiation. Your oracles are not worth ours: and the proof that our sect is the only good one, is that your own oracles predicted all that we are teaching you, and all that our Lord Jesus Christ has done. Have you not heard of the Sibyls?—Yes, reply the pagan disputants to the Galilean disputants; all the Sibyls have been inspired by Jupiter himself; their predictions are all true.—Very well, reply the Galileans, we will show you verses of the Sibyls that clearly announce Jesus Christ and then indeed it will be necessary for you to give in."

Immediately they set themselves to fabricating the worst Greek verse ever composed, verse similar to that of our Grub Street, of Blackmore and Gibson. They attributed them to the Sibyls, and for more than four hundred years they did not cease to base Christianity on this proof, which was equally within reach of the cheaters and the cheated. The first step being taken, we see the childish forgers lay at the Sibyls' door even acrostic verse which began with all the letters of the name of Jesus Christ.

Lactantius has preserved a great part of these rhapsodies as authentic evidence. To these myths they added miracles which they

---

They say that Paul and Barnabas found at Paphos a Jewish magician, named Bar-Jesus, who wished to prevent the Propraetor Sergius from becoming Christian; it is in Chapter 13. Following this they say that Bar-Jesus called himself Elymas, and that Paul and Barnabas turned him blind for several days, and that this miracle caused the propraetor to become a Christian. We sense well enough the worth of such a story. We have only to read the discourse that Paul held with Sergius to see that Sergius would have been able to comprehend none of it.

The chapter finishes by saying that Paul and Barnabas were driven from the island of Cyprus. How would Sergius, who was the master, permit them to be driven out when he had embraced their religion? But also why would Sergius, being the principal dignitary on the island, and in consequence no imbecile, all at once become a Christian?

Are not all these *Tales of a Tub* a palpable absurdity?

Let us note above all that in the Acts of the Apostles and in all of Paul's discourses, Jesus is only a man, and that there is not a single authentic text where there may be a question of his claimed divinity.—*Voltaire*

performed sometimes even in public. True, they did not revive the dead like Elisha; they did not halt the sun like Joshua; they did not pass through the sea dry-footed like Moses; they did not, like Jesus, have the Devil transport them to the summit of a small mountain in Galilee from which the whole world could be observed; but they cured a fever when it was on the decline, and also the itch when the afflicted had been bathed, bled, purged, and scrubbed. Above all they chased out demons; this was the primary purpose of the Apostles' mission. It is stated in more than one Gospel [Matt. 10:1; Mark 3:15; Luke 9:1] that Jesus sent them out expressly to drive out demons.

It was an ancient prerogative of the people of God. There were, as we know, exorcists in Jerusalem who cured the possessed by putting a bit of the root *barath* under their noses, while muttering some words taken from the *Clavicle of Solomon*. Jesus himself says that the Jews had such a power. Nothing was easier for the Devil than to enter into the body of a beggar, for a consideration of one or two shillings. A Jew or a Galilean could with little trouble chase out ten devils per day for a guinea. The devils never dared to take possession of a governor of a province, a senator, or even a centurion: it was always those who possessed nothing at all who were possessed.

If the Devil ought to have seized anyone it was Pilate; however he never dared approach him. For a long time the mob has been exorcised in England and still more elsewhere; but although the Christian sect is established for precisely this, the custom has been abolished nearly everywhere except in the States in the obedience of the pope and in some rustic areas of Germany unfortunately subjected to bishops and monks.

Governments were right to abolish primitive Christian customs: baptism of nude adult girls, in vats, by men; the dreadful baptism of the dead; exorcism, possession by the Devil, inspiration; love feasts which fostered so much immorality; all that is destroyed, yet the religion lives on.

Thus, for a century, the Christians gained credit with the common people. They were left alone; they were looked upon as a sect of Jews, and Jews were tolerated. Neither Pharisees, Sadducees, Therapeutae, Essenes, nor Judaites were persecuted; there was even more reason to leave those little known Christians to crawl about in obscurity. They were so unimportant, that neither Flavius Josephus, nor Philo, nor Plutarch deigns to mention them; and if Tacitus mentions them at all, he does so by confusing them with the Jews, and denouncing them with withering scorn. Therefore, they had little difficulty in spreading their sect. Under Domitian they were investigated somewhat. Some were punished under Trajan, and it was then they began to mix a thousand false martyrdoms with some that were only too true.

## CHAPTER XV—How the Christians Conducted Themselves with the Jews: Their Ridiculous Explanation of the Prophets

The Christians could not prevail over the Jews as they did over the Gentiles. While they continued to live according to the Mosaic law, as Jesus had done all his life, to abstain from so-called impure meats and not to proscribe circumcision, they were regarded only as a special society of Jews, such as were the Sadducees, Essenes, and Therapeutae. They said that it was wrong to have hanged Jesus, who was a holy man sent from God and who was resurrected.

This kind of talk, in fact, was punished in Jerusalem; it cost Stephen his life, they say; but elsewhere the schism produced only altercations between the dogmatic Jews and the half-Christians. They argued; the Christians believed they found in the Scriptures some passages that they could twist in favor of their cause. They claimed that the Jewish prophets had predicted Jesus Christ; they cited Isaiah [7:14–20] who said to King Ahaz:

"A girl, or young woman (*Alma*)[1] will become great with child, and shall take to her bed with a son who shall be called Immanuel; he shall eat butter and honey, so that he knows to reject evil and choose the good. The land that you abhor shall be delivered of its two kings and the Lord shall whistle to the flies which are in the uttermost parts of the rivers of Egypt, and to the bees of the land of Assyria. He shall take a hired razor and shall shave the head, the pubic area [sic], and the beard of the king of Assyria."*

"And the Lord said to him: Take a great book and write in visible letters: *Maher-shalal-hash-baz, seize quickly the spoils. And I lay with the prophetess, and she was with child and she brought a son into the world and the Lord said to me: Call him Mahar-shalal-hash-baz, seize quickly the spoils.*"

You see clearly, said the Christians, that all this signifies the advent of Jesus Christ. The girl who had a child is the Virgin Mary; *Immanuel* and *seize quickly the spoils*, they are Our Lord Jesus. As for the borrowed razor with which the pubic area of the king of Assyria is shaved, that is another matter. All these explanations resemble perfectly that of Lord Peter in the *Tale of a Tub* of our dear Dean Swift.

The Jews replied: "We do not see as clearly as you that *seize quickly the spoils* and *Immanuel* signify Jesus, that Isaiah's young wife is a virgin, and that *Alma*, which expresses equally a girl or a young woman, means Mary"; and they laughed at the Christians.

When the Christians said: "Jesus was foretold by the patriarch Judah, because the patriarch Judah had to bind *his foal unto the vine and his ass's colt unto the choice vine; he washed his garments*

---

[1] By what impudent bad faith have the *christicoles* contended that *Alma* always meant virgin? There are in the Old Testament twenty passages where *Alma* is taken for wife, and even for concubine, as in the Song of Solomon. Until the Abbot Trithème, there had been no doctor of the Church who knew Hebrew, except Origen, Jerome, and Ephraim, who were from that country.—*Voltaire*. The Vulgate does not say *Alma* but *Vergo*.—*Beuchot*

* This rendition of Isaiah disagrees materially with the Douay, King James, and Vulgate versions.—*kwa*

*in wine, and his clothes in the blood of grapes* [Gen. 49:11]; and
Jesus entered Jerusalem upon an ass; thus Judah is the figure of
Jesus": then the Jews laughed even louder over Jesus and his ass.

If they claimed that Jesus was the Shilo who was bound to come
when the scepter would no longer be in Judea, the Jews confounded
them by saying that since the Babylon captivity the scepter or rod
[verge] between the legs had never been in Judea, and even at the
time of Saul the rod had not been in Judea. Thus the Christians,
far from converting the Jews, were scorned and detested by them,
and still are. They were regarded as bastards who wished to despoil
the son of the house by fabricating false titles. They renounced
then the hope of drawing the Jews to them and addressed
themselves solely to the Gentiles.


## CHAPTER XVI—On False Citations and False Predictions in the Gospels


In order to encourage the first catechumens, it was well to quote
ancient prophesies and to make up new ones. Ancient prophesies
were cited left and right in the Gospels. Matthew or he who took
his name says [2:23]: "[Joseph] dwelt in a city called Nazareth:
that it might be fulfilled which was spoken by the prophets. He
shall be called a Nazarene." No prophet had said these words;
Matthew spoke then at random. Luke dares to say in Chapter 21
[25–32]: "There will be signs in the moon, and in the stars;* and
upon the earth distress of nations, with perplexity; the sea and
waves roaring; men's hearts failing them from fear shall await
what must happen to the whole world. The powers of heaven shall
be shaken; and then they shall see the Son of Man coming in a
great cloud with power and great glory. . . . Verily I say to you
that the present generation shall not pass before all that has been
fulfilled."*

* Text as cited here exemplifies Voltaire's omissions.—*kwa*

Generations passed, and if none of these things took place it is not my fault. Paul said almost the same in his letter to the Thessalonians [Thess. 4:17]: "We which are alive *and* remain shall be caught together with them in the clouds, to meet the Lord in the air."

Let each person ask himself here: could it be possible to see imposture and the stupidity of fanaticism pushed further? When it was seen what gross falsehoods had been put forward, the Fathers of the Church asserted that Luke and Paul had meant, by these predictions, the fall of Jerusalem. But what connection is there, I ask you, between the taking of Jerusalem, and Jesus coming in the clouds with great power and great majesty?[1]

In the Gospel attributed to John there is a passage which makes it apparent that the book was not composed by a Jew. Jesus said: "A new commandment I give unto you, That ye love one another" [8:34]. This commandment, far from being new, is found expressly in a much stronger statement in Leviticus: "Thou shalt love thy neighbor as thyself" [19:18].

Finally, whoever will take the trouble to read attentively, will find in all those passages where the Old Testament is cited, only an obvious abuse of words, and the seal of falsehood on almost every page.

## CHAPTER XVII—On the End of the World, and the New Jerusalem

Not only has Jesus been introduced upon the scene predicting the end of the world in his own time but such was the fanaticism of all those who are called apostles and disciples. Peter Barjona in the First Epistle attributed to him says that: "the Gospel [was]

---

[1] Preoccupation with the expectation of the end of the world went on so long that in the sixth, seventh, and eighth centuries, a great many of the charters and donations to the monasteries began thus: "Christ reigning, the end of the world approaching, I, for the remedy of my soul, etc."—*Voltaire*

preached also to them that are dead . . . But the end of all things is at hand" [4: 6, 7].

The Second Epistle states [3: 13]: "We look for new heavens and a new earth."

The First Epistle attributed to John says formally [2: 18]: "Even now are there many Antichrists; whereby we know that it is the last time."

The Epistle which is credited to Thadeus, surnamed Jude, proclaims the same mania [15: 14, 16]. "Behold the Lord who is about to come with millions of saints to judge men."*

This ridiculous idea survived century after century. If the world did not end under Constantine, it had to end under Theodosius; if the end had not come under Theodosius, it had to occur with Attila. And up to the twelfth century this idea enriched the monasteries; because to reason correctly, according to the monks, since there will be no longer men or lands, all lands must belong to the monks.

Finally, upon this madness was founded another madness of a new city of Jerusalem that was bound to descend from heaven. Revelation announced this next development [21: 2]; all the *christicoles* believed it. New sybilline verses were concocted in which this Jerusalem was predicted; it seemed surely the new city where the *christicoles* were to live during the thousand years after the world conflagration. It descended from heaven in forty consecutive nights. Tertullian saw it with his own eyes. A time will come when people will ask: "Is it possible that so much time has been wasted to refute this *Tale of a Tub*"!

Behold then for what opinions half the earth has been ravaged! Behold what has given principalities and kingdoms to unscrupulous priests, and what still every day throws imbeciles into the dungeons of the cloisters among the Papists! It is with these cobwebs that are woven the bonds which hold us; the secret of changing them into chains of iron has been found. Great God! for this nonsense

---

* A condensed and inaccurate citation of verses 14–15.—*kwa*

Europe has swum in blood and our King Charles I died upon the scaffold! O destiny! When some half-Jews wrote their shallow impertinences in their barns, did they foresee that they prepared a throne for the abominable Alexander VI, and for that rascal Cromwell?

## CHAPTER XVIII—On Allegories

Those whom we call the Fathers of the Church thought up a strange way to strengthen the catechumens in their new creed. Disciples who reasoned a little were found in the course of time. They were told that the Old Testament was only an image of the New. The small piece of red cloth that the lewd Rahab placed in her window to signal Joshua's spies signifies the blood of Jesus shed for our sins. Sarah and her servant Hagar, the bleary-eyed Leah and the beautiful Rachel, are the Synagogue and the Church. Moses raising his hands when he gives battle to the Amalechites is evidently the cross, because one has the form of a cross when extending his arms to the right and left. Joseph sold by his brothers is Jesus Christ; the manna is the Eucharist; the four winds are the four Gospels; the kisses on the mouth, etc., that the Shulamite gives in the Song of Solomon are evidently the marriage of Jesus Christ with his Church. The bride has not yet a dowry, she was not yet well established.

No one knew what he ought to believe; no exact dogma had yet been formulated. Jesus had written nothing. He was a strange lawgiver, a man from whose hand they had not a single line. It was therefore necessary to write for him; they thus abandoned themselves to the "good news," that is, the Evangels [The Gospels], to those acts of which we have already spoken; and they turned all of the Old Testament into allegories of the New. It is not astonishing that the catechumens, fascinated by those who wanted to organize a sect, let themselves be seduced by these images which always please the common people. This method contributed more than any other thing to the propagation of Christianity, which secretly extended itself from one end of the empire to the other, without interference from the authorities.

Ridiculous and foolish fancy, to make out of the history of a band of beggars the symbol and prophecy of all that must happen in the entire world for centuries to come.

## CHAPTER XIX—On Falsifications and False Books

In order to better seduce the catechumens of the first centuries, it was suggested that the sect had been respected by the Romans and by the emperors themselves. It was not enough to forge a thousand documents that were attributed to Jesus; Pilate too was made to write. Justin and Tertullian cite these documents; they were incorporated in the Gospel of Nicodemus. Here are some passages from Pilate's first letter to Tiberius; they are curious.

"He arrived just awhile ago, and I have verified that by their envy the Jews have incurred a cruel condemnation: their God promised them to send from on high his holy one, who would have just title to be their king, and He promised that he would be the son of a virgin; the God of the Hebrews did in fact send him while I was chief officer in Judea. Jewish leaders denounced him to me as a magician; I believed it; I ordered him well whipped, I turned him over to them: they crucified him; they put guards before his tomb; the third day he was resurrected."

This very old letter is of great importance in that it makes clear that at first the Christians did not yet dare imagine that Jesus was God; they called him only the envoy of God. If he had been thought to be God, Pilate, whom they caused to speak, would not have failed to say so.

In the second letter, he says that, had he not feared sedition, perhaps this "noble Jew" would still be alive, *Fortasse vir ille nobilis viveret*. Another forgery, this time of a more detailed account by Pilate.

Eusebius of Caesarea, in Book VII of his *Ecclesiastical History*, assures us that the woman with the bloody flux cured by Jesus Christ, was a citizen of Caesarea: he saw her statue at the feet of that of Jesus Christ. About the base there are herbs that cure all sorts of maladies. There has been preserved a request from the afflicted woman whose name was, as we know, Veronica; in it she gave Herod an account of the miracle that Jesus Christ had performed on her. She asked Herod for permission to erect a statue to Jesus; but it is not in Caesarea, it is in the city of Paniada; and that is sad news for Eusebius.

There was circulated an edict, claimed to have been by Tiberius, ranking Jesus among the gods. They fabricated letters from Paul to Seneca, and from Seneca to Paul. Emperors, philosophers, Apostles, all were laid under tribute; it is an uninterrupted chain of frauds, some are merely fanatic, others are political. A fanatical falsehood, for example, is to have written Revelations under the name of John, which is absurd; a political falsehood is the book of constitutions* attributed to the Apostles. In it they point out in Chapter 25 of Book II, that they want the bishops to collect tithes and the first fruits; and, in Chapter 26, bishops are called "kings": *Qui episcopus est, hic vester rex et dynastes.***

It is a must, Chapter 28, when love feasts are given,[1] to send the best dishes to the bishop if he is not at table. The priest and the deacon must receive double portions. The portions of the bishops have since been augmented, above all that of the Bishop of Rome.

---

\* Evidently a reference to the *Credo* [Creed] of the Apostles—*kwa*
\*\* "He who is bishop is your king and ruler".—*kwa*

[1] Many Christian societies are accused of having turned the love feasts into scenes of the most infamous dissoluteness, accompanied by mysteries. And we must note that the Christians accused one another. Epiphanius was convinced that the Gnostics, who were the only learned society among them, were the lewdest.— *Voltaire*

In Chapter 34, the bishops are ranked well above emperors and kings, a precept from which the Church has deviated as little as possible: *Quanto animus praestat corpore, tantum sacerdotium regno.** There is the hidden origin of the terrible power that the bishops of Rome have usurped during so many centuries. All the supposed books, all the lies which they have dared to call pious, were only in the hands of the faithful. It was an enormous sin to communicate them to the Romans, who for two centuries had almost no knowledge of them; thus the flock grew larger every day.

## CHAPTER XX—On the Principal Impostures of the First Christians

One of the oldest impostures of these devilish innovators was the *Testament of the Twelve Patriarchs*, which we still have complete in a Greek translation by John, surnamed St. Chrysostom. This ancient book, from the first century of our era, is obviously by a Christian, since Levi is made to say, in Article 8 of his *Testament*; "The third shall have a new name, because he shall be a king of Judea, and he shall be perhaps of a new priesthood for all nations, etc"; this designates their Jesus Christ, who could only be designated by such impostures. Further on, Jesus is clearly predicted in all of Article 18, after Levi is made to say in Article 17 that the priests of the Jews commit the sin of lust with animals.[1]

There were concocted testaments of Moses, Enoch and of Joseph, their ascension or assumption into heaven, and those of Abraham, Elda, Moda, Elias, Zephaniah, Zacharias, and Habakkuk.

* "Just as the mind takes precedence over the body so does the priesthood over the realm"—*kwa*

[1] It is an astonishing thing that bestiality among the Jews is always mentioned. We have among the Roman authors, only one verse from Virgil, *Bucolics*, 3, 8:
*Novimus et qui te . . . .*
and passages from Apuleius where there is talk of this infamy—*Voltaire*

Forged at the same time was the famous book of Enoch which is the sole foundation of the whole mystery of Christianity, since it is in the book alone that is found the story of the angels in revolt who sinned in paradise and who became devils in hell.[2] It is demonstrated that the writings attributed to the Apostles were composed only after the myth of Enoch, written in Greek by some Christian in Alexandria: Jude, in his epistle, quotes Enoch more than once; he uses his very words; he is so devoid of good sense as to assure us that Enoch, *seventh man after Adam, has written these prophecies.*

Here then are two gross deceptions, that of the Christian who invents the books of Enoch and that of the Christian who invents the Epistle of Jude, in which the words of Enoch are reported; there was never a cruder lie.

It is altogether useless to attempt to discover the principal author of these imperceptibly accepted fabrications; but there is some evidence that it was a certain Hegesippus, whose fables were widely circulated, and who is cited by Tertullian and ultimately copied by Eusebius. It is this Hegesippus who relates that Jude was of the lineage of David, and that his grandsons lived under the Emperor Domitian. This emperor, if Hegesippus is to be believed, was terrified on learning that there were descendants of the great King David, who had an incontestable right to the throne of Jerusalem, and in consequence to the throne of the entire universe. He caused these illustrious princes to be brought before him; but having seen what they were—some ragamuffins from the waterfront—he dismissed them without harm.

As for Jude, their grandfather, who is placed in the ranks of the Apostles, at times he is called Thadeus, and at others Lebbeus, like our cutpurses, who always have two or three aliases.

A letter that it was claimed Jesus Christ wrote to a supposed minor king of the city of Edessa, which at that time had no king,

---

[2]The myth of the sin of the angels comes from India, from whence all comes to us; it was known to the Jews of Alexandria, and to Christians, who adopted it very late. It is the cornerstone of the edifice of Christianity.—*Voltaire*

and the journey of this same Thadeus to the court of this king, had a vogue among the early Christians for four hundred years.

Whoever wrote a gospel, or whoever devoted himself to teaching his newly formed flock, imputed to Jesus discourses and actions which are not mentioned in the four Gospels. Thus, in the Acts of the Apostles [20:35], Paul cites these words of Jesus: *Macharion esti didonai mallon e lambanein*. It is more blessed to give than to receive. These words are found in neither Matthew nor Luke nor John.

Peter's journeys, the Apocalypse of Peter, the Acts of Peter, the Acts of Paul, of Tekla, the Letters of Paul to Seneca and of Seneca to Paul, the Acts of Pilate, the Letters of Pilate, are well known to scholars; and it is not worthwhile to rummage in these archives of falsehood and absurdity.

The height of the ridiculous is reached with the writing of a biography of Claudia Procula, the wife of Pilate.

One wretch named Abdias, who without argument was accepted as having lived with Jesus Christ, and as having been one of the more famous disciples of the Apostles, has furnished us with a history of the struggle between Peter and Simon—the alleged magician—so famous among the first Christians. It is solely upon this imposture that was founded the belief that Peter went to Rome; it is to this myth that the popes owe all their grandeur, so disgraceful to humanity; and which would suffice to make their grandeur ridiculous, if a multitude of crimes had not rendered it odious.

Here then is the account of this Abdias, who claims that he was an eyewitness. Simon Peter Barjona having come to Rome under Nero, Simon the magician came there also. A young man, a close relative of Nero, had died; of course a relative of the emperor had to be resurrected; the two Simons offered their services in the matter. Simon the magician stipulated that the one of the two who could not succeed should die. Simon Peter accepted, and the other Simon began his performance; the dead shook his head; the people uttered cries of joy. Simon Peter demanded silence and said:

"Gentlemen, if the dead man is really alive, let him arise, walk and talk with us." The dead kept to himself; then Peter said from a distance: "My son, arise, our Lord Jesus Christ heals you." The young man arose, spoke, and walked; and Simon Barjona returned him to his mother. Simon, his adversary, went to Nero to complain, and told him that Peter was only a miserable charlatan and an ignorant man. Peter appeared before the emperor and whispered in his ear: "Believe me, I know more than he, and to prove it to you, cause me to be given secretly two barley loaves; you will see that I shall divine his thoughts and that he will not divine mine." The two loaves were brought, he hid them in his sleeve. Immediately Simon caused two great dogs to appear—his guardian angels: they wanted to devour Peter, but the sly one threw them his two loaves of bread; the dogs ate them, and did no harm to the Apostle. Says Peter: "Well, you see that I knew his thoughts, and that he did not know mine."

The magician demanded revenge; he promised that he would fly in the air like Daedalus; he was assigned a day; he in fact flew, but St. Peter prayed God with so many tears that Simon fell and broke his neck. Nero, enraged over having lost so good a mechanic through the prayers of Simon Peter, immediately had the Jew crucified head downward.

Who would believe that this story is narrated not only by Abdias, but by two other contemporary Christians: Hegesippus of whom we have already spoken, and Marcellus? But Marcellus adds some nice particulars in his own fashion. He resembles the writers of the Gospels, who contradict one another. Marcellus puts Paul in the act; he adds only that Simon the magician, in order to convince the emperor of his ability, says to this prince: "Do me the favor of cutting off my head, and I promise you to come to life again on the third day." The emperor agreed, cut off the magician's head; he reappeared before Nero on the third day with the world's most beautiful head on his shoulders.

Let us think this over together, reader. Suppose that the three

imbeciles—Abdias, Hegesippus, and Marcellus—who recount
these miserable stories, were less clumsy, that they had invented
more probable tales about the two Simons; would they not now be
regarded as undeniable Fathers of the Church? Would not our doctors continuously cite them as irreproachable witnesses? Would not
the truth of their writings be proved at Oxford and in the Sorbonne
by the analogy to the Acts of the Apostles; similarly, the truth of
the Acts of the Apostles would be proved by these same writings of
Abdias, Hegesippus, and Marcellus? Their stories are assuredly as
authentic as the Acts of the Apostles and the Gospels; they have
come down to us century after century in the same manner, and
there is no more reason to reject the ones than the others.

I pass over in silence the rest of this story, the wonderful deeds
of Andrew, of James the Elder, John, James the Younger, Matthew, and Thomas. Let who will read these absurdities. The same
fanaticism, and the same imbecility have dictated all of them; but
so long a foolishness is too insipid.[3]

---

[3] Lord Bolingbroke is right. It is the utter boredom that one experiences in
reading such books that saves them from an examination which they would be
unable to survive. Where are the magistrates, the warriors, the merchants, the
farmers, and even the men of letters, who have ever heard of the Deeds of the
blessed Apostle Andrew, of the letter of St. Ignatius the Martyr to the Virgin
Mary, and of the response of the Virgin? Would we know a single one of the books
of the Jews and of the first Christians, if the men hired to make them valuable did
not din them in our ears, and if they did not create a patrimony out of our
credulity? Is there anything in this world more ridiculous and more gross than the
fable of Simon Barjona's journey to Rome? Yet it is upon this impertinence that the
throne of the pope was founded: what has plunged all the bishops of his communion
into dependence upon him; this is what requires them to obtain the permission of
the Holy See in order to take the title of bishop, although by the laws of their
Church they are equal to him. Finally this is what has given to the popes the
domains of the emperors in Italy and has despoiled thirty Italian lords in order to
enrich this idol.—*Voltaire*

## CHAPTER XXI—On the Dogmas and Metaphysics of the Christians of the First Centuries—On Justin

Justin, who lived under the Antonines, is one of the first to show some evidence of what is called philosophy; he was also one of the first who gave credit to the oracles of the Sibyls, to the new Jerusalem, and to the sojourn that Jesus Christ had to make upon earth for a thousand years. He claimed that all the science of the Greeks came from the Jews. He certifies, in his second apology for the Christians, that the gods were only devils who came in the form of incubi and succubi, to sleep with men and women, and that Socrates was given the hemlock only for having preached this truth to the Athenians.

Nobody before him had spoken of the mystery of the Trinity as it is spoken of today. If his work has not been falsified, he clearly says in his explanation of the faith "that in the beginning there was only one God in three persons who are the Father, the Son, and the Holy Ghost; that the Father was not begotten, and that the Holy Ghost proceeds."[1] But to explain the Trinity in a different manner from Plato, he compares the Trinity to Adam. Adam, says he, was not begotten. Adam may be identified with his descendants; in the same way the Father may be identified with the Son and the Holy Ghost. Then Justin wrote against Aristotle, and it may be asserted that what Aristotle did not understand, Justin understood no better.

He asserts in Article 43 of his responses to the orthodox, that

[1] It is very probable that these words have in fact been added to Justin's text, because how could it be that Justin, who lived so long a time before Lactantius, had spoken thus of the Trinity when Lactantius always spoke only of the Father and the Son.

As for the rest it is clear that the Christians promoted the dogma of the Trinity only with the aid of the Platonists of their sect. The Trinity is one of Plato's doctrines, and is certainly not that of Jesus, who had never heard anyone speak of it in his village.—*Voltaire*

men and women will come to life again with their organs of procreation, since such organs will continually remind men and women that without them they would have never known Jesus Christ, for they would not have been born. All the Fathers without exception reasoned much like Justin; and in order to lead the mob, better reasoning is not necessary. Locke and Newton would not have created religion.

Besides, Justin and all the Fathers who followed him believed as did Plato, in the preexistence of souls; admitting that the soul is spiritual, a kind of wind, a puff, invisible air, they made it in fact a composition of subtle matter. "The soul is manifestly composed," said Tatian in his *Discourse to the Greeks*, "else how could it make itself known without body?" Arnobius speaks yet more positively of the corporality of souls. He asks, "Who does not see that what is immortal and simple can suffer no grief? The soul is nothing other than the ferment of life, the electuary of a dissolvable thing": *Fermentum vitae, rei dissociabilis glutinum*.

### CHAPTER XXII—On Tertullian

The African Tertullian appeared after Justin. The metaphysician Malebranche, celebrated in his country, applies to him without reserve the epithet of madman; and the writings of the African justify Malebranche. The sole work by Tertullian that is read today is his *Apology for the Christian Religion*. Abbadie and Houteville,[1] regard it as a masterpiece, without quoting any passage from it. This masterpiece consists of insulting the Romans in place of con-

---

[1] Were not Abbadie and Houteville as mad as Tertullian?—*Voltaire*

Contemporary with Voltaire's early years these men apparently incurred his criticism by their praise of the Christian religion. Abbadie produced a *Treatise on the Truth of the Christian Religion* and Houteville, *The Truth of the Christian Religion Proved by the Facts.*—*kwa*

ciliating them, of imputing crimes to them, and of making petulant assertions which he does not support with the slightest proof.

He reproaches the Romans (Chapter 9) that in secret the people
of Carthage sometimes still sacrificed children to Saturn, in spite of
the emperor's express prohibitions under pain of death.[2] Here was
an opportunity to praise Roman wisdom, not to insult it. He reproached them with the combats of the gladiators who were forced
to fight ferocious animals, acknowledging that only condemned
criminals were thus exposed. It was a means afforded them to save
their lives by their courage. He ought rather to have praised the
Romans for it, and condemned the combats of the volunteer
gladiators, but of them he does not speak.

He works himself up (Chapter 23) to the point of saying: "Bring
me your celestial virgin who promises rain, and your Aesculapius
who conserves life in those who must lose it some time after: if
they do not confess that they are devils (not daring to lie before a
Christian), spill the blood of such a reckless Christian. What is
more evident? What is more proven?"

To all that, a wise reader responds: "What is more extravagant
and more fanatic than this discourse? How could some statues
have confessed to the first Christian to come around that they were
devils? At what time, in what place has anyone witnessed such a
prodigy? Since he dared say such foolishness, it must have been
that Tertullian was very sure that the Romans would not read his
absurd apology, and that they would not give him statues of Aesculapius to exorcise."

---

[2] Can anyone witness anything more ridiculous than Tertullian's censure of the
Romans, that the Carthaginians eluded the wisdom and goodness of their laws, in
sacrificing children secretly?

But what is more repulsive, is his claim in this same Chapter 9, that many Roman
women swallowed their lovers' sperm. What tie could this strange lewdness have
with religion?

Tertullian was really mad; his book, *The Mantle,* is proof of this. He says that he
has quit the robe for the mantle, because serpents change their skins and peacocks
their plumes. With similar reasons he proves his Christianity. Fanaticism desires no
better reasons.—*Voltaire*

His Chapter 32, to which attention has never been paid, is quite remarkable. He states, *"We pray God,* for the emperors and the empire; but it is because we know that the general dissolution that menaces the universe and the consummation of the centuries will be retarded by them."

Wretch! Thou wouldst not have prayed for thy masters if thou hadst known that the world would continue on without such prayers.

What does Tertullian wish to say in his barbarous Latin? Does he mean the reign of a thousand years? Does he mean the end of the world announced by Luke and Paul, and which had not yet arrived? Does he mean that a Christian can, by his prayer, hinder God from putting an end to the universe, when God has resolved to destroy his work? Do we not have here the idea of a fanatic, however we interpret it?

A much more important observation is that at the end of the second century, there were always very rich Christians. It is not astonishing that in two hundred years their ardent and indefatigable missionaries had finally attracted to their sect people from respectable families. Excluded from honors, because they did not want to assist in ceremonies established for the prosperity of the empire, they engaged in business as the Presbyterians and other nonconformists have done in France and our country; they became rich. Their feasts were great banquets; already they were reproached for luxury and high living. Tertullian admits it (Chapter 39); he says: "Yes; but in the mysteries of Athens and of Egypt, do they not live sumptuously also? Whatever the expense incurred, it is useful and pious, because the poor benefit." *Quantiscumque sumptibus constet, lucrum est pietatis, siquidem inopes refrigerio isto juvamus.*

Finally the fiery Tertullian complains that the philosophers are not persecuted, and the Christians are suppressed (Chapter 56). He asks: "Is there anyone who forces a philosopher to sacrifice to, or swear by your gods?" *Quis enim philosophum sacrificare aut de-*

*jerare,* etc. This difference evidently proves that the philosophers were not dangerous and that the Christians were. Both the philosophers and the magistrates derided popular superstitions, but they did not comprise a party, a faction in the empire, whereas the Christians had begun to organize a faction so dangerous that in the end it contributed to the destruction of the Roman Empire. We see, from this characteristic alone, that they would have been most cruel persecutors if they had been the masters: their unsociable, intolerant sect only awaited the moment of being fully at liberty to ravish the liberty of the rest of humanity.

Already Rutilius, prefect of Rome,[3] said of this half-Jewish, half-Christian sect:

> *Atque utinam nunquam Judaea subacta fuisset*
> *Pompeii bellis, imperioque Titi!*
> *Latius excisae pestis contagia serpunt;*
> *Victoresque suos natio victa premit*[4]

Would the gods that Titus, that Pompey,
Had never conquered this infamous Judea!
Its poisons have spread among us;
The oppressed victors will surrender to the vanquished.

---

[3] Here Lord Bolingbroke is mistaken. Rutilius lived more than a century after Justin; but that in itself proves how all good Romans were irritated with the growth of this superstition. It made tremendous advances in the third century; it became a state within a state; and it was a tremendous political move on the part of the Constantius Clorus and his son, to place themselves at the head of a movement that had become so rich and powerful. It was not the same in Tertullian's time. His *Apologetica,* made by so obscure a man in Africa, was no more known to the emperors than the trifles of our Presbyterians have been known in the reign of Queen Anne. No Roman has mentioned Tertullian. What the Christians of today relate with so much pomp was then ignored. The sect has prevailed; so be it: it is indeed necessary that some sect surpass all the others of a country. But at the very least let it not be tyrannical; or if it insists on despoiling our goods and bathing in our blood, let us place restraints upon its avarice and its cruelty.—*Voltaire*

[4] The verse is found in the first book of a poem by Claudius Rutilius Numatianus, entitled *Itinerarium* or *De reditu.* The author was a Gaul, and lived at the beginning of the fifth century. Only the first book and sixty-eight verses of the second remain of his work. J. J. Le Franc de Pompignan has translated it into French.—*Beuchot*

It is seen from this verse that the Christians dared display the frightful dogma of intolerance. They cried out everywhere that the old religion of the empire must be destroyed, and it became clear that there was no longer a middle ground between the necessity of exterminating them or of being soon exterminated by them. However such was the indulgence of the senate that it had very few condemned to death, as Origen confesses in his response to Celsus, in Book III.

We will not here analyze the other works of Tertullian. We shall not examine his book which he entitles *Scorpion* because the Gnostics he claims sting like scorpions; nor his book about cloaks which Malebranche has ridiculed enough. But let us not pass over in silence his work about the soul: not only does he search to prove that it is material, as all the Church Fathers of the first three centuries had thought; not only does he bring to his support the authority of the great poet Lucretius,

*Tangere enim ac tangi, nisi corpus, nulla potest res.*[5]

but he assures us that the soul has form and color. Such are the champions of the Church: such are its fathers. Furthermore, let us not forget he was both priest and husband; these two estates were not yet sacramental and marriage was not forbidden to priests by the Bishops of Rome until they were powerful enough and ambitious enough to have, in a part of Europe, a militia that, being without family or without country, was submissive to their orders.

[5] *Lucretius,* Liber I, Verse 305.—*Voltaire*
  "Nothing but a body can touch or be touched."—*kwa*

### CHAPTER XXIII—On Clement of Alexandria

Clement, a priest of Alexandria, always called the Christians Gnostics. Was it one of the sects that divided the Christians and that will always divide them? Or was it that the Christians took then the title of Gnostics? Be that as it may, the sole thing in his works that can instruct and please is the profusion of verse from Homer, Orpheus, Musaeus, Hesiod, Sophocles, Euripides, and Menander, which he quotes in all truth scarcely pertinently, but which are always reread with pleasure. He is the only one of the Church Fathers of the first three centuries who wrote in this vein; he displays in his *Exhortation to the Nations* and in *Stromateis* a great knowledge of ancient Greek works, and of Asiatic and Egyptian rites; he argues but little, which is so much the better for the reader.

His greatest fault is to always accept the fables invented by the poets and storytellers as the basis of Gentile religion, a fault common to the other Fathers, and to all the polemical writers. The more a person imputes absurdity to his adversaries, the more he believes himself free of it, or rather he compensates with ridicule. He says: "If you find it unacceptable that our Jesus is the son of God, you have your Bacchus, your Hercules, your Perseus who are sons of God: if our Jesus was transported by the Devil onto a mountain, your giants have thrown mountains at the head of Jupiter.

"If you do not wish to believe that our Jesus changed water into wine at a village wedding feast, we will not believe that the daughters of Aeneas changed all that they touched into wheat, wine, and oil." The parallels are very long and very exact on both sides.

The most singular miracle of all pagan antiquity, reported by

Clement of Alexandria in his *Exhortation*, is that of Bacchus in hell. Bacchus did not know the road; a certain Prosymnus, whom Pausanius and Hyginus call otherwise, offered to show him the way on the condition that on his return Bacchus (who was a very handsome fellow) would pay him in favors, and that he would allow him to do what Jupiter did to Ganymede, and Apollo to Hyacinth. Bacchus made it a bargain; he went to hell; but on his return he found Prosymnus dead; he wished not to break his promise; and, encountering a fig tree in the vicinity of the tomb of Prosymnus, he very neatly carved a branch into a phallus; he penetrated himself, in the name of his benefactor, in that part destined to fulfill his promise, and had nothing with which to reproach himself.

Similar excesses, common to nearly all the ancient religions, prove irrefutably that whosoever has been away from true religion, from true philosophy which is to worship one god without any room for others; whosoever, in a word, has been able to devote himself to superstitions, is unable to utter anything sensible.

But in all truth were these Milesian myths the religion of Rome? Did the Senate ever raise a temple to Bacchus sodomizing himself? to Mercury pilfering? Did Ganymede have temples? Hadrian, it is true, erected a temple to his friend Antinoüs, just as Alexander had to Haephestion; but did they do them honor in their rôle of nances? Was there a medallion, a monument whose inscription was to Antinoüs the pederast? The Fathers of the Church made merry at the expense of those whom they called Gentiles: but the Gentiles had some retorts to make! there was the matter of a so-called Joseph who was made a member of the grand confraternity by an angel; and that of a carpenter God whose grandmothers were guilty of adultery, incest, and prostitution; and that of a Paul journeying to the third heaven; and that of a husband[1] and wife beaten to death for not having given their all to Simon Barjona. Such points furnished the Gentiles with terrible weapons! Were not the

---

[1] Ananias, cf., Acts of the Apostles, Chapter 5.—*Beuchot*

angels of Sodom equivalent to Bacchus and Prosymnus, or to the myth of Apollo and Hyacinth?

Clement's good sense equals that of his colleagues. According to him, God created the world in six days, and rested on the seventh because there are seven wandering stars; because Ursa Minor is composed of seven stars, just as the Pleiades; because there are seven principal angels; because the moon changes its face every seven days; because the seventh day is critical in sicknesses. Therein is what they call true philosophy, *ten alethe philosophian gnostiken.** Behold, yet again, the people who prefer themselves to Plato and Cicero; and we must now revere all those obscure pedants whom the indulgent Romans permitted to spread their fanatical ravings in Alexandria, where Christian dogma was principally formulated!

## CHAPTER XXIV —On Irenaeus

The truth of the matter is that Irenaeus knows neither science, nor philosophy, nor eloquence; he limits himself nearly always to repeating what Justin, Tertullian, and others said; he believed with them that the soul is a light and airy form; he was persuaded of the reign of a thousand years in the new Jerusalem descended to earth from the sky. He explains in his fifth book, Chapter 33,** what an enormous quantity of flour each grain of wheat will produce, and how many casks there must be for each bunch of grapes in the new beautiful city.[1] He awaits the Antichrist at the end of a thousand years, and explains marvelously the number 666, which is the mark

* "The true gnostic philosophy." The excerpt of Clement's ideas is from *Stromateis.—kwa*
** This discourse is based on Irenaeus' *Adversus Haereses.—kwa*

[1] Each vinestock produced ten thousand bunches; each bunch ten thousand grapes, each grape ten thousand pitchers.—*Voltaire*

of the beast. We avow that in all of this he differs not at all from the other Fathers of the Church.

But one very important thing, one on which perhaps we have not been sufficiently enlightened, is that he assures us that Jesus died after fifty, and not at thirty-one, or thirty-three, as can be inferred from the Gospels.

Irenaeus calls upon the Gospels to support this point of view; as witnesses he calls upon all the old men who lived with John and with the other Apostles. He declares positively that only those who came too late to know the Apostles could be of a contrary opinion. And contrary to his habit, he even adds conclusive enough reasoning to his factual proofs.

The Gospel of John has Jesus say: "Your father Abraham has been exalted to witness my days; he has seen them and he has rejoiced in them"; and the Jews answered him: "Art thou a madman? Thou are not yet fifty years and thou boast of having seen our father Abraham?"

Therefore Irenaeus concluded that Jesus was near his fiftieth birthday when the Jews spoke to him thus. In fact, if Jesus had been thirty at the most, no one would have spoken of fifty. Since Irenaeus seeks testimony from all the Gospels and all the old men who had such scripture in their hands, the Gospels of that time were not the same as those that we have today. They have been altered, like so many other books. But since they changed them, they ought to have rendered them a little more reasonable.

## CHAPTER XXV—On Origen and the Trinity

Clement of Alexandria had been the first scholar among the Christians. Origen was the first thinker. But what philosophy it was in his time! He was in the ranks of celebrated children, and at a very early age taught in that great city of Alexandria where the Christians maintained a public school: the Christians in Rome did not have one. And in fact, among those who took the title of the Bishop of Rome, there was not counted a single illustrious man; which is very remarkable. The Church, which afterward became so powerful and so proud, took everything from the Egyptians and the Greeks.

Without doubt there was a great deal of folly in Origen's philosophy, since he got the notion of cutting off his testicles. Epiphanius wrote that a prefect of Alexandria had given him the choice of being either a Ganymede to an Ethiopian, or of sacrificing to the gods, and that he made the sacrifice in order not to be sodomized by an ugly Ethiopian.[1]

Whether that was the reason that determined him to make himself a eunuch, or there was some other reason, I leave to scholars writing a history of eunuchs; I confine myself here to the history of the absurdities of the human mind.

He was the first to make fashionable the nonsense and the balderdash about the Trinity which had been forgotten since Justin From then on, the Christians dared to consider the son of Mary as God, as an emanation from the Father, as the first *Eon*, as identified in some way with the Father; but the Holy Ghost had not yet been made a God. No one had yet thought to falsify I don't know what epistle attributed to John, in which someone inserted these ridiculous words [First Epistle of St. John 5:7]; "There are three who give witness in heaven: the Father, the Word, and the Holy Ghost."* Would this be the way to speak of three substances or divine persons together composing God the creator of the world? Would it be said that they gave testimony? Other copies carry the yet more ridiculous words: "There are three who render testimony on earth, the spirit, water, blood, and the three who are only one."[2] Again there is added in other copies: "and the three are

---

* Voltaire omitted: "and these three are one."—*kwa*

[1] Epiphanius, *Haereses*, 64 Chapter 2.—*Voltaire*

[2] The question of whether or not these are John's words is very disturbing. Those *christicoles* who reject them follow the ancient Vatican manuscript, in which the words are not found; those who accept them make use of later manuscripts. But

one in Jesus." None of these passages, each different from the others, is found in the ancient manuscripts, none of the Fathers of the first three centuries cites them; moreover, what reward could accrue to those who admitted such falsifications? How could they understand that the spirit, water, and blood make up the Trinity and are only one? Is it because it is told [Luke 22:44] that Jesus sweated blood and water, and gave up the spirit? What connection is there between these things and a God in three hypostases?

Plato's trinity was of another kind; it is little known. What there is of it can be found in his *Timaeus*. The eternal Demiurgos is the first cause of all that exists; his idea of archetype is second; the universal soul, which is his contribution, is the third. There is some sense in Plato's concept. God conceived the idea of the world, God made it, God animated it; but never was Plato insane enough to say that his idea encompassed three persons in God. Origen was a Platonist; he took what he could from Plato, he made a Trinity after his own fashion. This concept remained so obscure in the first centuries that Lactantius, in the time of the Emperor Constantine, speaking for all Christians, explaining the beliefs of the Church, and addressing the emperor himself, says not a word about the Trinity; on the contrary, here is how he speaks, in Chapter 29 of Book 4 of his *Institutiones*: "Perhaps someone will ask me why we

---

without entering into such a useless discussion, either these lines are by John or they are not. If they are, John ought to have been incarcerated in the Bedlam of the time, if there was one. If he is not the author, they are an absurd and audacious falsehood.

It must be acknowledged that nothing was more common among the first *christicoles* than such barefaced imaginings. Falsity could not be discovered, so rare were the mendacious works, so carefully had the nascent sect stolen from those who were not initiated into their mysteries!

We have already remarked that the most terrible crime in the eyes of this sect was to show Gentiles what it called holy books. What an awful contradiction existed among these misguided people! They said: "We must preach Christianity in the whole earth"; and they showed to no one the scriptures in which Christianity is contained. What would you say of a dozen ragamuffins who would come into Westminster to claim the property of a man who died in Wales, and who will not show the dead man's testament?—*Voltaire*

adore one God, while we assure them that there are two, the Father and the Son; but we do not distinguish them, because the father cannot be without his son, nor the son without his father."

The Holy Ghost was entirely forgotten by Lactantius, and some years after it was briefly commemorated, and for mere form's sake, at the Council of Nicaea; for, after having made a declaration of its dogma as solemn as it is unintelligible, that the Son is consubstantial with the Father, the Council contents itself with declaring simply, "We believe also in the Holy Ghost."[3]

We can say that Origen laid the first foundations of that chimerical metaphysics which has only been a source of discord, and which was absolutely useless to morality. It is evident that one can be as honest a man, as wise, as moderate, with one hypostasis as with three, and that these theological inventions have nothing in common with our duties.

Origen attributes a body to God, as well as to the angels and all souls; and he says that God the Father and God the Son are two different substances; that the Father is greater than the Son, the Son greater than the Holy Ghost, and the Holy Ghost greater than the angels. He says that the Father is sufficient of himself, but that the Son is not sufficient of himself; that the Son is not the truth in regard to his Father, but the image of truth in regard to us; that it is not the Son but the Father who should be adored; that it is to the Father alone that our prayers ought to be addressed; that the Son brought from heaven the flesh with which he clothed himself in the womb of Mary, and that while ascending to heaven he left his body in the sun.

[3] How unfortunately ambiguous is this Holy Ghost, this *agion pneuma* of which the *christicoles* have made a third god! The word meant only breath. You shall find in the Gospel attributed to John (20:22): "When he said this, he breathed on them, and saith unto them, Receive ye the Holy Ghost."

Take note that this was an ancient ceremony of magicians, to breathe into the mouth of those whom they desired to bewitch. There, then, is the origin of the third god of these maniacs; is there fundamentally anything more blasphemous or impious? and are not the Muslims right in regarding them as infamous idolaters?— *Voltaire*

He asserts that the Virgin Mary while giving birth to the Son of God, was delivered of an afterbirth like other women; this obliged her to purify herself in the Jewish temple; because it is well known that nothing is as impure as an afterbirth. The harsh and petulant Jerome reproached him sharply, about one hundred fifty years after his death, for many similar opinions which are worth as much as Jerome's opinions; because from the moment that the first Christians entangled themselves with dogma, they abused each other, and proclaimed the civil wars which would desolate the world in the course of arguments.

Let us not forget that Origen distinguished himself above all others in interpreting the deeds of the Scriptures as allegories; we must confess that the allegories are quite amusing. The drippings from the sacrifices are the soul of Jesus; the tail of a sacrificial animal is perseverance in good works. If it is said in Exodus [23] that God placed Moses in the cleft of a rock, so that Moses could see God's buttocks, but not his face, this cleft in the rock is Jesus Christ, through whom God the Father is seen from the rear.[4]

The above should, I think, suffice to make known the Fathers, and to reveal the foundation on which was built the most monstrous edifice that has ever dishonored reason. Reason that has said to all men: Religion must be clear, simple, universal, within the reach of all souls, because it is fashioned for every heart; its morality must not be suppressed by dogma, no absurdity must disfigure it. In vain has reason employed such language; fanaticism has outshouted it. And what evils has fanaticism not produced?

---

[4] There was a very old superstitious belief among nearly all peoples that no one could look upon the gods just as they are, without dying. That is why Semela was consumed for having wished to lie with Jupiter just as he was. One of the greatest of the innumerable contradictions, in which the Jewish books abound, is found in Exodus [33:23]: "Thou canst behold only my back." The Book of Numbers [12:8] says expressly that God made himself visible to Moses as one friend to another; and that he saw and talked with God face to face.

Our poor theologians extricate themselves by saying that we must understand a passage in its proper sense and another in its figurative sense. Would it not be necessary to present them with pigs' bladders under their noses, in the figurative sense and in the proper sense?

## CHAPTER XXVI—On the Martyrs

Why did the Romans never persecute any of the wretched, abhorred Jews for their religion,[1] never oblige them to renounce their superstitions, permitted them their rites, their laws, and synagogues in Rome, counted them among the citizens to whom they gave gifts of wheat? And how is it possible that these same Romans, so indulgent, so liberal toward the wretched Jews, were in about the third century, more severe toward the worshippers of a Jew? Is it not because the Jews, occupied in selling old clothes and love-potions, did not have a mania for exterminating the religion of the empire, a mania that possessed the intolerant Christians?

Some of the more fanatical ones were punished in the third century; but so small was their number that no Roman historian bothered to speak of them. The Jews revolted under Vespasian, Trajan, and Hadrian, and were always cruelly chastised as they merited. they were forbidden to go into their small city of Jerusalem, the name of which was even obliterated, because it had always been a center of revolt; but they were permitted to circumcise their infants under the walls of the Capitol, and in all the provinces of the empire.

The priests of Isis were punished in Rome under Tiberius. Their temple was destroyed because it was a market of prostitution and a

---

[1] There is certainly nothing to reply to Lord Bolingbroke's assertion. It is demonstrated that the ancient Romans persecuted none for his dogma. This execrable horror has been committed only by the Christians and above all by the modern Romans. Even today there are still ten thousand Jews in Rome who are well protected, although it is known that they consider Jesus an impostor. But if a Christian dares to announce in the Church of St. Peter, or in the Piazza Navona, that three make three, and that the Pope is not infallible, he will inevitably be burned.

I assert as a fact that the Christians were never persecuted except as factious destroyers of the laws of the empire; and the proof that they wanted to commit such a crime is that they committed it.—*Voltaire*

den of thieves; but the priests and priestesses were permitted to carry on their work everywhere else. They went with impunity in procession from one town to another; they performed miracles, healed the sick, told fortunes, danced the dance of Isis with castanets. We can observe this amply in Apuleius. Let us remark here that these same processions have been perpetuated up to our time. There are still in Italy some remnants of those ancient vagabonds who are called *Zingari,* and among us Gypsies, an abbreviation of Egyptians, and who are, I believe, called Bohemians in France. The sole difference between them and the Jews is that the Jews, having like the Banyans always carried on commerce, were like the latter able to maintain themselves, and that the followers of Isis, being a very small number, are nearly extinct.

The Roman magistrates, who gave so much freedom to the Isiacs and Jews, treated all other sects in the same manner. Each god was welcome in Rome:

*Digna Roma locus, quo deus omnis eat.*[2] All the gods of the earth had become citizens of Rome. No sect was so insane as to wish to subjugate the others; thus all lived in peace.

The Christian religion was the only one that, toward the end of the second century of our era, dared to proclaim that it wished to exclude all other rites in the empire, and that it must not only dominate, but annihilate all religions; *christicoles* ceaselessly insisted that their God was a jealous God: a nice definition of the Being of beings: to impute to him the basest of vices!

The enthusiasts, who preached in their congregations, fashioned a population of fanatics. It was impossible that among so many hotheads there would not be found madmen who insulted the priests of the gods, who disturbed public order, who committed punishable indecencies. We have seen this happen to members of European sects, who all, as we shall prove, have had infinitely more martyrs slain by our hands than ever had the Christians under the emperors.

[2] Ovid, *Fasti,* Book 4, verse 270.—*Voltaire*
    "Noble Rome is a place in which every god may live."—*kwa*

Excited by popular complaint, the magistrates could sometimes be carried away with infamous cruelties; they could sentence women to death, although such a barbarity has certainly not been proven. But who dares to tax the Romans with having been too severe, when we see the Christian centurion Marcel throw his military belt and command baton into the midst of the Roman eagles, while crying seditiously: "I wish to serve only Jesus Christ, the Eternal King; I renounce the emperors!'"? What army would have permitted so pernicious an insolence to go unpunished? You may be sure that I would not have permitted it when I was Secretary of War,* and the Duke of Marlborough would have tolerated it no more than I.

If it is true that Polyeuctes, in Armenia, the day when thanks were rendered to the gods in the temple for a signal victory, chose this moment to overturn the statues and throw the incense upon the ground, would this not everywhere be considered a maniac's crime?

When the deacon Laurentius refuses before the prefect of Rome to contribute to the public charges; when, having promised to give some money from the Christian treasury, which was considerable, he only brings some beggars in place of money, is that not an insult to the emperor, is he not guilty of *lèse-majesté*? It is very doubtful that anyone made a six-foot grill on which to cook Laurentius, but he certainly merited punishment.

The bombastic Gregory of Nyssa eulogizes St. Theodore who decided to burn the temple of Cybele in Amazea just as Erostratus was said to have burned the temple of Diana. They have dared to make a saint of this arsonist who certainly merited the greatest punishment. They hold up for our adoration what we punish with execution.

Furthermore, all the martyrdoms that so many writers have copied century after century so much resemble the *Golden Legend*, that truthfully there is not one of the stories that isn't pitiful. One

* Bolingbroke was Secretary of War in the British government, 1704–1708.—*kwa*

of the first is that of Perpetua and Felicita. Perpetua sees a ladder
of gold which reaches up to heaven. (Jacob had only seen one of
wood; that marks the superiority of the new dispensation.) Perpetua climbs the ladder; she sees in a garden a tall white shepherd
who milks his sheep, and who gives her a spoonful of curdled milk.
After three or four such visions, Perpetua and Felicita are exposed
to a bear and a cow.

A French Benedictine named Ruinart,** believing to reply to
our learned compatriot Dodwell, has collected supposed acts of
martyrdom, and he calls them the *Actes sincères*. Ruinart begins
with the martyrdom of James, older brother of Jesus, narrated in
the *Ecclesiastical History* of Eusebius, three hundred years after
the event.

Let us never cease to observe that God had human brothers. The
older brother they say, was a very devout Jew; he did not cease to
pray or to sacrifice in the Jewish temple even after the descent of
the Holy Ghost; therefore he was still not a Christian. The Jews
referred to him as *Oblia the Just*: they begged him to take the platform in the temple to declare that Jesus was an impostor. The Jews
were then so foolish as to address themselves to the brother of
Jesus. He did not fail to declare upon the platform that his younger
brother was the savior of the world, and was stoned.

What shall we say about the conversation of Ignatius with the
Emperor Trajan who asked him: "Who art thou, impure spirit?";
and of the blessed Symphorosa, who was denounced to Emperor
Hadrian by her household gods? And of Polycarpus whom the
flames of a fagot dared not touch, but who was unable to with-
stand the edge of a sword? And of the shoe of St. Epipoda the
Martyr, which cured a nobleman of a fever?

And of St. Cassienus, a schoolmaster who was flogged by his
students? And of St. Potamiena who, not wanting to go to bed with

** Dom Henri Ruinart (1657–1709) compiled the *Acta Primorum Martyrum
Sincera* to refute Oxford professor Dodwell's assertion that there were not nearly as
many martyrs as claimed.—*kwa*

the governor of Alexandria, was for three hours entirely submerged in a pot of boiling pitch, and came out with her skin whiter and finer?

And of Pionius who remained safe and sane in the midst of flames, and who died I don't know how?

And of the actor Genestus, who became a Christian while playing a farce[3] before the Emperor Diocletian, and who was condemned by the emperor at the time that he most favored the Christians? And of a Theban legion that was sent from East to West, to suppress rebellion among the Bagaudes, who were already suppressed, and who were martyrized, one and all, at a time when no one was martyrized, and in a place where four hundred men cannot be sent into battle; and about which the public was informed in writing, two hundred years after that fine event.

It would be insupportably boring to report all these so-called martyrdoms. However I cannot restrain myself from a glance at some of the more famous.

Nilus, eyewitness to the facts, but who is unknown (more's the pity), assures us that his friend St. Theodotus, a tavern-keeper by occupation, performed every miracle that he willed. He could change water into wine; but he liked better to heal sickness with the touch of his fingertips. Theodotus the tavern keeper encountered, in a meadow, a priest of the city of Ancyra; they found the meadow an appropriate site for building a temple in a time of persecution. "I certainly wish to," said the priest, "but I have no relics."—"What you may not have," said the saint, "you shall have immediately; and here is my ring that I give you as bond." He was very sure of himself, as you shall see.

Soon seven Christian virgins of Ancyra, each seventy years old, were condemned *to be delivered over to the brutal passions of the*

---

[3] He feigned illness, says the *Sincere Acts*. "I feel heavy," said Genestus.—"Do you wish someone to massage you?" "No, I wish to be given the extreme unction of the Christians." Immediately two actors anointed him, and he was converted on the spot. Please note that in the time of Diocletian, extreme unction was absolutely unknown in the Latin Church.—*Voltaire*

*young men of the city.* The legend notes that the maidens were very wrinkled; and what is most astounding is that the young men made not the least advances, with the exception of one, whose physical make-up permitted him to overlook this point, wished to undertake the adventure, and was shortly nauseated. The governor, highly irritated because the seven virgins had not undergone the torture that he designed for them, made them priestesses of Diana, which the Christian virgins readily accepted. They were appointed to wash the statue of Diana in the nearby lake; they were completely nude; doubtlessly because it was the custom that the chaste Diana should be attended only by naked girls, although those who approached her always wore a large veil. Two choruses of Maenads and Bacchantes, armed with thyrses, preceded the chariot, according to the judicious account of the author, who here mistakes Diana for Bacchus; but since he was an eyewitness we cannot gainsay him.

St. Theodotus trembled at the thought that the seven virgins might succumb to some temptation. He was at prayer when his wife came to give him the news that someone had just thrown the seven old women in the lake; he thanked God for having thus saved their chastity. The governor mounted a tight guard around the lake in order to keep the Christians, who had a habit of walking on water, from coming to steal their bodies. The holy tavern-keeper was in despair: he went from church to church, because beautiful churches were everything during these frightful persecutions; but the cunning pagans had closed all their doors. So the tavern-keeper decided to take a nap. One of the old ladies appeared to him in his dream; you know already who it was: St. Thecusa, who addressed him in fitting words: "My dear Theodotus, will you allow our bodies to be eaten by fish?"

Theodotus awakes; he resolves to fish the saints from the bottom of the lake at the risk of his life. At the end of three days he acts, having given the fish time to eat them, he runs out to the lake one dark night with two brave Christians.

A celestial horseman places himself at their head, carrying a great torch before them so as to keep the guards from discovering them: the horseman takes his lance, falls upon the guards, puts them to flight; he was, as everyone knows, St. Soziandrus, old friend of Theodotus, who had been martyred not too long before. That's not all; a violent storm, accompanied by thunder and lightning and a torrential rain, had dried up the lake. The seven old ladies were fished out and properly interred.

You may well believe that Theodotus' crime was discovered shortly; the celestial horseman could not stand in the way of his being scourged and put to the question. When Theodotus had been well beaten, he cried out to the Christians and the idolaters: "See, my friends, what favors Our Lord Jesus heaps upon his servants! He causes them to be whipped to the point where they have no more skin, and then gives them the strength to support it all." Finally, he was hanged.

His friend Fronton the priest then proved that the saint was a tavern-keeper; having previously received from him some bottles of excellent wine, he got the guards drunk, and carried away the hanged man, who said to him: "Father, I promised you relics, I have kept my promise."

This admirable tale is one of the most authentic. Who could doubt it after the testimony of the Jesuit Bollandus* and the Benedictine Ruinart?

These old wives' tales disgust me; I shall say no more of them. I admit that some Christians were in fact tortured to death at various times, as subversives who had the insolence to be intolerant and to insult the government. They wore the crown of martyrdom and deserved it well. Those whom I pity were the poor stupid women seduced by these nonconformists, who were guilty of abusing the faculties of such feeble creatures, and turning them

* Jean Bollandus (1596–1665) began the compilation of the tremendous *Acta Sanctorum*. Dom Henri Ruinart (1657–1709) gathered the *Acta Primorum Marytrum Sincera* that Voltaire labels here the *Actes sincères.—kwa*

into fanatics; but the judges who put some of these women to death were barbaric.

Thank God that there were few of these executions. The pagans were far from practicing upon these fanatics the cruelties that we have since practiced on each other for so long a time. It seems that above all the Papists have manufactured so many imaginary martyrs of the first centuries in order to justify the massacres with which their church is befouled.

A proof, strong indeed, that there never were great persecutions of the first Christians is that Alexandria, which was the center, the headquarters of the sect, openly maintained a school of Christianity, like the Lyceum, the Stoa, and the Academy at Athens. There was a succession of Christian professors. Pantenus succeeded publicly to a certain Mark, who is mistaken for Mark the Apostle. After Pantenus came Clement of Alexandria whose chair was next occupied by Origen who left a host of disciples. As long as they merely split hairs, they were left in peace; but when they rose against the laws and public order, they were punished. They were curbed especially in the reign of the Emperor Decius: even Origen was put in prison. Cyprian, bishop of Carthage, does not hide the fact that the Christians brought persecution on themselves. In his book *On the Fallen*, he says: "Each of them runs after goods and honors with an insatiable fury. The bishops are without religion, the women without modesty; knavery reigns; they swear, they break faith, animosities divide the Christians; bishops abandon their pulpits to run to the fairs and to enrich themselves in business transactions; we please only ourselves, and we displease the rest of the world."

It is not astonishing that these Christians had violent quarrels with partisans of the religion of the empire, that self–interest entered into the quarrels, that they often caused violent trouble and that in the end they brought on persecution. The famous jurist Ulpian regarded the Christians as a very dangerous faction that could someday be instrumental in the ruin of the state; in that he was not at all mistaken.

## CHAPTER XXVII—On Miracles

After the Oriental marvels of the Old Testament; after those stories in the New, in which God, carried onto a mountain by the Devil [Matt. 4:8; Luke 4], descended from it to change the vessels of water into wine [John 2:9]; withered a fig tree [Matt. 21:19; Mark 11:13] because the tree had no figs at the end of winter; sent devils [Matt. 7:23; Mark 5:13; John 2:9] into the bodies of two thousand pigs; after, I say, we have witnessed all these fine things, it is not astonishing that they were imitated.

Peter Simon Barjona did well in resurrecting the dressmaker Dorcas; it was the least one could do for a girl who patched the garments of the faithful, *gratis*. But I do not overlook Simon Peter Barjona's having caused [Acts 5] Ananias and his wife Saphira to die a sudden death, two good souls, who were supposed to have been so foolish as to give all their possessions to the Apostles. Their crime was to have retained what supplied their pressing needs.

Oh Peter! Oh disinterested Apostles! So! Already you persuade those under your directions to donate their goods to you! By what right do you ravish the whole of a family fortune? Is this not then the first example of depredation by your sect, a most punishable depredation? Come to London to play the same tricks, and you will see if the anger of the heirs of Saphira and Ananias will not rise against you, and if the grand jury will let you go unpunished. With goodwill they gave their money! But you have misled them in order to despoil them with their consent! They have kept something for themselves! Slothful ravishers, you dare to make it a crime to have kept that which was necessary to prevent death from hunger! They lied, you say? Were they obliged to tell you their secret? If a swindler comes to ask me: "Have you some money?" I shall certainly reply: "No, I haven't." There, in a word, is the most abominable miracle that can be found in the legend of miracles. None of all those performed since can begin to compare; if the thing were true it would be the most execrable of all true things.

It is nice to have the gift of languages; it would be more so to have common sense. The Fathers of the Church had at least the gift of language; because they talked a great deal, but they had among them only Origen and Jerome who knew Hebrew. Augustine, Ambrose, John Chrysostom, did not know a word of it.

We have already seen the marvelous miracles of the martyrs who always let their heads be cut off as a last marvel. Origen, it is true, in his first book against Celsus says that Christians have visions, but he dares not claim that they resurrect the dead.

Christianity always worked great deeds in the first centuries. St. John, for instance, interred at Ephesus, turned continually in his grave. This useful miracle endured until the time of the bishop of Hippo, Augustine. Predictions and exorcisms were never lacking; Lucian himself gives witness. Here is the way he glorifies truth in the chapter about the death of the Christian Peregrinus, who had the vanity to immolate himself: "As soon as a skillful juggler becomes a Christian, he is sure to make a fortune at the expense of the fanatical fools with whom he associates."

The Christians every day performed miracles of which no Roman ever heard. Those of Gregory the Thaumaturge,* or the Marvelous, are indeed worthy of his surname. Firstly a handsome old man descends from heaven to dictate the catechism which he must teach. On the way he writes a letter to the Devil; the letter is delivered and the Devil does not fail to do what Gregory ordered.

Two brothers are in dispute over a pond; Gregory dries up the pond and causes it to disappear in order to abate the quarrel. He encounters a charcoal burner and makes him a bishop. "The faith of a *charbonnier*" has since become proverbial.[1] But this is not a

---

* Bishop of Neo–Caesarea, converted that city to Christianity by his many miracles. He died about 272 A.D.—*kwa*

[1] Alexander, Bishop of Comana.—*Beuchot*
   The expression means "simple faith."*kwa*

great miracle; I have seen some bishops[2] in my travels who knew no more than Gregory's charcoal burner. A more extraordinary miracle occurred when one day the pagans chased Gregory and his deacon, intending to give them a bad time; suddenly both of them changed themselves into trees. The miracle maker was a true Proteus. But what name shall we give those who wrote these absurdities? And how can it be that Fleury copied them in his *Ecclesiastical History*? Is it possible that a man who had some sense, and who reasoned tolerably well on other subjects, seriously reported that God made a lunatic of an old woman in order to prevent Felix de Nole from being found during the persecution?[3]

The reply will be that Fleury confined himself to transcribing, and I would rejoin that he did not have to transcribe such stupidities injurious to the Divinity; that he was culpable if he copied them without believing them, and that he was an imbecile if he did believe them.

## CHAPTER XXVIII—On the Christians from Diocletian to Constantine

The Christians were so much more often tolerated, and even protected, that they endured no persecutions. For eighteen whole years, the reign of Diocletian was a reign of peace and of signal favors to them. The two principal officers of the palace, Gorgonius

[2] Biord, grandson of a mason, bishop of Annecy.—*Beuchot*

[3] See, for all these miracles, Fleury's books VI and VII. See also the *Collection of Miracles Performed at Saint-Médard in Paris*, presented to the king of France, Louis XV, by a certain Carré de Montgeron, counselor in the *Parlement* of Paris. Epileptics had done or seen more than a thousand miracles. Did not Fatio and Daudé claim to have resurrected a corpse here in 1707? Does not the Roman Curia canonize every day, for money, saints who worked miracles which it cares nothing about? And how many miracles did our monks perform, before the implements of their abominable impostures were displayed in the public square under Henry VIII?—*Voltaire*

and Dorotheus, were Christians. It was no longer required that they sacrifice to the gods of the empire in order to enter into public employ. Finally, Prisca, wife of Diocletian, was a Christian; and they enjoyed greater advantages. They built superb temples after having said in the first centuries that neither temples nor altars were necessary to God; and, passing from the simplicity of a poor and obscure church to the magnificence of a church, opulent and full of ostentation, they displayed vessels of gold and dazzling ornaments; some of their temples were raised on the ruins of old, abandoned pagan peripteros. Their temple in Nicomedia dominated the imperial palace; and as Eusebius remarks, such prosperity had produced insolence, usury, indolence, and moral depravity. Eusebius said that envy, slander, discord, and sedition were rampant.

It was this spirit of treason that exhausted the patience of the Caesar, Galerius Maximianus. The Christians irritated him at precisely the time when Diocletian had published his fulminating edicts against the Manicheans. One of the edicts of this emperor begins thus: "We have recently learned that the Manicheans, coming out of Persia our ancient enemy, inundate our world."

The Manicheans had not yet caused any trouble; they were numerous in Alexandria and in Africa; but they only spoke up against the Christians; there was never the least evidence of a quarrel between the religion of the ancient Romans and the sect of the Manes. The various Christian sects, on the contrary, Gnostics, Marcionites, Valentinians, Ebionites, Galileans—opposed to each other and to the dominant religion—spread confusion throughout the empire.

Is it not quite probable that the Christians had enough influence in the palace to obtain an edict from the emperor against the Manicheans? This sect, which was a mixture of the ancient religion of the Magi and of Christianity, was very dangerous to the nascent Church, especially in the Orient. The idea of bringing together the

Christian sect and what the Orient held most sacred had already made a great impression.

The obscure and sublime theology of the Magi, mixed with the no less obscure theology of the Christian Platonists, was just right for luring romantic souls who were satisfied with words. Finally, since a hundred years later the famous pastor of Hippo was a Manichean, it is obvious that this sect had charms for excitable imaginations. Manes had been crucified in Persia, if we believe Chondemir about it; and the Christians, in love with their crucifixion, did not want a second one.

I know that we have no proof that the Christians obtained the edict against Manicheanism; but there followed a bloodletting, and it was not against the Christians. What then happened to cause the Christians to fall into disgrace in the last two years of the reign of an emperor philosophic enough to abdicate the throne, to live in retirement, and to never regret it?

The Christians were attached to Constantius the Pale, father of the celebrated Constantine, who was born to a servant named Helen.[1]

Constantius always protected them openly. It is not known whether the Caesar Galerius was jealous of the preference given by the Christians to Constantius the Pale instead of him, or if he had some other reason to complain of them; but he took it very ill that they built a church which dwarfed his palace. He tried for a long time to persuade Diocletian to tear down the church, and to prohibit the practice of the Christian religion. Diocletian resisted him; finally, he assembled a council made up of the principals of the empire. I remember having read in the *Ecclesiastical History* by Fleury that: "The emperor had the trick of not consulting when he wished to do something good, and of consulting when there was a

---

[1] This Helen who was made a saint, was *stabularia* (overseer of the stable) for Constantius Chlorus, as testify Eusebius, Ambrose, Nicephorus, Jerome. The *Chronicle of Alexandria* classifies Constantine as a bastard; Zosimus certifies it; and certainly no one would offer this affront to the powerful imperial family, if there had been the least doubt about his birth.—*Voltaire*

question of doing something bad." What Fleury calls trickery, seems to me the greatest praise for a sovereign. Is there anything more exhilarating than doing good by oneself? At such moments a noble heart consults no one; but in severe actions a just and wise man does nothing without counsel.

The church in Nicomedia was finally demolished in 303; but Diocletian contented himself with a decree that Christians should no longer be elevated to the offices of the empire; this was to withdraw his good graces, but not to persecute. A Christian had the insolence to publicly pull down the emperor's edict, to tear it up, and to trample it underfoot. This crime was rightfully punished by the death of the culprit. Then Prisca, wife of the emperor, no longer dared protect the seditious; she even renounced the Christian religion when she saw that it led only to fanaticism and revolt. Thus Galerius was fully at liberty to wreck vengeance.

There were at the time a great many Christians in Armenia and Syria; they fomented uprisings; the Christians were even accused of setting fire to Galerius' palace. It was quite natural to believe people who had publicly torn up the imperial edicts, and who had burned temples as they often did, had also burned the palace; however it is entirely false that there was a general persecution of them. Legal severity was necessary only with recalcitrants, since Diocletian ordered that the executed be interred, which he would not have done if persecution were carried on without formal process. No edict is found which inflicts the death penalty solely for declaration of the Christian faith. That would have been as senseless, as horrible, as the St. Bartholomew massacre, as the massacres in Ireland, and as the crusade against the Albigensians; because by that time a fifth or a sixth of the empire was Christian. Such persecution would have forced this sixth part of the empire to take up arms, and the despair that armed it would have made it terrible.

Some such as Eusebius of Caesarea and those who followed him, generally said that an incredible number of Christians were immolated. But how is it that the historian Zosimus says not a word about it? Why does not Zonarius, a Christian, name any of the famous martyrs? How is it that ecclesiastical exaggeration has not preserved the names of fifty Christians put to death?

If the supposed massacres, attributed vaguely to Diocletian by the Legend, were examined with critical eyes, the tales would be seen as greatly exaggerated; there would be the deepest scorn for such deceptions, and Diocletian would no longer be considered a persecutor.

In fact it is under this prince that are placed the ridiculous stories of Theodotus the tavern-keeper, the Theban legion that was claimed to have been immolated, the young Roman born a stammerer, who spoke with incredible fluency as soon as the emperor's doctor, turned torturer, cut out his tongue; and twenty other similar adventures that doting old women in Cornwall would be ashamed to tell their grandchildren.[2]

---

[2] If in the fourth century of our ridiculous computation, there were some Christians punished for crimes and abominations that were imputed to them, must we be astonished? Have we not seen that the bishops reproached them with the most monstrous acts? The scholar Hume brought to our attention the most horrible abomination, that Lord Bolingbroke had forgotten, and which is narrated by St. Epiphanius. You will find it in the Paris edition of 1564, page 185. It is a matter of a society of Christians who sacrificed a pagan infant to the infant Jesus, killing him by jabbing him with needles. I confess that I am not astonished at this refinement of horror, after the incredible excesses which the Papists carried on against the Protestants in the massacres in Ireland. Superstition is capable of anything.—*Note by Decroix*

    Jacques Decroix and Caron de Beaumarchais co-edited the Kehl edition (1774–1780) of *Les Oeuvres Complètes de Voltaire.* This footnote does not appear there. Both the footnote and its attribution to Decroix would seem to be ideas that occurred to Voltaire later than 1774.—*kwa*

## CHAPTER XXIX—On Constantine

What man who has received a tolerable education does not know what Constantine was like? He has himself acclaimed emperor by a small body of foreign troops in the depths of England: had he more right to the empire than Maxentius, elected by the Senate or by the Roman armies?

Sometime thereafter he goes into Gaul and rallies the Christian soldiers serving his father; he crosses the Alps, constantly increasing his army; he attacks his rival who falls into the Tiber in the midst of the battle. It is even mentioned that there was a miracle in his victory, that in the clouds were seen a banner and a celestial cross on which was written in Greek: *In this sign shall ye conquer.* Obviously the Gauls, Bretons, Allobroges, and Insubri, who followed along in his train, all understood Greek perfectly, and God preferred to speak Greek to them rather than Latin.

However in spite of the dramatic miracle that he himself spread, he did not yet become a Christian; as a good political tactic, he remained content to declare liberty of conscience for everyone; and he so openly professed paganism that he took the title of grand pontiff: thus it is seen that he had two religions; it was a prudent way to behave in the first years of his tyranny. I do not scruple to make use here of the word tyranny, because I am not accustomed to recognizing as sovereign a man who has no other rights to the title than force; and I am too human not to call tyrant a barbarian who had his father-in-law, Maximian-Hercules, assassinated in Marseilles, on the flimsiest of pretexts, and the Emperor Licinius, his brother-in-law, killed in Thessalonica through the basest perfidy.

Without reservations I call a tyrant the man who had his son, Crispus, killed and strangled his wife, Fausta, and who, besmirched with murders and parricides, and displaying a most revolting pomp, delivered himself over to every pleasure in a most infamous manner.

Let cowardly ecclesiastical flatterers shower him with eulogies while at the same time admitting his crimes; let them see in him, if they wish, a great man, a saint, because he allowed himself to be immersed three times into a vat of water; a man of my nation and of my character who has served a virtuous sovereign, will never defile himself by pronouncing the name of Constantine without horror.

Zosimus reports, and it is very probable, that Constantine, as weak and cruel as he was, intermingling superstition with crime like so many other princes, believed he would find in Christianity the expiation of his misdeeds. In good time the interested bishops made him believe that the God of the Christians would pardon him everything and be thankful for having been given money and honors. As for me, I would not have deemed God one who would have pardoned a heart so deceitful and inhuman; only priests would canonize the assassin of Uriah among the Jews, and the murderer of his wife and his son among the Christians.

The character of Constantine, his pomp and his cruelties, are well enough expressed in these two verses that one of his wretched courtiers named Ablavius affixed to the door of the palace:

> *Saturni aurea saecla quis requirat?*
>
> Who can regret Saturn's golden century?
>
> *Sunt haec gemmea, sed Neroniana!*[1]
>
> It is of gems, but it is Nero's.

But what would Ablavius have been able to say of the Christians' zeal for charity when from the time they were fully liberated

---

[1] These two lines, which have been preserved by Sidonius Apollinarus, Book v, Epistle vii, are all that remain of Ablavius.—*Beuchot*

by Constantine, they assassinated Candidian, son of the Emperor
Galerius, an eight-year-old and a seven-year-old daughter of the
Emperor Maximian; they drowned the children's mother in the
Orontes? For a long time they pursued the aged Empress Valeria,
widow of Galerius, who fled their vengeance. They caught up with
her in Thessalonica, murdered her, and threw her body in the sea.
Thus they signalized their evangelical kindness; and they complain
of having had martyrs.

## CHAPTER XXX—On Christian Quarrels Before Constantine and During His Reign

Before, during, and after Constantine, the Christian faith was
forever divided into many sects, factions, and schisms. How could
a people who had no consistent system, who did not even have the
small Credo[1] so falsely attributed to the Apostles, who differed
among themselves as to nation, language, and customs, be united
in the same faith?

Saturninus, Basilides, Carpocrates, Euphrates, Valentinus,
Cerdo, Marcion, Hermogenes, Hermas, Justin, Tertullian, Origen
all had contrary opinions; and while the Roman magistrates sometimes attempted to curb the Christians, one saw them enraged with
one another, excommunicating and anathematizing each other, and
fighting one another in the depths of their prisons: there, surely,
was the most tangible and deplorable effect of fanaticism.

[1] The Credo, a creed called the Apostles Creed, has no more to do with them
than with the bishop of London. It was composed in the fifth century by the priest
Rufinus. The whole Christian religion has been made up of bits and pieces; it is
there that it is stated that Jesus, after his death, descended into hell. There was, in
the time of Edward VI, a great dispute to settle whether Jesus had descended in
both body and soul; it was decided that the soul alone had gone to preach in hell,
while his body was in sepulcher: as though in fact he was placed in a sepulcher,
having been executed, when the usage was to throw onto a dump heap. What was
his soul doing in hell? We were fools indeed in Edward VI's time.—*Voltaire*

The drive to dominate opened another source of discord: with the same passion and fraudulence that have since marked the schisms of forty anti-popes, they disputed among themselves what to name the rank of bishop. They were as desirous of commanding a small obscure populace as the Urbans, the Johns, have been to give orders to kings.

Novatus disputed the first Christian office in Carthage with Cyprian, who was elected. Novatian contested the bishopric of Rome with Cornelius; each of them received the assignation from bishops in his own faction. They were already daring to trouble Rome; and theological compilers dare today to be astonished that Decius* punished some of these agitators! However Decius, under whom Cyprian was executed, punished neither Novatian nor Cornelius; such obscure rivals were left to declare war on one another, much as dogs are left to fight among themselves in the courtyard, provided that they do not bite their masters.

In Constantine's time there was a similar schism at Carthage; two African anti-popes, or anti-bishops, Cecilian and Majorin, disputed the See, which was beginning to become an object of ambition. There were women on each side. Donatus succeeded to Majorin, and organized the first of the bloody schisms that would defile Christianity. Eusebius reports that they beat each other with clubs, because Jesus, they said, had ordered Peter to replace his sword in its scabbard [John 18:11]. Thereafter they were less scrupulous; the Donatists and the Cyprianists fought with steel. At the same time, three hundred years of carnage opened up with the quarrel of Alexander and Arius, of Athanasius and Eusebius, to determine if Jesus was exactly of the same substance as God, or of a substance similar to God.

---

* Decius, Roman emperor, 249–251 A.D., lost his life in battle with the Goths who had seriously breached the empire's defenses. Praised by pagan writers and execrated by Christian writers, Decius instituted systematic prosecution of Christians on the grounds that they were subversives who weakened the defense of the empire by preaching peace.—*kwa*

## CHAPTER XXXI—Arianism and Athanasianism

That a Jew named Jesus may have been similar to God, or consubstantial with God is equally absurd and impious.

That there may be three persons in one substance is just as absurd.

That there are three gods in one god is also just as absurd.

Nothing of all this was a Christian system, since nothing of it is to be found in any Gospel, the only known foundation of Christianity. It was only when they wished to platonize it that they became lost in these chimerical ideas. The more that Christianity spread, the more its scholars belabored themselves to render it incomprehensible. Subtleties saved whatever was in essence low and gross.

But what good are all these metaphysical fancies? What does it matter to human society, morality, and duties that there is one person in God, or three, or four thousand? Will a man be any better for pronouncing words that he does not understand? Does religion, which is submission to Providence and the love of virtue, need to become ridiculous in order to be adopted?

For a long time the nature of the *Logos*, the unknown Word, was disputed when Alexander, pope of Alexandria, aroused the ire of many popes by preaching that the Trinity was a monad. Of course the title of pope was then given indiscriminately to bishops and to priests. Alexander was bishop: the priest Arius placed himself at the head of the malcontents. Two violent parties were formed; and the question having immediately changed direction, as so often happens, Arius upheld the view that Jesus had been created, and Alexander that he had been engendered.

This hollow dispute was reminiscent of that which afterward caused division in Constantinople: whether the light that the monks saw on their navels was that of Tabor, and if the light from Tabor and their navels was created or eternal.

There was no longer a question of three hypostases among the disputants. The Father and the Son occupied minds [esprit] and the Holy Spirit was neglected.

Alexander had Arius excommunicated. Eusebius, bishop of Nicomedia, protector of Arius, assembled a small council that declared erroneous the doctrine that is today orthodox; the quarrel became violent; the bishop Alexander and the deacon Athanasius, who was already noted for his inflexibility and his intrigues, stirred the whole Church. The Emperor Constantine was despotic and hard, but he had good sense; he sensed the ridiculousness of the dispute.

The famous letter that he ordered Osius to carry to the chiefs of the two factions is well known. It said: "These questions arise only out of slothful curiosity; you are divided over an insignificant subject. Such conduct is low and puerile, unworthy of sensible men." The letter exhorted them to peace; but he did not yet know theologians.

The venerable Osius advised the emperor to assemble a great number in council. Constantine, who loved fanfare and pomp, convoked the assembly at Nicaea. He appeared in triumph in the imperial robe, wearing the crown, and covered with jewels. As the oldest of the bishops, Osius presided. The historians of the Papist Church have since claimed that Osius presided only in the name of the pope at Rome, Sylvester.* This notorious falsehood, which must be placed beside that of the Donation of Constantine, is confounded enough by the names of Sylvester's deputies—Titus [or Vitus] and Vincent—charged with his proxies. Actually the Roman popes were regarded as bishops of the imperial city, and as the metropolitans of the suburbicarian towns in the province of Rome;

---

* St. Sylvester I, A.D. 314–335, according to legend baptized Constantine and cured him of leprosy. The Roman Church credits him with calling the first ecumenical council, that of Nicaea in A.D. 325.—kwa

but they were far from having any authority over the bishops of the Orient and Africa.

The council, by a large plurality, established a formula in which the Trinity was not specifically named. "We believe in one God and in one Lord Jesus Christ, the only son of God, begotten of the Father, but not consubstantial with the Father." After these inexplicable words, they placed in supererogation: "We believe also in the Holy Spirit"—without defining what the Holy Spirit is, whether it is begotten, made, created, proceeds, or is consubstantial. Finally they added: "Anathema to those who say that there was a time when the Son was not."

But the most amusing thing about the Council of Nicaea was the decision about some canonical books. The Fathers found it difficult to make a choice of Gospels and other writings. They finally decided to pile them on an altar and pray the Holy Spirit to throw on the ground all those that were not legitimate. The Holy Spirit did not fail to grant the Fathers' request immediately.[1] A hundred volumes fell of their own accord under the altar; it is an infallible means of ascertaining the truth; that is what is reported in the *Appendix of the Acts of the Council*; it is one of the best confirmed events in ecclesiastical history.

Our learned and wise Middleton has discovered an Alexandrian chronicle, written by two patriarchs of Egypt, in which it is stated that not only seventeen bishops but also two thousand priests protested the decision of the council.

The winning bishops obtained from Constantine the exile of Arius and three or four other losing bishops; but afterward, Athanasius having been elected bishop of Alexandria and having very much abused his office, the exiled bishops and Arius were recalled, and Athanasius was exiled in his turn. There can be only one of two conclusions: either the two parties were equally wrong or Constantine was very unjust. The truth of the matter is that the

[1] The above is reported in the *Appendix of the Acts of the Council*, a document that has always been reputed to be authentic.—*Voltaire*

disputants of that time were conspirators like those of the present, and that the princes of the fourth century resemble ours, who understand nothing of the matter—neither they nor their ministers—and who exile capriciously. Fortunately, we have taken away from our kings the power to exile; and though we have not been able to cure our priests of a passion for conspiracy, we have rendered this passion useless.

A council was held at Tyre where Arius was rehabilitated and Athanasius condemned. Eusebius of Nicomedia intended to have his friend Arius enter the church at Constantinople with pomp; but a Catholic saint, by the name of Macarius, prayed so fervently and tearfully that Arius would die of apoplexy, that God, who is good, granted his wish. They say that the bowels of Arius came out through the anus; that is difficult; those people were not anatomists. But St. Macarius having forgotten to ask for the peace of the Christian church, God never gave it. Sometime after Constantine died in the arms of an Arian priest; apparently St. Macarius had further forgotten to pray God for the salvation of Constantine.

## CHAPTER XXXII—On Constantine's Children, and Julian the Philosopher, Called the Apostate by the Christians

The children of Constantine were as Christian, as ambitious and as cruel as their father; there were three who partitioned the empire, Constantine II, Constantius, and Constans. The Emperor Constantine I had left a brother, named Julius, and two nephews, to whom he had given some lands. They began by killing the father, in order to round out their parts of the empire. They were at first united by the crime, but soon fell apart. Constans had Constantine, his older brother, assassinated, and following that he himself was killed.

Constantius remained sole master of the empire; he had exterminated nearly all of the rest of the imperial family. Julius, whose death he had caused, left two sons, one named Gallus, and the other the celebrated Julian. Gallus was killed, and Julian was spared because, having a taste for seclusion and for study, it was decided that he would never be dangerous.

If there is something of truth in history, it is that the first two Christian emperors, Constantine and his son Constantius, were monsters of despotism and cruelty. It can be as we have already insinuated, that in the bottom of their hearts they believed in no god; and that mocking equally pagan superstitions and Christian fanaticism, they unfortunately persuaded themselves that the Divinity does not exist, because neither Jupiter the Cretan, nor Hercules the Theban, nor Jesus the Jew, are gods.

It is possible also that tyrants, who nearly always combine cowardice and barbarity, have been seduced into and encouraged in crime, by the belief held then by all Christians without exception—that three immersions in a vat of water before death would efface all penalties and take the place of all the virtues. This unfortunate belief has been more pernicious for the human race than the blackest passions.

Be that as it may, Constantius declared himself orthodox, that is to say Arian because Arianism prevailed then in the whole Orient against the doctrines of Athanasius; and the Arians, previously persecuted, were now persecutors.

Athanasius was condemned in a council of Sardinia, in another held in the city of Arles, in a third held in Milan. He roamed all of the Roman Empire, sometimes followed by his partisans, sometimes exiled, sometimes recalled. Always, everywhere the trouble lay in a single word *consubstantial.** Here was a scourge that had never been known in the history of the world until then. The ancient religion of the empire, which still existed in some splendor,

* According to the Roman Church, first pronounced by Sylvester I.—*kwa*

drew from all these divisions advantage in its struggle against Christianity.

However Julian, whose brother and family Constantius had assassinated, was obliged to outwardly embrace Christianity, just as our Queen Elizabeth was at one time forced to dissimulate her religion under the tyrannical reign of our infamous Mary, and as in France Charles IX forced the great Henry IV to go to mass after the St. Bartholomew massacre. Julian was a Stoic, a sect at once philosophical and religious which produced so many great men and which never knew a criminal, a sect more divine than human, in which are seen the asceticism of the Brahmans and of some monks—without their superstition; in short, the faith of Cato, Marcus Aurelius, and Epictetus.

It was shameful and deplorable that this great man saw himself reduced under Constantius to hiding all his talents, as the first Brutus did under Tarquin. He feigned being Christian and nearly imbecilic in order to save his life. He was even forced for a time to enter monastic life. Finally Constantius, who had no children, declared Julian a Caesar, but he sent him to Gaul as into a kind of exile; he was almost without troops and without money, surrounded by spies, and with almost no authority.

Different German tribal groups often crossed the Rhine and ravaged the Gauls, as they had done before Caesar, and as they did often after, up until the time that they finally invaded them, and that the single small nation of the Franks easily subjugated all these provinces.

Julian organized his troops, disciplined them, and won their love; he led them to Strasbourg, crossed the Rhine on a bridge of boats, and at the head of an army very weak in numbers—but fired with his courage—defeated a prodigious multitude of barbarians, took their chief prisoner, pursued them to the Hercynian forest, forced them to return Roman and Gallic captives, all the spoils that the barbarians had taken, and imposed tribute upon them.

To the conduct of a Caesar he added the virtues of Titus and

Trajan, bringing in wheat to feed the people of devastated areas, fostering cultivation of the fields, rebuilding cities, encouraging the population, the arts, and the talented by privileges, effacing himself and working day and night for the welfare of men.

As a reward, Constantius resolved to separate him from the Gauls who loved him so; he demanded two legions that Julian himself had trained. The indignant army opposed the move; it proclaimed Julian emperor in spite of himself. The earth was freed of Constantius when he marched against the Persians.

Julian the Stoic, so foolishly labeled the Apostate by the priests, was unanimously recognized as emperor by the peoples of the Orient and the Occident.

The force of truth is such, that Christian historians are obliged to admit that on the throne he lived as he had in Gaul. His philosophy never weakened. He began by reforming the luxury of Constantine and Constantius in the palace at Constantinople. The emperors, at their coronation, received heavy crowns of gold from all of the cities; he reduced such onerous presents to almost nothing. The frugal simplicity of the philosopher subtracted nothing from the majesty and justice of the sovereign. The abuses and the crimes at court were reformed; but in all only two public peculators were executed.

It is true that he renounced his baptism, but he never renounced virtue. He is reproached with superstition, but such reproach only acknowledges that he was religious. Why shouldn't he have chosen the religion of the Roman Empire? Why should he have been blamed for conforming to that of Scipio and of Caesar, rather than to that of Gregory of Nazianzus and of Theodoret? Paganism and Christianity divided the empire. He gave preference to the faith of his fathers, and with good political reason, since under the old religion Rome had triumphed over half the earth and under the new had everywhere fallen into decadence.

Far from persecuting the Christians he wished to soothe their shameful quarrels. I wish to adduce as proof only his fifty-second letter. "Under my predecessor many Christians have been hounded, imprisoned, and persecuted; a great number of them called heretics have been massacred in Samothrace, Paphlagonia, Bythynia, Galatia and many other provinces; they have been pillaged, their cities ruined. Under my regime, on the contrary, those banished have been recalled, confiscated goods have been returned. However, they are so furious that they complain of no longer being permitted to be cruel, or to tyrannize each other."

Does not this single letter suffice to confound the calumnies with which the Christian priests overwhelmed him?

There was in Alexandria a bishop named Georgius, the most seditious and the most fanatic of the Christians; he gathered a following of satellites; he beat the pagans with his hands; he demolished their temples. The people of Alexandria killed him. Here is how Julian speaks to the Alexandrians in his tenth epistle:

"Hear ye! In place of informing me of your outrage you have let yourselves be carried away by anger! You have delivered yourselves unto the same excess that you reprobate in your enemies! Georgius merited his treatment, but it was not for you to be his executioners. You have laws, you must ask for justice," etc.

I do not intend to repeat here or to refute what is written in the *Ecclesiastical History*,* that the spirit of party and of faction have dictated. I pass on to the death of Julian, who lived too short a time for the glory and welfare of the empire. He was killed in the midst of his victories over the Persians, after having crossed the Tigris and Euphrates at the age of thirty-one; he died as he had lived, with stoic resignation, thanking the Being of beings, who was about to join his soul with the universal and divine soul.

We are filled with indignation when reading in Gregory of Nazianzus and in Theodoret that Julian spurted all his blood toward the sky, saying: "Galilean, thou hast conquered." What a

---

* By Eusebius of Caesarea (264–340). His *History* relates the development of the Christian church from the Apostles to the Emperor Constantine whom he praised in a manner that many historians consider excessive.—*kwa*

miserable story! what a travesty! Did Julian fight against Jesus? And was Jesus the god of the Persians?

We cannot read without horror the discourse that the impetuous Gregory of Nazianzus delivered against him after his death. It is true that had Julian lived Christianity ran the risk of being abolished. Surely Julian was a greater man than Muhammed, who destroyed the Christian sect throughout Asia and Africa; but all submit to destiny; and an illiterate Arab wiped out the sect of an illiterate Jew, something which a great emperor and philosopher could not do. But Muhammed lived long enough, and Julian too little.

The *christicoles* have dared to say that Julian lived only thirty-one years as punishment for his impiety; and they do not recall that their supposed God did not live any longer.


## CHAPTER XXXIII—Considerations Concerning Julian

Julian, a Stoic in practice and of a virtue even superior to that of his own sect, was a Platonist in theory: his sublime spirit had embraced Plato's sublime idea, taken from the ancient Chaldeans, that God, existing through all eternity, had created eternal beings. God, immutable, pure, immortal, could only form beings similar to himself, images of his splendor whom he ordered to create mortal substance: thus God created the gods, and the gods created man.

This magnificent system was not proven; but such an imagination is no doubt worth more than a garden which included the sources of the Nile and the Euphrates, though they are eight hundred leagues apart; a tree which gives knowledge of good and evil; a woman taken from the rib of a man; a serpent who speaks; a cherub who guards the door; and all the disgusting fantasies with which Jewish grossness had stuffed this myth borrowed from the

Phoenicians. It must be observed in Cyril with what eloquence Julian confounded these absurdities. Cyril was arrogant enough to report Julian's arguments, and to believe that he answered them.

Julian deigns to make it clear how unlike the nature of God it is to have placed in the garden of Eden fruit that gave a knowledge of good and evil, and then to have forbidden the eating of it. On the contrary as we have already remarked, it must be recommended to man that he nourish himself on this necessary fruit. The distinction between good and evil, justice and injustice, was the milk with which God must nourish the creatures that came forth from his hands. It would have been better to have put out their two eyes than to have obstructed their understanding.

If the writer of the Asiatic novel Genesis had had the least spark of imagination, he would have envisioned two trees in Paradise; the fruits of the one would nourish the soul and inspire a knowledge and love of justice; the fruits of the other would inflame the darkest passions of the heart: man neglected the tree of knowledge, and attached himself to that of cupidity.

At least here was an appropriate allegory, a visible image of the frequent abuse that men make of their reason. I am astonished that Julian did not propose it; but he was too disdainful of this book to descend to correcting it.

With very good reason Julian scorned the famous Decalogue that the Jews regarded as a divine code: it was, in fact, a mild law in comparison with the Roman laws that forbade robbery, adultery, and homicide. Among what barbaric peoples has not nature dictated such laws with a much greater scope? What a pity to make the Lord descend in the midst of thunder and lightning, upon a small barren mountain, in order to teach that one must not be a robber! Yet it can be said that it was not for this God—who had ordered the Jews to rob the Egyptians, and who proposed that they practice usury with foreigners as their best recompense, and who had rewarded the robber Jacob—to forbid larceny.

With great wisdom the worthy emperor destroyed the supposed

Jewish prophecies on which the *christicoles* founded their fantasies, and the rod of Judah which would not be lacking between his legs, and the girl or woman who will bear an infant, and above all these words attributed to Moses [Deut. 18:5], which concerned Joshua, and which were so inappropriately applied to Jesus: "God will raise up unto thee a Prophet from the midst of thee . . . like unto me." Surely a prophet like Moses does not wish to say God and the son of God. Nothing is so palpable, nothing panders more to the grossest of minds.

But Julian believed, or pretended to believe, for the sake of politics, in divinations, in auguries, and the efficacy of sacrifices: after all, the people were not philosophers; he had to choose between the insanity of the Christians and that of the pagans.

I think that if this great man had lived he might have, in time, disengaged religion from the crudest of its superstitions, and he might have accustomed the Romans to the recognition of a God who was the creator of gods and of men, and to pay him all homage.

But Cyril and Gregory, and other Christian priests profited from his seeming need to profess the pagan religion publicly, to discredit him among the fanatics. The Arians and the Athanasians united against him; and the greatest man who may ever have lived, became useless to the world.*

* Voltaire's admiration for Julian inspired his *Discourse of the Emperor Julian Against the Christians 1767* (Discours De L'Empereur Julien Contre Les Chrétiens, Hâchette edition, v. 21, p. 172; Moland XXXI, 101) based upon Julian's *Against the Galilaeans* (The Works of the Emperor Julian, 3 v., Loeb Classical Library, Cambridge and London, 1961, v. 2, p. 319). Many of Voltaire's comments on the Old Testament and the Christians closely parallel those of Julian, who was conversant with Celsus, third century pagan critic of Christianity, and the fourth century Neo-Platonists Porphyry and Iamblichus.—*kwa*

## CHAPTER XXXIV—On the Christians up to Theodosius

After the death of Julian, the Arians and the Athanasians whose fury he had suppressed, began again to trouble the empire. The bishops of the two camps became nothing but leaders of sedition. Fanatical monks poured in from the deserts of the Thebaid to fan the flames of discord, mouthing extravagant miracles such as may be found in the history of the *papas* of the desert; insulting the emperors, and foreshadowing the monks of the future.

There was a wise emperor who—in order to extinguish, if possible, all the quarreling—decreed entire liberty of conscience, and partook of it himself; he was Valentinian I. In his time all the sects lived at least for some years in an outward peace, confining themselves to anathema without massacre, pagans, Jews, Athanasians, Arians, Macedonians, Donatists, Cyprianists, Manicheans, Apollinarists, were all astonished at their tranquility. By this example Valentinian taught all those who are born to rule that while two sects may tear the state apart, thirty tolerated sects leave the state in repose.

Theodosius did not think so, and was on the point of losing everything; he was the first to take the part of the Athanasians, and by his intolerance fostered the rebirth of discord. He persecuted the pagans and alienated them. He then felt himself obliged out of cowardice to give whole provinces on the right bank of the Danube to the Goths; and because of this unfortunate precaution taken against his own people, he precipitated the dissolution of the Roman Empire.

The bishops, imitating the emperor, abandoned themselves to the fury of persecution. There was a tyrant who, having dethroned and assassinated a colleague of Theodosius named Gratian, made himself master of England, the Gauls, and Spain. I know that Priscillian in Spain, having dogmatized like so many others, and having said that souls were emanations of God, some Spanish bishops, who knew no more of whence came the soul than Priscillian, reported him and his principal followers, to the tyrant Maximus. This monster, to curry favor with the bishops whose help he needed to maintain his usurpation, condemned Priscillian and seven of his partisans to death. A bishop named Itacus was barbarous enough to order them put to the rack in his presence. In Bordeaux, the people, always foolish and always cruel when their superstition is given free rein, stoned a woman of the nobility who was said to be a Priscillianist.

This condemnation of Priscillian is more confirmed than that of all the martyrs, about whom the Christians had made so much noise under the first emperors. The unfortunate wretches thought they pleased God by sullying themselves with the very crimes of which they themselves had complained. The Christians from that time on were like dogs that have sighted their quarry; they were eager for carnage, not in defense of the empire—which they permitted to be invaded by twenty barbarian nations—but rather in the persecution of the followers of the old Roman religion, and sometimes their brothers who did not think as they did.

Is there anything more horrible or more cowardly than the deed of the priests of the bishop Cyril, whom the Christians call St. Cyril? There was in Alexandria a young woman celebrated for her beauty and her mind; her name was Hypatia. Brought up by the philosopher Theo, her father, she took in 415, the chair that he had occupied, and was applauded for her knowledge as much as honored for her morality; but she was a pagan. Cyril's tonsured mastiffs, followed by a gang of fanatics, attacked her in the street when she was returning from her teaching, dragged her by the hair, stoned her and burned her; Cyril the Saint in no way reprimanded them, nor did the young Theodosius and the devout Pulcheria, his sister—who governed him and shared the empire with him—condemn this excess of inhumanity. Such a contempt for the law might have seemed less astonishing under the rule of their grandfather Theodosius I, who had steeped himself so cowardly in the blood of the citizens of Thessalonica.[1]

## CHAPTER XXXV—On the Sects and Misfortunes of the Christians up to the Establishment of Muhammedanism

Disputes, anathemas, persecutions did not cease to inundate the Christian church. It was not enough to have united in Jesus the divine nature and the human: someone decided to raise the question of whether Mary was the mother of God. The title of Mother of God seemed a blasphemy to Nestorius, bishop of Constantinople. His opinion was the most credible; but since he had been a persecutor he found some bishops persecuting him. He was driven from his seat at the council of Ephesus, but thirty bishops of this same council also deposed the mortal enemy of Nestorius, St. Cyril; and the whole Orient was divided.

This was not enough; it had to be known precisely if Jesus had two natures, two persons, two souls, two wills; if when he

[1] Nothing better characterizes the Christian priests than their fulsome praises of Theodosius and Constantine over so long a time. It is certain that Theodosius—surnamed the Great and sometimes the Saint—was one of the most evil men who had ever governed the Roman Empire; because, after having for six months promised complete amnesty to the citizens of Thessalonica, this Cantabrian, as perfidious as he was cruel, in 390, invited the citizens to the public games, in which he caused to be massacred men, women, and children without a single one escaping. Is it possible not to be violently indignant at the panegyrists of such a barbarian, who went into ecstasies at his penitence? They said that truly, he went many months without attending mass. Is it not an insult to all humanity to dare to speak of such expiation? If the authors of the Irish massacres had let six months go by without attending mass, would they have satisfactorily expiated their crimes? Is a person cleansed of them because he did not assist at a ceremony as idolatrous as it is ridiculous, when he is sullied with the blood of his fatherland?

As for Constantine, I am of the mind of the consul Ablavius, who declared that Constantine was another Nero.—*Voltaire*

performed the animal functions of man, the divine part was or was not involved. Such questions merited treatment only by Rabelais, or by our dear Dean Swift, or by Punch.[2] Now there were three parties in the empire, owing to the fanaticism of a certain Eutyches, a miserable monk, enemy of Nestorius and fought by other monks. There could be seen in all these disputes, monastery opposed to monastery, devotee to devotee, eunuch to eunuch, council to council, and often emperor to emperor.

While the descendants of Camillus, Brutus, Scipio, and Cato, mixed with Greek and barbarian, wallowed thus in the mire of theology, and while a spirit of frenzy spread over the face of the Roman Empire, spoilers from the north who knew only combat, came to dismember this great colossus now become feeble and ridiculous.

When they had conquered, they had to govern a fanatical people; they had to take their religion, and lead these beasts of burden by the halters that they had created for themselves.

The bishops of each sect strove to entice their conquerors; thus the princes of the Ostrogoths, Visigoths, and Burgundians were converted Arians; the Frankish princes were Athanasians.[3]

The Roman Empire of the destroyed Occident was divided into blood-soaked provinces that continued to anathematize one another with a reciprocal sanctity. There was as much confusion and vile abjection in religion as there was in the empire.

The contemptible emperors of Constantinople still affected to claim over Italy and provinces they no longer held, rights that they

[2] Let us call things by their name. Blasphemy has been pushed to such a point that it is an article of faith that God came to defecate and urinate on earth; that he was hanged and now we eat him; that we defecate and urinate him. And it is gravely disputed whether it was the divine nature or the human which defecated or urinated! Good God!—*Voltaire*

[3] What an Athanasian, what a good Catholic that Clovis, who caused to be murdered three kings, his neighbors, in order to rob them of their cash! What good Catholics, those sons of his, who with their own hands cut the throats of their nephews in the cradle. *By God!* [in English] Reading the history of the first Christian kings is like reading the history of the kings of Judah and Israel, or that of highway robbers.—*Voltaire*

believed they had. But in the seventh century a new religion appeared which soon ruined the Christian sects in Asia, Africa, and a large part of Europe.

Muhammedanism was without a doubt more sensible than Christianity. It did not adore a Jew while abhorring Jews; it did not fall into the extravagant blasphemy of asserting that three gods make one god; it did not call a Jewish woman mother of god; and it did not eat the god whom it adored, nor render its creator on the stool. To believe in one all-powerful god was its sole dogma; and if it had not been added that Muhammed was its prophet, it would have been a religion as pure, as beautiful as that of the Chinese men of letters. It was a simple theism, a natural religion, and in consequence a true one. Muslims can be excused for calling Muhammed the spokesman of God, since in fact he had taught the Arabs that there is only one God.

The Muslims, by arms and by word, silenced Christianity to the very gates of Constantinople; and the Christians, restricted to some provinces of the Occident, continued to dispute and tear one another apart.

## CHAPTER XXXVI—Summary Discourse on Papal Usurpations[1]

The barbarian inundation reduced Europe to a deplorable state. Only the reigns of Theodoric and Charlemagne were marked by some good laws; yet Charlemagne—half Frank, half German—committed barbarities with which no sovereign today would dare besmirch himself. Only cowardly writers of the Roman faith could

[1] Milord does not say enough about the tyranny of the popes. Gregory, surnamed the Great, burned all the Latin authors that he could find. There still is extant a letter from him to the bishop of Cagliari in which he says: "I want all the pagans of Sardinia to be forced to become converts."—*Voltaire*

praise this prince for having massacred half the Saxons in order to convert the other half.

The Bishops of Rome, at the time of the decadence of Charlemagne's family, began to try to attribute a sovereign power to themselves, and to resemble the caliphs who united the power of the throne and the altar. Divisions among the princes and popular ignorance soon favored their enterprise. The Bishop of Rome, Gregory VII, was the one who revealed his audacious designs with the utmost insolence. Fortunately for us, William of Normandy, who had usurped our throne, no longer distinguishing the glory of our nation from his own, curbed Gregory's insolence, and forbade the payment of Peter's pence, which at first we had given as alms and which the bishops of Rome exacted as tribute.

All our kings have not possessed the same tough fiber; and when the popes, so powerless in their small territory, became the masters of Europe by means of the Crusades and the monks, when they had deposed so many emperors and kings, and when they had made religion a fearful weapon that pierced all sovereigns, our island witnessed the wretched King John Lackland declare himself on his knees a vassal of the pope, take an oath of fidelity at the feet of Pandolfo the legate, and obligate himself and his successors to pay the Bishops of Rome an annual tribute of one thousand marks,[2] nearly the revenue of the crown. Since one of my ancestors had the misfortune to sign this treaty, the most infamous of treaties, I ought to speak of it with more abhorrence than someone else; it is an honorable amend that I owe to the dignity of debased human nature.

---

[2] The legate trampled the money before carrying it away. Our island was then an obedient country. We were in reality serfs of the people. What an infamous slavery! Good God! We are not enough avenged. We have sent vessels of war to Gibraltar, but we have not sent them to the Tiber!—*Voltaire*

## CHAPTER XXXVII—.On the Dreadful Excesses of the Christian Persecutions

It must not be doubted that new dogma invented every day contributed mightily to fortifying the usurpations of the popes. The *hocus pocus*,[1] or the transubstantiation, which name is ridiculous, became established little by little, after having been unknown in the first centuries of Christianity. We can estimate what veneration a priest or a monk attracted who made a god with four words, and not only one god but as many as he wished: with what respect bordering on adoration must he be regarded who had made himself absolute master of all the god–makers? He was the sovereign of priests—and of kings; he was a god himself; and in Rome still, when the pope officiates, they say: "The venerable carries the venerable."

However, from this slime in which the human species was plunged in Europe, men rose up who protested these novelties. They knew that in the first centuries of the Church no one claimed to change bread into a god at the Lord's supper; that Jesus had made a meal of lamb cooked with lettuce; that it resembled in no way the communion of the mass; that the first Christians had loathed images; that as late as Charlemagne, the famous Council of Frankfort had proscribed them.

Many other articles of belief revolted them; they even dared to doubt sometimes that the pope, as much god as he was, could by divine right depose a king for having espoused his godmother, or a relative seven times removed. Thus they rejected secretly some

---

[1] We call a juggler's tricks and palming by a charlatan *hocus pocus*. They are two abridged, or rather maimed Latin words derived from the Latin mass, *hoc est corpus meum.—Voltaire*
The Latin is: "this is my body."—*kwa*

points of the Christian faith, but accepted others no less absurd; they were similar to the animals that were at one time claimed to have been formed from the mud of the Nile, and which had life in one part of their bodies while the other was still mud.

But when they wished to speak out, how were they treated? In the Orient, ten centuries of persecution were employed in the extermination of the Manicheans; and under the regency of one empress, Theodora, devoted and barbarous,[2] one hundred thousand persons or more were put to death by torture. The Occidentals, having heard reports of the butcheries, became accustomed to call Manichean anyone who disputed any dogma of the Papist Church, and to pursue them with the same barbarity. Thus it was that a certain Robert of France had his wife's confessor and several priests burned before his eyes.

When the Vaudois and the Albigensians appeared they were labeled Manicheans to make them more odious.

Who does not know of the horrible cruelties inflicted in the southern provinces of France on those unfortunates whose crime was to deny that God can be made with words?

Later when the disciples of our Wycliff, of John Hus, and then those of Luther and of Zwingli wished to throw off the papal yoke, we know that nearly all of Europe was divided into two sorts: one the executioners, the other the executed. The reformers next did what the Christians of the fourth and fifth centuries had done; after having been persecuted, they in their turn became persecutors. If we wished to count the civil wars that disputes over Christianity have incited, we should see that there were more than a hundred.

[2] Is it possible that this horrible proscription, this forerunner of St. Bartholomew, is so little known? It is lost in the mob. However Fleury does not omit this hideous thing in his Book XLVIII, under the year 850; he relates it as an ordinary event. Bayle, in the article *Paulicians*, should have made some mention of it; so much the more since the Paulicians who escaped from the massacre joined with the Muslims and aided them to destroy that detestable empire of the Orient that knew proscription, but knew no longer how to do battle. But what caps this Christian atrocity is that this fanatic Theodora was declared a saint and for a long time after was celebrated with a feast day in the Greek church.—*Voltaire*

Our Great Britain has been ravaged: the massacres in Ireland are comparable to those of St. Bartholomew; and I don't know whether there were more abominations committed, more blood shed in France than in Ireland. The wife of Sir Henry Spotswood,[3] sister of my great-grandmother, was killed with her two daughters. So in this study, I have to avenge both the human race and myself.

What shall I say about the Tribunal of the Inquisition that still exists? The sacrifices of human blood with which we reproach ancient nations were rarer than those with which the Spaniards and the Portuguese have sullied themselves in their acts of faith.

Does someone now wish to compare this massive destruction and carnage to the martyrdom of St. Potamiena, St. Barbara, St. Pionius, and St. Eustache? For centuries we had weltered in blood like raging tigers, and we dare to brand a Trajan and an Antoninus as persecutors!

Now and then I have chanced to represent to priests the enormity of all the desolation of which our grandfathers were the victims; they coldly answered me that it was a good tree which had produced bad fruit: I would say to them that it was a blasphemy to claim that a tree that carried so many and such horrible poisons had been planted by the hands of God himself. Truly there is not a

---

[3] Lord Bolingbroke is right in comparing the Irish massacres to those of St. Bartholomew in France; I believe that the number of murders in Ireland even surpassed that of French murders.

It was proven juridically by Henry Shampart, James Shaw, and others, that the Catholic confessors pronounced excommunication and eternal damnation on Catholics, if they did not kill every Protestant including women and children, that they could put to death; and the same confessors enjoined them not to spare the cattle belonging to the English for the purpose of better resembling the holy Jewish people, when God delivered Jericho to it.

When Lord Macguire was taken, there was found in his pocket a bull of Pope Urban VIII, of May 25, 1643, which promised the Irish remission of all crimes and relieved them of all their vows, except that of chastity.

Clarendon and Temple said that from the autumn of 1641 to the summer of 1643 there were one hundred and fifty thousand Protestants killed and that neither women nor children were spared. An Irishman named Brooke, an Irish patriot, claims that only forty thousand were massacred. If we take an average of the two figures, we have ninety-five thousand victims in twenty-one months.—*Voltaire*

priest but who ought to lower his eyes and blush in the presence of any decent man.

## CHAPTER XXXVIII—Excesses of the Roman Church

Only in the Roman Church do we see—combined with the ferociousness of the descendants of the Huns, Goths, and Vandals— such a continuous series of scandals and barbarities unknown to priests of the other religions of the world.

Because they are men, priests have everywhere taken advantage of their situations. Among the Brahmans there were and still are rascals and scoundrels, although this ancient religion is unquestionably the most virtuous of all. The Roman Church has surpassed in crime every religion in the world, because it has had wealth and power.

It has surpassed others in obscene debaucheries, because, in order to better govern men, it has interdicted within its ranks marriage, which is the greatest curb on lasciviousness, lewdness, and pederasty.

I will mention only what I have seen with my own eyes and what went on a few years before my birth. Was there ever a criminal who less respected the public faith, the blood of men, and the honor of women, than Bernard Van Galen, bishop of Muenster, who hired himself out to the Dutch against his neighbors as well as to Louis XIV against the Dutch? All his life he intoxicated himself with wine and blood. He went from the beds of his concubines to the fields of death, like a carnivorous animal in rut. However the ignorant people fell on their knees before him and humbly received his benediction.

I have seen one of his bastards who, in spite of his birth, found the means to become canon of a collegiate church; he was more wicked than his father, and much more dissolute: I know that he murdered one of his mistresses.

I ask if it is not probable that the bishop, married to a virtuous German woman, and his son, born in legitimate wedlock and well brought up, would not have both led less abominable lives. I ask if there is anything in this world more capable of moderating our fury than the concern of a spouse and a respected mother, and if the duties of a head of the family have not nipped a thousand crimes in the bud.

How many murders committed by priests in Italy in the last forty years have I not seen? I am not exaggerating; few were the days when a Corsican priest, after having said mass, did not go out into the bush to shoot an enemy or a rival: and if the one assaulted was still breathing, the priest would offer to confess him and to give him absolution. Thus it was that those whom Pope Alexander VI ordered to be murdered so that he could seize their wealth, asked him for *unam idulgentiam in articulo mortis.**

I was reading yesterday what is related in our histories about a bishop of Liège, at the time of our Henry V. The bishop was called only *Iohn without pity*. He had a priest who served him as an executioner; and after having employed him to hang, to break on the wheel, and to disembowel more than two thousand persons, he had him hanged.

What shall I say about the archbishop of Upsala named Troll who, in conjunction with the king of Denmark, Christian II, had ninety-four senators massacred in his presence and gave up the city of Stockholm to pillage, a papal bull in his hand?**

There is not a Christian state where the priests have not committed similar scenes.

I will be told that I speak only of ecclesiastical crimes and pass over in silence secular ones. That is because the abominations of the priests, above all those of the Papist priests, make the greatest

* "An indulgence in the throes of death."—*kwa*
** See footnote, p. 49—*kwa*

contrast with what they teach the people; because to the mass of their misdeeds they join a crime no less hideous—if that is possible—that of hypocrisy; because the more pure their conduct ought to be the more sinful it is. They insult humanity; they persuade some imbeciles to bury themselves alive in a monastery. They exhort people to take the habit, they administer their oils; and then they plunge into voluptuousness or carnage; thus has the Church been governed from the upheavals of Athanasius and Arius to our own day.

Let them speak to me in the same good faith with which I explain myself; do they think that a single one of these monsters believed the impertinent dogma that he preached? Was there a single pope who, with the little common sense that he possessed, believed in the incarnation of God, the death of God, the resurrection of God, the Trinity of God, the transubstantiation of the bread into God, and all those odious chimeras that have placed the Christians below the beasts? Surely they have believed none of all this, and because they have sensed the horrible absurdity of Christianity, they imagine that there is no God. Here is the origin of all the horrors with which they are tainted; let us beware, it is the absurdity of Christian dogma that makes atheists.


## CONCLUSION


I conclude that all sensible men, all honest men must hold the Christian religion in dread. "The great name of Theist, that is not revered enough"[1] is the sole name that we should take. The only Gospel that we ought to read is the great book of nature, written by the hand of God and sealed with his seal. The only religion that we ought to profess is to *adore God and be an honest man*. It is

---

[1] These words are taken from *Characteristics* by Lord Shaftesbury.—*Beuchot*

just as impossible for such a pure and eternal religion to produce evil as it is impossible for Christian fanaticism not to produce it.

No one could ever say to the natural religion: *I came not to send peace, but a sword* [Matt. 10:34]. However, that is the first confession of faith put in the mouth of the Jew they called the Christ.

Men are surely blind and singularly unfortunate to prefer an absurd and bloody religion, supported by hangmen and surrounded with pyres; a religion that can only be approved by those to whom it gives power and riches; a restricted religion that is received in only a part of the world, to a simple and universal religion, that the *christicoles* themselves confess was the religion of mankind in the time of Seth, Enoch, and Noah. If the religion of their first patriarchs is true, then the religion of Jesus is false. Sovereigns have submitted to this sect, believing that they made themselves dearer to their people by taking on themselves the same yoke that burdened their people. They have not seen that they made of themselves the first slaves of priests, and they have not in half of Europe succeeded in freeing themselves.

And what king, I ask you, what magistrate, what family head would not prefer to be master in his own house than to be a slave to a priest?

What! the innumerable ordinary citizens, excommunicated, reduced to beggary, murdered, thrown into the sewers, the number of princes dethroned and assassinated, have not yet opened the eyes of men! And if we open them a little, that still does not overthrow the sinister idol!

What shall we put in its place? You say: what? A ferocious animal has sucked the blood of my near-and-dear ones? I tell you to get rid of the beast, and then you ask me what we shall put in its place! You ask me that! You, a hundred times more detestable than the pagan pontiffs, who calmly contented themselves with their ceremonies and sacrifices, who did not claim to chain minds with dogma, who never disputed the power of the magistrates, and who did not introduce discord among men. You have the effrontery to ask what can replace your myths! I reply to you God: truth, virtue, law, punishment, and reward. Preach probity and not dogma. May you be the priests of God and not of man.

After having weighed Christianity in the scales of truth before God, we must weigh it in those of policy. Such is the miserable human condition, that the truth is not always advantageous. There would be danger and little sense in wishing to all at once make of Christianity what has been made of Papism. I believe that in our island we must permit the hierarchy established by an act of Parliament to exist, subordinating it always to civil legislation and preventing it from being harmful. Without doubt it would be desirable to overturn the idol and offer the purest homage to God; but the people are not yet worthy of it. For the present, it suffices that our Church be contained within its bounds. The more the laity becomes enlightened, the less harm the priests will be able to do. Let us try to enlighten them, to make them blush for their misdeeds and, little by little, to bring them up to be citizens.[2]

---

[2] It is not possible for the human mind, however depraved it may be, to reasonably contradict what Lord Bolingbroke has said above. I have myself, with one of the greatest mathematicians of our island, attempted to imagine what the *christicoles* could allege as plausible, and I have been able to find nothing. This book is a thunderbolt that crushes superstition. All that our *divines* (*divine* means in English a theologian) have to do is to consistently preach morality, and to consistently render Papism execrable to all nations. For that they will be dear to ours. Let them cause God to be adored, and let them cause to be detested an abominable religion founded on imposture, persecution, rapine, and carnage; the enemy of kings and of peoples, and above all the enemy of our constitution, the most inspired constitution in the universe. It has been given to Lord Bolingbroke to destroy theological insanities, as it has been given to Newton to annihilate errors in physics. May the whole of Europe soon bask in this light. *Amen*. London. March 18, 1767. *Mallet**

* David Mallett published in 1754 a five-volume edition of the *Works* of Bolingbroke that Dr. Samuel Johnson characterized as the gun charged against Christianity. The language of the footnote is distinctly that of Voltaire who may have reasoned that associating the name of Bolingbroke's publisher with the *Important Study* would aid in establishing its authenticity.—*kwa*

# INDEX